Demand-Driven Inventory Optimization and Replenishment

Wiley & SAS Business Series

The Wiley & SAS Business Series presents books that help senior-level managers with their critical management decisions.

Titles in the Wiley & SAS Business Series include:

Agile by Design: An Implementation Guide to Analytic Lifecycle Management by Rachel Alt-Simmons

Analytics in a Big Data World: The Essential Guide to Data Science and Its Applications by Bart Baesens

Bank Fraud: Using Technology to Combat Losses by Revathi Subramanian

Big Data Analytics: Turning Big Data into Big Money by Frank Ohlhorst

Big Data, Big Innovation: Enabling Competitive Differentiation through Business Analytics by Evan Stubbs

Business Analytics for Customer Intelligence by Gert Laursen

Business Intelligence Applied: Implementing an Effective Information and Communications Technology Infrastructure by Michael Gendron

Business Intelligence and the Cloud: Strategic Implementation Guide by Michael S. Gendron

Business Transformation: A Roadmap for Maximizing Organizational Insights by Aiman Zeid

Connecting Organizational Silos: Taking Knowledge Flow Management to the Next Level with Social Media by Frank Leistner

Data-Driven Healthcare: How Analytics and BI are Transforming the Industry by Laura Madsen

Delivering Business Analytics: Practical Guidelines for Best Practice by Evan Stubbs

Demand-Driven Forecasting: A Structured Approach to Forecasting, Second Edition by Charles Chase

Demand-Driven Inventory Optimization and Replenishment: Creating a More Efficient Supply Chain by Robert A. Davis

Demand-Driven Inventory Optimization and Replenishment, Second Edition: Creating a More Efficient Supply Chain by Robert A. Davis

Developing Human Capital: Using Analytics to Plan and Optimize Your Learning and Development Investments by Gene Pease, Barbara Beresford, and Lew Walker

The Executive's Guide to Enterprise Social Media Strategy: How Social Networks Are Radically Transforming Your Business by David Thomas and Mike Barlow

Economic and Business Forecasting: Analyzing and Interpreting Econometric Results by John Silvia, Azhar Iqbal, Kaylyn Swankoski, Sarah Watt, and Sam Bullard

Financial Institution Advantage and The Optimization of Information Processing by Sean C. Keenan

Financial Risk Management: Applications in Market, Credit, Asset, and Liability Management and Firmwide Risk by Jimmy Skoglund and Wei Chen

Foreign Currency Financial Reporting from Euros to Yen to Yuan: A Guide to Fundamental Concepts and Practical Applications by Robert Rowan

Fraud Analytics Using Descriptive, Predictive, and Social Network Techniques: A Guide to Data Science for Fraud Detection by Bart Baesens, Veronique Van Vlasselaer, and Wouter Verbeke

Harness Oil and Gas Big Data with Analytics: Optimize Exploration and Production with Data Driven Models by Keith Holdaway

Health Analytics: Gaining the Insights to Transform Health Care by Jason Burke

Heuristics in Analytics: A Practical Perspective of What Influences Our Analytical World by Carlos Andre, Reis Pinheiro, and Fiona McNeill

Hotel Pricing in a Social World: Driving Value in the Digital Economy by Kelly McGuire

Human Capital Analytics: How to Harness the Potential of Your Organization's Greatest Asset by Gene Pease, Boyce Byerly, and Jac Fitz-enz

Implement, Improve and Expand Your Statewide Longitudinal Data System: Creating a Culture of Data in Education by Jamie McQuiggan and Armistead Sapp

Killer Analytics: Top 20 Metrics Missing from your Balance Sheet by Mark Brown

Mobile Learning: A Handbook for Developers, Educators, and Learners by Scott McQuiggan, Lucy Kosturko, Jamie McQuiggan, and Jennifer Sabourin

The Patient Revolution: How Big Data and Analytics Are Transforming the Health Care Experience by Krisa Tailor

Predictive Analytics for Human Resources by Jac Fitz-enz and John Mattox II

Predictive Business Analytics: Forward-Looking Capabilities to Improve Business Performance by Lawrence Maisel and Gary Cokins

Retail Analytics: The Secret Weapon by Emmett Cox

Social Network Analysis in Telecommunications by Carlos Andre Reis Pinheiro

Statistical Thinking: Improving Business Performance, Second Edition by Roger W. Hoerl and Ronald D. Snee

Taming the Big Data Tidal Wave: Finding Opportunities in Huge Data Streams with Advanced Analytics by Bill Franks

Too Big to Ignore: The Business Case for Big Data by Phil Simon

The Value of Business Analytics: Identifying the Path to Profitability by Evan Stubbs

The Visual Organization: Data Visualization, Big Data, and the Quest for Better Decisions by Phil Simon

Trade-Based Money Laundering: The Next Frontier in International Money Laundering Enforcement by John Cassara

Understanding the Predictive Analytics Lifecycle by Al Cordoba

Unleashing Your Inner Leader: An Executive Coach Tells All by Vickie Bevenour

Using Big Data Analytics: Turning Big Data into Big Money by Jared Dean

Visual Six Sigma, Second Edition by Ian Cox, Marie Gaudard, Philip Ramsey, Mia Stephens, and Leo Wright

Win with Advanced Business Analytics: Creating Business Value from Your Data by Jean Paul Isson and Jesse Harriott

For more information on any of the above titles, please visit www.wiley.com.

Demand-Driven Inventory Optimization and Replenishment

Creating a More Efficient Supply Chain

2nd Edition

Robert A. Davis

WILEY

Published by John Wiley & Sons, Inc., Hoboken, New Jersey.
Published simultaneously in Canada.

For general information on our other products and services or for technical support, please contact our Customer Care Department within the United States at (800) 762-2974, outside the United States at (317) 572-3993 or fax (317) 572-4002.

Wiley publishes in a variety of print and electronic formats and by print-on-demand. Some material included with standard print versions of this book may not be included in e-books or in print-on-demand. If this book refers to media such as a CD or DVD that is not included in the version you purchased, you may download this material at http://booksupport.wiley.com. For more information about Wiley products, visit www.wiley.com.

Library of Congress Cataloging-in-Publication Data:

Names: Davis, Robert A., 1947–
Title: Demand-driven inventory optimization and replenishment : creating a
  more efficient supply chain / Robert A. Davis.
Description: Second edition. | Hoboken : Wiley, 2015. | Series: Wiley and SAS
  business series | Revised edition of the author's Demand-driven inventory
  optimization and replenishment, 2013. | Includes index.
Identifiers: LCCN 2015036768 (print) | LCCN 2015041898 (ebook) |
  ISBN 9781119174028 (hardback) | ISBN 9781119220404 (ePDF) |
  ISBN 9781119220411 (ePub)
Subjects: LCSH: Business logistics. | Inventory control. | Delivery of
  goods—Management. | Customer services—Management. | Supply and demand. |
  BISAC: BUSINESS & ECONOMICS / Decision-Making & Problem Solving. |
  BUSINESS & ECONOMICS / Decision-Making & Problem Solving.
Classification: LCC HD38.5 .D38 2015 (print) | LCC HD38.5 (ebook) | DDC
  658.7/87—dc23
LC record available at http://lccn.loc.gov/2015036768

Cover Design: Wiley
Cover Images: Network © mattjeacock/Getty Images, Inc.;
Shiny pattern © Ralf Hiemisch/Getty Images, Inc.

Printed in the United States of America

10 9 8 7 6 5 4 3 2 1

Contents

Preface

I grew up in a town called Bremerton, Washington. The town is situated on the Kitsap Peninsula right in the middle of Puget Sound. Given its location so close to the ocean, there are a lot of navel installations in the vicinity. The majority of the residents worked at the Trident Missile Base (nuclear missiles), the Keyport Underwater Warfare Base (torpedoes), or the Puget Sound Naval Shipyard (ship repair). This type of employment created a huge middle class. In addition to these blue-collar workers, Bremerton had a supporting cast of people there to help with every need. Doctors, lawyers, shopkeepers—you name it—they were there to support the town and the surrounding area.

One of the residents, a lawyer, had a huge house built on property overlooking one of the great views of Puget Sound and Mt. Rainier. It was a beautiful home fit for the very successful family. In addition to the home, the property sported landscaped gardens, elegant trees, and garages designed for 6 to 10 cars. People from Bremerton would take visitors on drives around the town and, invariably, swing by the lawyer's house to have everyone gawk at the fancy house on the hill.

Oddly, over the years, very few, if any, people ever saw the inside of the house. If anyone was allowed on the property, it was to tend to the gardens or clean the various fixtures. If there was a gathering of friends, the entertaining was done on the grounds, not in the house. This type of behavior got everyone to wonder what wonderful treasures were inside. It led to a mystique about how fancy it must have to be to keep others out. How else would such privileged people live? Everyone could see how successful the family was. Who could hold it against them to be so private? They lived in luxury, as everyone could see, and everyone aspired to have the trappings of success just like the lawyer's family.

Now why, you must be wondering, would I bring up a story about a house in Bremerton, Washington, in a book about demand-driven distribution? Something happened to that house that I will explain at the end of the book. The house has become a metaphor for when I examine highly regarded and not so highly regarded companies and their supply chains.

Let's face it, companies like to dress themselves up. Just like the people of Bremerton, Washington, executives see other highly regarded organizations from the outside and wish their companies could be just like the lawyer's house in my story—the envy of all who see it.

While the outside might be awe-inspiring, it is the guts of the organization that make the products. Many C-level executives look at supply chain as the underbelly of their company. The black hole, if you will, of activities where products are pushed out and revenue comes back in the form of a balance sheet and/or income statement. In my 35-plus years of working in and around supply chains I find executives treating supply chains like our lawyer friend in my story—as something inside the organization that is not to be seen by the outside world.

With that said, please enjoy the book and wait until the end to find out what happened to our Bremerton, Washington, lawyer and how it relates to demand-driven distribution.

Acknowledgments

I have had the great fortune of being in contact with many people much smarter than myself. I guess one of my strengths is to be able to understand that when smart people speak it is best for me to stop talking and learn. People wax on about having a mentor in order to be successful. I'm lucky enough to have many mentors over the years who have taken time out to teach me. I am eternally grateful that they took time for me even though I was not always receptive!

- If JoAnne McBride had not told me to put up or shut up about ordering, I never would have had the opportunity to become a buyer.

- Bob Larson and Pat Smith spent many hours going over what made good buying decisions while supporting turn volume and promotional volumes.

- Nick Gazzard took the time to teach me about supply chain cost analysis and the ability to see beyond the numbers when researching problems.

- Radhika Kulkarni, Jinxin Yi, Tugrul Sanli, and Xinmin Wu practiced supreme patience as they helped me understand the technical side of Operations Research and Inventory Optimization.

- Anders Richter showed me and just about every other inventory optimization practitioner how to successfully deliver a solution on time and under budget.

- Vinay Chaturvedi has been my close confidant, friend, and sounding board for many, many years. I can't imagine dealing with complex supply chain issues without having Vinay working with me to better understand customer needs.

- Scott Nalick gave me countless hours of time to show how time-phased business analysis reports could be provided to wary C-level decision makers in a manner that is both professional and personal. Indeed, Scott's "I've got one more question" queries could rival any episode of "Colombo," and I am forever grateful for his thoroughness.

■ Ed Katz could provide many sanity checks during my research when I was ready to jump out of my skin. Over the last 15 years, Ed has acted like a big brother. He was always ready to smack me upside the head when I did wrong, but help me up and dust me off when he made his point.

■ Charlie Chase always believed I could be a writer and had something to say about the subject of inventory optimization. Charlie was the one who told me not all books about optimization have to be written by PhDs and have algorithms plastered all over the page. Yes, Charlie, executives want to learn too!

■ Lora Cecere has been there for me for the last 7–8 years as I have pushed my learning envelop. I remember when I first met Lora after dealing with her on the phone. I told her, "I'm 6'4" tall and weight 250 lbs., but you scare me!" Lora doesn't suffer fools so she taught me to always be prepared!

■ Mark Demers, my boss! You believed in me and supported me as I dug deep into the subject of inventory optimization. You are one of those great managers who take joy in the success of those who work for you.

Finally, over the years I have had the great fortune to have been welcomed into many companies who have been looking for ways to improve their supply chains. In virtually every occasion I am floored by the intelligence, professionalism, and grit these supply chain practitioners have in doing their jobs. I thank these wonderful people for sharing with me their successes and their not so successful endeavors. If these people are any indication, the supply chains of now and the future are in good hands.

About the Author

Robert A. Davis

Over the past 35 years I have had a unique practitioner's view into inventory and replenishment optimization. This pathway has led me from humble purchasing, to an eye-opening supply chain cost analysis career, to, finally, helping some of the largest companies in the world drive huge inefficiencies out of their supply chains.

Starting in the mid-1980s, while working as a key account manager for a large grocery manufacturer, a harried, overworked co-op wholesale buyer asked me take over the purchasing of my own products as a way of lightening her load. That's right. I was a practicing vendor-managed inventory (VMI) manager 20 years before it was in vogue. Over the next three years, I was able to learn all of the tricks of the replenishment trade and balanced my selfish vendor goals with some of the highest inventory turns in the company. Three times, I was asked to join the staff as a full-fledged buyer, but felt my skills were better served in sales and business management. However, that grounding in replenishment and the fascination with supply chain relationships continued to tug at me until 2000.

Efficient consumer response (ECR) and its stepchild, collaborative planning, forecasting, and replenishment (CPFR), were sweeping through forward-thinking supply chain companies in the late 1990s, and I was able to immerse myself in those movements with my efforts as product manager for an award winning solution called value chain analytics (VCA). ECR Europe had just promoted VCA as the cost analysis tool to use in collaborative engagements. This allowed me entry to study some of the most famed supply chains in the world, like Kimberly Clark, 3M, and Kroger and Rona of Canada. It also thrust me onto the stage as a supply chain cost expert with featured speaking opportunities with CGIT, VICS, IBF, ABC User Group, SASs User Group, and Rochester Institute of Technology Operations Conference.

At SAS the natural progression would be to move from performance/cost analysis into inventory optimization product management. Over the past eight years I have had the privilege of leading the development of SAS inventory optimization solution from a single install to engagements listing some of the largest companies in their respective industry verticals. I have literally helped save millions and increase revenues by tens of millions. However, in the process I have gotten to experience, first hand, how unknown shortcomings in enterprise resource planning (ERP) systems and reliance on ancient replenishment methodologies have pushed some of the best buyers and inventory control managers to the breaking point.

I have found, through my experiences, that when you understand the shortcomings of the present inventory systems you embrace the benefits of inventory and replenishment optimization. It can be a leap of faith, but it does not have to be a black-box leap of faith. You can have a tremendously positive effect on an organization and personnel. Inventories come under control, buyers have more time to spend on value-added activities, and the top-line revenues and bottom-line costs of the company dramatically improve. Anyone can ratchet down days of supply over the short run to meet a number, but when an organization right-sizes an inventory for best results you might even get a buyer to smile.

CHAPTER 1

Creating Demand-Driven Supply

When people talk about inventory optimization I am always surprised at the number of definitions that are rolling around out there. Most C-level executives know it has something to do with reducing or right-sizing inventories and that it really helps control supply chain costs. The career path of that C-level executive can morph her viewpoint about where that optimization resides. Indeed, the closer you get to the customer, the more optimization means replenishment. This means a retail executive has a far different view of optimization compared to that of a manufacturing executive.

For many, the focal point of supply chain efficiency projects is to uncover and exploit cost discrepancies positioned by supply chain partners in the name of "optimization." For instance, in the article "Optimizing Replenishment Policies Using Genetic Algorithms for Single Warehouse/Multi-retailer System," W. Yang, T. Felix, S. Chan, and V. Kumar cite how huge savings can be achieved by adhering to a methodology of quantity discounts in transportation cost models.[1] This technique of uncovering supply chain inefficiencies to fill the void with cost savings shifts costs onto another portion in the supply chain. It is rampant inside companies and between external trading partners in almost all industries. Obviously, the whole point of optimization is to take advantage of every opportunity of cost savings, not just taking advantage of trading partner inefficiencies. Optimization is not simply shifting the costs from one location to another. Optimization is all about the actual elimination of costs and the savings enjoyed by either the network as a whole or the end customer satisfaction.

This is why we oftentimes find supply chain executives perplexed about where to start in developing a fact-based pathway to better supply chain dynamics. There seem to be a million different definitions of what inventory optimization is, depending on what flavor of optimization is in vogue. At one time the flavor might be *network design* to drive best positioning at the moment of a warehouse. Another time it might be a *theory of constraints* project to uncover bottlenecks in the company supply chain that can be smoothed out. Conversely, it might even be a project about *SKU (stock keeping unit) rationalization* for overall portfolio profitability. I have heard them all batched under the banner of inventory optimization. However, nothing has created more confusion than a definition driven out of the just-in-time wave of supply chain efficiencies—the idea that a company that practices *pull supply chain* methodologies will suddenly enjoy massive inventory savings and replenishment nirvana. Nothing could be further from the truth.

There is nothing wrong with the assumption that replenishment is what drives supply. In fact, given my background I would almost wholeheartedly agree. Over the past 30 years supply chains are shifting from being supply-driven (push) to being demand-driven (pull). While the theory is easy to imagine, the devil is in the details. There are decades of supply-side or push-style supply chain practices in place throughout organizations. You can't simply flip a switch and make your supply chain work in a new way.

Originally, the thought of most companies was to make a complete shift from push to pull as a way to have a nimble and/or agile supply chain. In an article written back in 2003,[2] Erik Kruse talks about some of the disastrous results companies incurred when they took perfectly good operating systems that insured efficiencies when producing large quantities of standardized products and attempted to make smaller batches of products to quickly react to customer demand. He points out an AMR Research study that supports his claim of inefficiencies. In that study, it was shown that companies tend to reconfigure their physical networks without introducing new processes that would help in the transition. Kruse points out that if customers don't buy what the efficient operations are producing, then the efficiency metric isn't really measuring true efficiency.

This brings up an interesting paradox. If you only use supply-side/push methodology, your operations can be extremely efficient. Large amounts of standardized product can be positioned, but if the customer is not buying the product at the same rate, the real efficiency is lost. In turn, if you shift to a demand-side/pull methodology, you reduce the production cycle and produce just enough to satisfy customer demand. When this occurs, you lose your manufacturing efficiencies, and you run the risk of not fulfilling *unexpected* customer demand.

Various large-scale supply chain movements like just-in-time, efficient consumer response, and collaborative planning, forecasting, and replenishment have all been rolled out in the name of creating a more responsive organization. The introduction of enterprise resource planning (ERP) and supply chain management (SCM) solutions in the late

1990s helped these movements gain traction, as technology interacted with methodology. Oddly, as technology and methodology interconnected, it seemed as though the supply chain industry was simply creating a bigger, better, and faster replenishment engine as a way of having an optimized supply chain. What is becoming more and more apparent, though, is that replenishment can only do so much in an effort to become demand driven. In the end, replenishment can only attempt to compensate for out-of-balance inventories.

THE PATH TO DEMAND-DRIVEN SUPPLY

This book is designed to take business practitioners through the fundamentals of inventory optimization so that they can attain a demand-driven supply. If you are looking for a book that will spell out stochastic algorithms, you're in the wrong place. Virtually every book written on the subject of *inventory optimization* (IO) seems to be done by academics with complete focus on proving that the stochastic algorithms they used during their studies are sound and repeatable. The rest of the inventory optimization publications could be categorized as "snake oil" whitepapers. Why snake oil? From the early 2000s through 2010, various inventory optimization vendors tried to differentiate themselves by claiming their "math" was superior or they had proprietary algorithms no one else could provide. There was little wonder the industry had confused the market.

The business world has heard about the subject of inventory optimization, but has trouble linking the solution to the many supply chain problems they might have in their organization. My goal is to provide a business perspective on why current inventory systems suboptimize the supply chain and why faulty replenishment processes lead to wasted time and effort. In the end, I hope the reader would come away with a good understanding of why *optimized inventory and replenishment* helps overcome in-system weaknesses and deliver results. We've come a long, long way, and it seems as though we only have a few more hurdles to go before we become part of the end game known as demand-driven supply.

When I am in front of executives who think replenishment cures their supply chain, I often ask the question: "If replenishment takes care of inventory ills, what caused your inventory to be sick in the first place?"

Although it is not the only place of supply inefficiency, let's take a look at the grocery supply chain in the United States. Because of the normal interactions people have with their grocery stores, they can recognize some of these push-style methods that companies use to entice you to buy products you wouldn't otherwise have purchased in the name of pushing products through the supply chain.

SHIFTING FROM SUPPLY-DRIVEN TO DEMAND-DRIVEN METHODOLOGIES

Thirty-five years ago, just before the demise of the so-called push supply chain in grocery products, I made a personal transition from being a supply-driven buyer to being demand-driven buyer. First of all, at the time I didn't know what any of this supply–demand mumbo-jumbo meant, and, second of all, I never set out to be a buyer in the first place.

So You Think You Can Do Better?

I was working as a key account manager in Portland, Oregon. My job was to manage grocery headquarter accounts for best results in sales. It was getting close to the end of the fiscal year, and we were slightly below the numbers I needed to bring in. One of my accounts was a co-op wholesaler who supplied almost all of the large, independent grocery stores in the northwest region. My buyer, Joanne McBride, did not have any direct responsibility for the advertising, but purchased for both turn and promotional merchandise. I was good friends with her. I was also really needling her to order a little more so I could make my year-end numbers. What she did next changed my life forever.

She looked at me and said in a very tired and very sarcastic voice, "Bob, you think you're so hot stuff. Why don't you do it?"

I was stunned. Now what am I going to do? However, never being the one to back down, I said, "Okay," and picked up the two orders so that I could get the heck out of there. I went downstairs to the lunchroom with a calculator and a very sharp pencil. The only instructions I got from her that day were the following:

- There are four numbers that show the running "as-is demand" by week with the most recent on the left.
- If there are any ads planned for the product, they will show up above the order line with the price and the placement—feature or subfeature.
- The order suggestions are forecasted only for turn volume. You must figure out what needs to be ordered for the advertising.
- Once you have the total amount, make sure the goods can fit in a truck ranging from 38,000 to 44,000 pounds.

For the next two-and-a-half hours, I was sweating bullets. After using up the calculator batteries, most of the pencil, and the entire eraser, I was able to put together two trucks for the Portland warehouse and one truck for the Medford warehouse. I took the orders up to Joanne and handed them over for the judgment. She looked at them and said, "Not bad, but anybody can buy once. Let's see what you can do over the long haul."

Yep, you guessed it—I was suddenly doing vendor-managed inventory (VMI) 20 years before it was cool.

Let's not get ahead of ourselves here. I wasn't shifting the product ownership points or taking on an official role of a VMI person. I was just a key account manager who got handed the keys to a treasure chest. My job at that point was to go into the wholesaler, pick up the computer-generated ordering output for the two wholesaler warehouses in Oregon, and develop orders to cover general turn volume and major advertising.

At the time—remember, this was the mid-1980s—there were two completely different inventory management philosophies between a grocery vendor and a grocery wholesaler. Grocery vendors were graded on sheer volume. *Total shipments* was the key performance indicator (KPI), with little focus on the actual consumer consumption until after the fact with POS data from IRI or Nielsen. On the flipside, the grocery wholesaler focus was on efficient inventory turns out to the stores.

In the middle of this conflict was an old adage uttered by just about every grocer vendor in the business: "A happy buyer is a loaded buyer."

The crux of this statement was that in order for the grocery wholesalers to be efficient, you should keep them in an overstock situation so that they would have to do something to get rid of the stock. Moreover, if they were overstocked with your products, they couldn't do anything with a competitive product. Therefore, if you had an overstock on a product that was so far out of whack that a wholesaler had to run a feature ad, you ended up moving a lot of stock, and the ad was a bonus to get customers to buy your product. Interesting paradox—in order to drive volume through the wholesaler warehouse, the more inefficient you made them, the better the overall volume would be.

So, guess what happened?

I did what every red-blooded vendor rep would have done. I put in over three months of unneeded, redundant inventory in the blink of an eye to make my year-end numbers. Heck, my management thought I was the greatest buyer of all time. I had made my numbers, and now all I needed to do was set up a whole bunch of ads, and the excess product would disappear. There was a flipside to this elation.

I had betrayed Joanne's trust. As a "real buyer," I had dug myself a pretty deep hole. I knew I had screwed up badly, but I couldn't figure out how to get rid of the excess inventory. It was time for me to go eat some of that long-deserved humble pie and have a meeting with the real buyer. I had practiced the loaded buyer/happy buyer philosophy, but I wasn't very happy.

She took it pretty calmly. Actually, she was much calmer than I would have been if some dumb guy like me had messed with my inventory. She told me that I had made the same mistake many first-time buyers make and I had put my personal needs ahead of her company. (*Ouch*, that one hurt.) She sat me down for the next hour and taught me the basics of *rule-of-thumb inventory management*.

Rule-of-Thumb Inventory Replenishment Management circa 1985

- If you have a lead time of a week, always have one week's supply for the demand and one week for the safety stock.
- Never buy more than five weeks' supply at a time, unless you have committed orders.

- ■ If you have a subfeature ad, buy two weeks' supply.
- ■ If you have a feature ad, buy four weeks' supply.
- ■ Keep a close eye on products with pull dates.

I felt very conflicted as I left her office. Here was a seasoned buyer trusting me with $5+ million in yearly sales. On one side, the supply-side mentality from my company's management thought I was the fox in the henhouse, but on the other side, I could see there was a real art/science to this replenishment and inventory management. Nobody had ever told me about *pull supply chains*, but I could see there was something to the idea of naturally pulling products through instead of making myself miserable with overstocks. I just had this feeling that I could really make a difference.

It took me close to two months to reduce the inventory through bleeding off the excess stock and minimizing the buying. During that time, I spoke regularly with the advertising managers based at the wholesaler warehouse about their planning cycles and expected ad lifts from various advertising formats. They knew about my new role and took me under their wings. They must have seen the hangdog expression I had from doing the buying and gave me some pointers.

They started me down the pathway of calculating lift, profitability, and basic rules of category management. I had a few items that were giving me fits from the lack of inventory bleed, and I talked a few of the ad guys into running some subfeatures to help me get rid of product. Once I got the inventory into a manageable level, as shown in Figure 1.1, I went back to Joanne to better understand the connection I needed to have between buying and advertising to pull product through. If any of you out there have had to deal with a co-op wholesaler, you know there is little you can do besides being a merchandising conduit for the membership stores. You can certainly set up products to be promoted, but there is very little influence brought to bear on ad price or display activity at the retail stores. The co-op wholesaler just does not have the retail clout that a chain store merchandiser might have. Given that downside, it was also the perfect testbed for a dumb, newbie buyer managing his own products. I learned, pretty fast, that oversupplying for limited demand was a recipe for disaster. I guess I

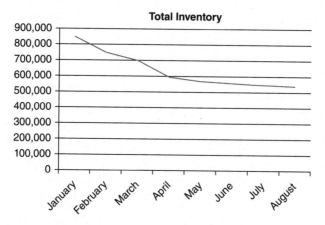

Figure 1.1 Inventory Bleed-Off of Davis Product Portfolio

needed to start acting like those big-boy chain stores and manage my demand.

Every quarter, I would attend a merchandising meeting with the brand managers from my company to plan out the promotion budgets. Up until that time, I would take what the brand managers felt I needed and present the packages to the ad managers at the accounts for the upcoming period. My normal acceptance rate was 50 to 60 percent, and I got so-so promotional lift and market share impacts from my merchandising. Well, now that I was a hotshot (and totally out of my league) buyer taking care of about 30 percent of the market volume, I just turned the tables on those brand managers.

Prior to my sitting down with the company brand managers, I went to each of the merchandising managers at the co-op wholesaler and discussed what I needed to do to plan out advertising on my key products. I had a pretty good stable of products, so I knew it was a win-win proposition. I didn't have any funds when I sat down with the merchandising managers, but we had an agreement that if we shook on it, I would get them the ad funds and unit costs required to support the plan. Now I could sit down in these quarterly planning meetings with the brand managers and lay out complete merchandising packages they could take to the bank. It didn't take long for word to get out about the guy up in Portland who managed his own products with 30 percent of the market's volume.

Inside of six months after taking on the responsibility of my products, my overall volume had increased by almost 15 percent. Remember, this was after digging a three-month overstock hole in the first weeks of the fiscal year. That being said, there were two key performance indicators I was even more excited about, which my company's managers didn't understand. My inventory turns were up by almost 30 percent, and my out-of-stocks were down to less than 2 percent. I had a few bumps in getting those brand managers to commit, but I was doing much better with using my trade funds. I was now at an 88 percent acceptance rate, and the market share on my portfolio had gone from 30 percent to 32 percent.

Around this time, I got my first offer (of three) to become a full-fledged buyer. You would not believe what a huge boost of confidence that gave me. I was getting the hang of this idea of pulling products through the system instead of shoving the product through, as most vendors in the grocery industry had practiced for 30 years. I turned down the offer, as I felt I had a lot more to give as a vendor rep, and I was just having too much fun breaking the mold as this newfangled vendor/buyer.

MOVING TO A DEMAND-DRIVEN SUPPLY

The better I got at managing my portfolio at the co-op wholesaler, the more pressure I got from my managers to push product into the account. The weird thing was that after being so indoctrinated in the push mentality, it was, suddenly, so easy to see through the faulty thinking.

Everything about a push supply chain has to do with what was described early in the chapter—make it inefficient by *packing somebody's pantry*. It didn't matter whose pantry, just pack it full. In essence, if you could create something so inefficient that you force someone else to fix it to get rid of the product, you were successful. With that kind of thinking, you are not focused on customer needs. You are just thinking about your quarterly sales quota. I was amazed at the lengths some participants would go to create inefficient push supply chains.

The late 1980s were a tough time to be a brand-new vendor management inventory practitioner. Don't worry, though, I was laughing all the way to the bank. While all the others were trying to continue their ways of pushing product through, I was learning more and more about pulling product through by catering to the customer's desires. It took 30 years for someone to put a name to what I was doing, but they now call it *demand-driven supply*.

I started looking into tweaking the inventory levels. Everyone was ratcheting down days of supply at the end of the quarter to make the numbers look better, but all I ever was able to do by practicing that was run out of stock on a boatload of items. I couldn't keep the inventory down very long without a lot of grumbling by the retail store owners and managers. I was getting ready for a yearly business review (funny, I was going to give myself a business review of my own buying activities for the year, but I was going to be giving it to my buyer/mentor Joanne). I noticed a strange set of problems:

- Approximately 70 percent of my products were in a constant overstock situation when using the one week for demand and one week for safety stock rule-of-thumb calculation.
- About 20 percent of my products seemed to be understocked using the same rule.
- Advertised items tended to have a very high probability of being out of stock using the rule-of-thumb ad-buying process.
- My company had a problem supplying highly advertised products in stock during heavy promotional months. It did not have good visibility into the advertising support in the field until it was too late to react.
- The entire product portfolio was backhauled by contractors to the co-op wholesaler, and therefore I was not responsible for the logistics. That being said, I did notice the backhaulers were delivering product anywhere between one and four days late on 30 to 40 percent of the shipment only needing two days' transit.

At the time I made my business review to "myself" (okay, Joanne was in the room, too), I recommended that we shift our thinking on the rule-of-thumb inventory management techniques from simple days of supply and begin to look at servicing the stores with a combination of demand, demand fluctuation, actual market data from Information Resources Incorporated (IRI), inventory costs, and logistics costs. Those recommendations came after I had just shown everyone that in the year I had been managing the product portfolio, I had gotten inventory turns up to some of the highest in the account. My overall volume was up by 30 percent in Portland and 40 percent in Medford. According to IRI numbers, I had increased the market share of stores covered by the co-op wholesaler from 5 to 10 percent on my products.

I was ecstatic and wholeheartedly agreed with myself, but Joanne had some reservations. Allowing a vendor this kind of access to competitive information could, potentially, compromise the wholesaler's market standing by allowing communication of ad events to other competitors. However, using upstream communications to my company would allow for better advertising performance on key items. It was decided that I would communicate long-term advertising schedules so that my company could gear up to support the ads I set with the accounts. My hope was that this visibility to the lower level of the supply chain would give me better ad support.

CREATING MY ISLAND OF EFFICIENCY

I was able to morph the simplified rule-of-thumb ordering processes to a forecast using IRI advertising lift information, coupled with a safety-stock add-on of one week's average demand. Over time I used this projection to get to within a 5 percent accuracy of the actual volume. The process really helped in controlling the infamous 20 percent of the portfolio that was always in an understock mode. Products getting advertised created a far higher fluctuation in forecast confidence, and, at the time, we had no real way of focusing on that demand.

However, the overall rule-of-thumb process of keeping two weeks of stock on hand was killing me. Whenever I tried to increase my store service level, my inventories soared. Conversely, when Joanne asked me to lower the inventories at the end of a quarter, my out-of-stocks increased. If I stayed in the status quo, I could handle the overall inventory situation.

There was one other thing that was driving me crazy. My company was horrible in terms of providing consistent lead times and shipping complete orders, even though I was providing much longer lead-time notice. I would call into our customer service representative and complain about orders showing up three days late from a distribution center only 500 miles away. In turn, Joanne would get calls from the customer service rep saying that products a, b, and c would be shorted, and did she want to backorder them? Joanne just took a message and gave it to me. Keeping a tight leash on inventories with a supplier noted for inconsistent delivery is a nightmare that I could not control.

This led me to a realization that no matter how hard I tried, in the current situation, I could only create efficiencies in my portfolio. I started to call myself the *island of efficiency*. In my own little world, I was able to bring inventories into a very lean position and increase my turns to the point of being in the top five of all portfolios, but no matter how hard I tried, I couldn't do any better because of the outside influences.

This put me into a position where 95 percent of all buyers in supply chains find themselves. First, we become prisoners of what we can see and the reactions to what we see. Depending on where you are in the supply chain, the vision is opaque. This is especially true the further up the chain you are from the original demand. In turn, the reaction is also blunted. At the end of the chain, the reaction to the demand is all-important. This is why replenishment becomes so important at this point. Smaller inventory quantities and fluctuating demand can put a strain on you to react. Since the immediate upstream location does not know of the demand until you order, the reaction could be delayed or nonexistent. The human response is to couch your replenishment "bet" with extra inventory, just in case you have a supply disruption. If you have never seen this kind of supply chain reaction to walled communications in a supply chain, I would strongly advise you to play the MIT Beer Game[3] to understand the effects of creating islands of efficiencies.

For those of you who don't know about the MIT Beer Game it is an experiential learning business simulation game created by a group of professors at MIT Sloan School of Management in the early 1960s to demonstrate a number of key principles of supply chain management. The game is played by teams of at least four players, often in heated competition, and takes at least one hour to complete.

The purpose of the game is to understand the distribution-side dynamics of a multiechelon supply chain used to distribute a single item, in this case, cases of beer.

WHAT IS AN ISLAND OF EFFICIENCY?

I have looked everywhere to find a generally accepted supply chain definition for the term *island of efficiency*. You see it everywhere in supply chains, but there is no simple explanation for the phenomenon. Given that state of affairs, let me take a stab at it.

The Intended Island of Efficiency

We will review this, at length, later in the book, but the Kanban system developed by Toyota is a classic example of creating an island of efficiency (see Figure 1.2). Kanban is not an inventory control system. It is a scheduling system that enables users to determine what to produce, how to produce it, and how much to produce. However, the technique helps drive the inventory into position where it is delivered *just in time* for it to be used. In Kanban, inventory is evil. Therefore, the less you hold, the better. The key to Kanban that Toyota quickly learned is the ability to communicate outside of the island. If you didn't communicate, the lean inventories could be quickly eaten up by unforeseen activities.

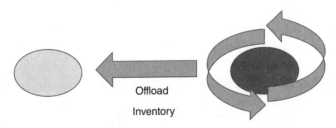

Offload

Inventory

Figure 1.2 The Kanban System

In my role as a pseudo-VMI buyer I was practicing a lot of Kanban techniques to ensure the inventory could be held at a lean level, but that I would still have the ability to shift strategy when needed. Communication was everything, and the goal of the intended island of efficiency was to make sure my little link in the chain would work as effectively as possible.

As we will soon see, it cannot be overemphasized how the Toyota Kanban production efficiencies have influenced modern distribution supply chain techniques in the last 40 years—for better and for worse.

The Unintended Island of Efficiency

In the intended island of efficiency, everyone working in their little link in the chain thinks they are pulling their own weight and effectively moving product to the final customer-facing location. As indicated in Figure 1.3, the arc data are severed so that very little immediate communication is actually propagated. What happens when there are barriers set up in technology that short-circuit the very best of human intentions and turn little links in the chain into what could best be described as inventory elephants on parade? Each chain link looks efficient, but when looked at as a whole, the supply chain takes on the appearance of bloated elephants. Each elephant is holding onto the tail of the one in front and blindly following the lead. More important, the further you get away from the initial customer demand, the more bloated the inventory gets. What would cause efficient links to turn

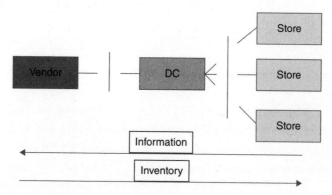

Figure 1.3 Unintended Island of Efficiency

into an inefficient chain? In almost every occurrence, it is a combination of technological shortcomings and human nature trying to correct it. In almost every instance, human intervention was to create a bigger and faster replenishment process.

In essence, an unintended island of efficiency is created when (1) the downstream demand has been accumulated and presented as an aggregated total, (2) there is a delay in the initial demand from the original customer, (3) your service level need is an average, and (4) the upstream supply is expected to be at a 100 percent service level.

1. The downstream demand has been accumulated and presented as an aggregated total.

   When demand is rolled up, the accumulated safety-stock calculations also get rolled up. This is the essence of the *bull-whip effect*. There will be larger and larger redundant stocks in place to cover this nonexistent demand variance.

2. There is a delay in the initial demand from the original customer.

   If the demand used for the link in the supply chain is not the initial customer demand, there is a delay to accumulate the demand at the upstream location. This accumulation creates a distortion of time so the forecasted demand is less and less accurate—and late in arriving.

3. Your downstream service level need is an average.

   Each downstream link in the chain might have a specific service level need, but there is little ability to discern differences between products and locations, so an average is used. You end up averaging to a small percentage of actually correct service level and leave the rest to fend for themselves.

4. The upstream supply is expected to be at a 100 percent service level.

   This is the bane of every buyer. A variance of demand creates a small to mid-size safety stock requirement, depending on the variance. A supply variance can be disastrous because instead of a small variance on one product, the supply variance makes for late arrival of lots of products. Several trucks showing up late by two days can put a whole product portfolio in jeopardy.

Late shipments and/or incomplete shipments take up most of the time a buyer spends on tactical activities. The natural reaction is to hold more stock to cover for the event of less than 100 percent service level.

These four issues have created massive problems for companies as they have tried to move to a more demand-driven supply model. During the period from 1995 to 2005, companies used their newly purchased ERP systems to help counter the problems encountered with supply chain issues. In turn, when it was found that new and better processes needed to be put in place, SCM systems continued to build out functionality. The efforts to overcome these inventory problems were most often focused on the great equalizer of out-of-balance inventories: supersizing the replenishment system with better and better transactional rigor. In hindsight, were we just trying to make a better and better bandage? In reality, the focus might have been better spent looking at why the inventories were out of balance in the first place.

How did we get to this place where technically "advanced global supply chains have added upward of 30 percent higher inventories than needed and actually reduced overall service levels"?[4]

NOTES

1. W. Yang, T. Felix, S. Chan, and V. Kumar, "Optimizing Replenishment Policies Using Genetic Algorithm for Single-Warehouse Multi-Retailer System," *Expert Systems with Applications: An International Journal Archive* 39(3) (2012): 3081–3086.
2. Erik Kruse, "From Push to Pull—Perfecting the Means," Supply Chain Resource Cooperative, September 4, 2003, http://scm.ncsu.edu/scm-articles/article/from-push-topull-perfecting-the-means.
3. MIT Beer Game: This game enables game players to simulate supply chain decisions.
4. Kruse, "From Push to Pull—Perfecting the Means."

CHAPTER 2

Achieving Timely and Accurate Responses to Customer Demand

P ush supply chain methodology: In 1640, Mary sits in front of the fire on a cold evening. She makes three candles and puts them in the corner of her dining room. The next day Linda, Martha, and Sally stop by Mary's house to share coffee and scones. They see the candles and decide to buy all three candles.

Pull supply chain methodology: While having coffee and scones in 1640, Linda, Martha, and Sally tell Mary they need candles. That night Mary sits in front of the fire and makes three candles and puts them in the corner of the dining room. Linda, Martha and Sally stop by the next day and buy the candles.

Not too tough to figure out, eh? In one example, Mary knew her friends needed candles, and in the other she had a good idea they needed candles. However, today's supply chains are in an identity crisis because of the demand-based definition of what "Mary knew her friends needed candles" really means.

PUSH AND PULL SUPPLY CHAINS

The original definitions of push and pull supply chains are pretty self-explanatory. The pull supply chain was predicated on known demand from specific customer needs. This was considered to be a build-to-order model. The classic view of a build-to-order supply chain was Mary's example of her friends asking her to make candles for them. A product was simply not built until it was ordered.

What was required for the pull model to work effectively?

- Customization of the product was paramount.
- Demand from orders was known.
- Customer did not expect the product to be immediately delivered.
- At every step of production and distribution, there were minimal inventory carrying costs.

The push supply chain was known as the built-to-stock model. This process was developed so products were manufactured in anticipation of customer needs. The idea was that the inventory could be built cost-effectively and delivered against potentially known demand. In this example, Mary builds some candles in anticipation of her friends needing some the next day.

What was required for the push model to work effectively?

- Customization was limited.
- Demand patterns were predicable.
- Customer expected to take ownership of the product quickly.
- There was an expectation of inventory costs somewhere in the supply chain.

If you look at the two models, the separation is predicated on customization, acceptable inventory, and understood or anticipated demand. Up until the Industrial Age, almost all supply chains were set up on the pull method except for the delivery of seasonal foodstuffs to market. In the early days, things were pretty much made to order. The Industrial Age, and especially the production capability of Henry Ford's Rouge Plant in Michigan, showed what kind of production savings could be had when a push model was enacted. By reducing the customization and giving customers an inexpensive, standardized product, Ford was able to get huge savings by driving long production runs with little or no downtime.

The automated production process with long runs gave customers products at low cost as long as they were willing to accept the standard output. As the old joke use to be told, "You can have a Model T in any color as long as it's black." With so many things being mass produced and the customer being dazzled with ever-increasing arrays of outputs, it was easy to accept the efficiencies of the push model. The problem that always becomes prevalent is that there are only a certain number of products that can be delivered to customers by having a lot of inventory built up by production. After a while, the need to have something that everyone else has is satisfied, and the consumer goes on to something else. If one looks at the Ford situation, the inexpensive Model Ts and Model As sold well until they had saturated the market for the inexpensive cars. Once that happened, the broad array of General Motors cars started taking over the market by giving the customer

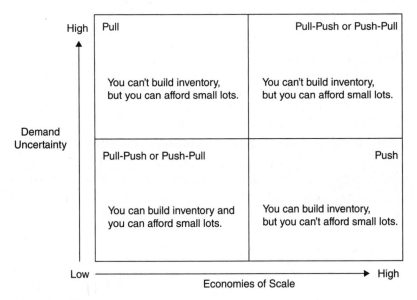

Figure 2.1 Push-Pull Quadrant
Source: Adapted from D. Simchi-Levi, P. Kaminsky, et al., Designing and Managing the Supply Chain: Concepts, Strategies, and Case Studies *(Boston: Irwin/McGraw-Hill, 2003).*

a choice. Even so, the choices were standardized, since GM cars were being produced on separate, smaller production lines.

The push-pull quadrants shown in Figure 2.1 demonstrates the problem facing manufacturing when dealing with the economies of scale and demand uncertainty. The simple cost of changing over a manufacturing line precludes small lot size production.

This tradeoff between efficient production runs and the distribution of nonstandardized products has been at the heart of the supply chain dilemma. The push model would dictate that production benefited as long as there was some kind of known or predictable demand pattern that the production could build to. The pull model would not be able to effectively compete except in an extremely volatile demand environment. Therefore, as long as demand was predictable the push model would win out as the most economical model.

ENTER TOYOTA AND THE KANBAN SYSTEM

In the late 1940s, Toyota of Japan was looking for ways to compete both domestically and internationally. It had seen the shift of consumer preferences in automobiles move away from the standardized, one-size-fits-all mentality to a market where consumers wanted a choice in makes, models, and most important, customized options.

If a car was to have choices in its makeup, a single production run was not feasible. The parts needed to accommodate those choices had to be on hand so production could nimbly shift back and forth between options. This flexibility required a lot more parts on the production floor, with no way to correctly anticipate the consumption until the car was moving down the assembly line.

Of all places for Toyota to look for guidance in operational efficiencies, a grocery supermarket in the United States called Piggly Wiggly would seem odd. However, both industries were morphing from a structured experience model to a new one centered on choices. At the time, the grocery industry was moving from a store model where the products were behind the counter to a model where products were right where the customer could pick and choose for themselves. Instead of dictating what the customer bought, the Piggly Wiggly grocer had to anticipate the demand and only carry what the customer wanted. This shift in paradigm in another industry caught Toyota's eye. Here, the grocer held just enough products to cover demand, and allowed customers to pick up what they needed and to proceed, unimpeded, to the checkout counter with their purchases. The idea was to understand that the granular demand was for the respective parts of an automobile and have just enough inventories to supply the production of the cars for the day.

Toyota developed a signaling process called Kanban that would work the same as a grocer seeing a bin of apples being consumed. *Kanban* literally means "signboard." The Kanban signboard is a card or ticket showing the consumption of a part. The Kanban becomes the pull or actual demand. The idea here is that the predictable demand is difficult to see so the production system needs to be very quick to react to a shift.

The Kanban card signaled a shift that propagated up through the supply chain. Therefore, the card not only told the production floor what to use, it signaled out both to manufacturing and raw materials that consumption had happened, and the reaction was systematic. Over time this card system developed into an electronic process that would signal everyone in the supply chain, from vendor onward, that demand was sensed, signaled, and acted upon. The Kanban system that started in Toyota is now used in such systems as SAP, Oracle, and Infor to signal actual demand so that Kanban triggers can be created for purchase orders to vendors and internal facilities. This methodology is known as "deterministic demand" and has been used in production planning for decades. Deterministic demand requires large amounts of historical information to come up with predictive models with little deviation of demand.

Now, before we get too far along in this story, what would have to be in place for a Toyota/Kanban system to be successful beyond just the place on the supply chain where it was practiced?

The answer to that is that the upstream supplier must know the actual demand with enough advance notice to be able to react to the demand efficiently. The problem with that premise is that the Kanban system is sending actual sales numbers. This number was fine as long as there were no unpredictable swings in the Kanban consumption. Given the long production run functionality and the fairly predictable demand for that production run, the Kanban consumption signal was fine. However, if there were any kind of deviation in that demand, there would be a huge burden placed on the immediate upstream supplier to that production point in the supply chain. Unpredictability is the nemesis of the Kanban system—and just about any other.

FROM KANBAN TO JUST-IN-TIME PRODUCTION

In a way, Kanban brought a sense of structure to the production side of the supply chain. By focusing on the direct correlation between demand and the need for a part or product, Kanban created the actual demand for consumption triggers in production. These triggers were constantly reviewed to increase efficiencies. By definition, inventories were considered the result of inefficiencies. Inventory, therefore, was evil in the Kanban system and needed to be done away with if the Kanban system was to be perfected.

Oftentimes, Kanban and just-in-time (JIT) inventory management strategies are considered to be one and the same. However, in actuality, Kanban is a way of achieving JIT strategies by way of signals for product availability and the speed it takes to replenish. The ability to measure availability, scheduling, and replenishment gives users the option for improvement of processes. The focus on improvement dovetails with the JIT philosophy of return on investment through reduction of in-process inventory and associated carrying costs. A quick notice of an inventory or stock reduction is at the heart of JIT.

The Kanban/JIT philosophy had strong influences on production scheduling all through the 1960s and 1970s and was a key component to similar movements such as lean manufacturing. All seemed well on the production side of the push supply chain. The lean manufacturing focus placed more and more efficiencies to the production side of the equation, but as was discussed earlier, this also created an island of efficiency problem in the organization. The effective application of JIT production capabilities cannot be done in a vacuum. Without the outward view into the whole organization the "opposite of the desired result" can occur.[1] The first opposite of the desired result issue centered on quality. It was one thing to have a part ready to be consumed. If that part is not acceptable, the entire system grinds to a halt, causing higher than expected downtime costs. In the situation of Toyota, Toyota engineers created a range of tolerance for product or part acceptance to overcome the quality issue. Parts had to constantly be tested for acceptability, and vendors had to be held to a high standard for the JIT system to work consistently and not have production slowdowns. Quite literally, supply disruptions in the JIT are almost worse than an unforeseen upward blip in demand.

Again, the production side seemed to have the lead in this supply chain efficiency process, but unless the whole organization supply chain was aligned, the potential for total efficiency could be jeopardized by simply moving inefficiencies to either the vendor or the downstream distribution system. On the vendor side, in order for

JIT to work there needs to be a strong collaboration for both demand signals and product quality. Toyota has done a good job at maintaining these strong collaborative relationships with its vendors. This is not always the case in vendor relationships. Vendors have a difficult role to play in the JIT supply chain because often they do not have any visibility into the actual demand and must rely on incomplete or intermittent information to make supply decisions. This can create problems in their own supply chains. Over the past 20 years, vendors involved in JIT supply chains often have charged a 5 percent surcharge to counter potential JIT supply chain costs shifted from the upstream customer to the vendor or supplier.[2]

Why did this happen?

WHAT IS NEEDED FOR A JIT SYSTEM TO WORK EFFICIENTLY?

Just-in-time inventories run on a pull supply chain philosophy. Kanban/JIT is based on actual demand measurements. As the production process occurs, parts are consumed, and the Kanban signals are alerting the system that the inventory is being depleted. As the depletion of parts proceeds to a specific point, the parts inventory is replenished by a vendor/supplier. Early adaptations of JIT/Kanban used simplistic demand models as a plan for inventory placement. In the instance of Toyota a last-year's sales history was the beginning point for production plans.

So, you've got a production-based supply chain set up with inventory positioned to support exactly what you did last year. You can imagine how difficult it is to supply this JIT/Kanban supply chain if (1) demand is more unstable than expected and (2) you are a supplier and you have to chase the actual consumption numbers provided by the Kanban signals. Now you see why whenever JIT management is discussed the ultimate need for the system to work is a *very compliant* supplier/vendor. By Toyota's own admission, the success of the JIT/Kanban system required vendors to be very reliable because to have any disruption of the JIT supply chain would result in costly production halts. In fact, most JIT practitioners winnow their suppliers

down to a select number of trusted suppliers who work as collabora-
tively as possible just as Toyota did years earlier.

A good example of this type of relationship would be the interaction between Dell Computer and its suppliers. Dell works on a JIT-pull
supply chain methodology where a customer can order a computer
with various options and Dell will build it to specifications. In order for
this JIT system to work, Dell cannot keep large amounts of computer
part inventories onsite, so it relies on a supplier network to react to
parts consumption just like that of Toyota. Dell expects the supplier to
provide a high service level and speed of replenishment in order to be
considered part of the Dell supplier system.

So what did the Dell suppliers do to accommodate the Dell
requirements? They did the same thing the Toyota suppliers did:
Position parts inventories as close to the Dell facilities as possible
and maintain larger than normal inventory levels to accommodate
potential demand volatility. This movement to the end of a supply
chain with extra inventory is a classic accommodation method for
suppliers needing high service levels, and it is done extensively in JIT-
pull situations.

Given the change of behavior by the suppliers to the JIT-pull environment, did the total supply chain become more efficient? Maybe,
but in most cases the costs of the JIT supply chain shifted to the suppliers, and the efficiencies went to the production system. Dell and
Toyota definitely realized an increase in efficiencies, but at what costs?
As indicated before, suppliers who understand JIT supply chains usually understand there is going to be a minimum of a 5 percent hike
in costs.[3]

As an aside, when one looks beyond the Dell & Toyota situation,
there is a specific industry that has taken this Kanban/JIT process to
the extreme. That would be the retail/consumer packaged goods (CPG)
industry where the retailer has become the "tail that wags the dog." In
virtually no other industry has a trading partner shifted more inventory
onto the vendor than in consumer packaged goods during the quest to
become "pull supply chain" centric. CPG vendors have a myopic view
of the final consumer, and it has grown over the past 30 years. Retailers in the space have actively reduced their inventory days of supply,

while the CPG vendor's inventory has grown. Indeed, the Kanban/JIT 5 percent inventory shift has occurred and, in many cases, has doubled to 10 percent. According to a recent Gartner study, the days of supply inventory split between retailers and vendors in CPG is at all-time highs and bigger than just about any other industry.[4]

Whether it is Toyota, Dell, or any other practitioner, the JIT-pull methodology was getting noticed. There is no denying the production efficiencies of keeping limited stock on hand and replenishing just what needed to be consumed sounded great. Indeed, it seemed like the perfect answer to all supply chain problems. From the mid-1980s through mid-1990, JIT was the new methodology of the moment in supply chain practices. It was during this time that many supply chain executives and academics were looking at how the production methodologies of JIT could be expanded into the distribution chain. This is also where the blurring of the lines between push and pull supply chain practices got out of control. Supply chain people were enamored with the concept of only making what was requested. Just as our puritanical concept at the beginning of the chapter suggests, if Mary knows what she needs to make, she doesn't need to have a lot of inventory. With the idea of only having to stock enough to supply known demand, like that found in a JIT-production system, the distribution supply chain could become super-efficient.

A BROADER VIEW OF JIT/KANBAN IN ACTION

Lora Cecere and Abby Meyer cite various industries in their article "What Drives Supply Chain Excellence," which discusses improvements in supply chain costs and responsiveness. In their research they look at six different industries: high-tech and electronics, consumer packaged goods, food, chemicals, industrial, and pharmaceuticals. Each of these industries has had variant levels of success in developing strong and responsible supply chains. There is an interesting factor in place when looking at these industries. In industries where there are strong retailing entities at the consumer-facing end of the supply chain, the industry tends to lag in supply chain metrics. In consumer packaged goods and food, the retail entities are practicing JIT/Kanban-type activities. In an effort to push costs back onto the vendor, the retailer is relieving itself of certain inventory carrying costs. The problem is that just like the production in JIT/Kanban the costs are shifted, but not eliminated. Over the past 10 years, according to Cecere and Meyer, the industries where the vendor has more influence with the end customer had better inventory control, as a whole, compared to industries that were retailer centric.[5] A supply chain that is dependent on reacting to customer demand must have visibility down to that customer. If it doesn't, it has to rely on a delayed and aggregate demand signal. This aggregate demand signal creates a bullwhip effect and is subject to shifts in cost burdens that flow up the chain. As the Cecere and Meyer article stresses, industries need to rethink their practices and gain organizational alignment to redefine supply chain excellence.[6]

THE KNOWN DEMAND BECOMES THE PREDICTABLE DEMAND

Push and pull supply chains go back to Mary and her candles.

At some point a supply chain makes a leap of faith from known demand to predicted demand. Known demand will be orders, but predicted demand is the forecast. Companies that rely on small lot sizes and orders can deal with a truly custom-based pull supply chain. Very few modern supply chains are built to sustain that kind of production schedule. Once we have production schedules and cost of change to production increases, there needs to be some kind of predictability to the demand stream. This allows for anticipation.

The tipping points between a full-blown built-to-order supply chain and a build-to-inventory supply chain fall into four categories. Let's take a look at Mary's situation.

1. How much customization is required?

   In the make-to-order/pull situation, there can be as much customization as required because each unit of production is based on a known order. Mary could be making specific candles for each of her friends based on what they requested of her. In modern-day situations, Dell is doing the same thing with computers. You won't see Dell computers in a retail store because each is built to specific criteria put forth on the order.

2. What are the delivery expectations?

The customer expects a lag in delivery with a make-to-order situation. The more customized it is, the more delay is usually expected. JIT morphs this a bit because production parts are expected to be delivered quickly. However, the actual parts to be delivered are pretty standardized and are not customized in the true sense of the pull environment.

3. What are the minimum inventory costs?

In Mary's candle situation, she is going to keep on hand just enough inventories to make, on average, enough candles for the next day's customer orders. In a production environment, the known finished goods inventory dictates how much raw material inventory needs to be on hand.

4. What is the known demand?

Mary knows she has three orders she needs to fill for her friends. Does she expect someone to just show up at her doorstep tomorrow and demand a candle? Not likely, as she will tell the demanding interloper that he will have to wait until she can make that candle.

Mary's husband, George, comes downstairs after listening to the conversation between Mary and the interloper asking for a candle at the door. He says to Mary, "What if you make two or three candles and put them in the corner just in case someone comes to the door asking for a candle? How many more candles could you sell in a month?"

Mary says, "Well, I get two to three people a week coming by asking me for a candle that they need immediately. Given that, I would say I could sell eight to ten more candles."

George gets to thinking for a minute and asks, "Mary, are they picky about what the candle looks like, or would they just take the normal candle you make?"

Mary laughs and says, "They would take whatever is on hand."

Between Mary and George, they figure out that Mary hardly needs any additional raw materials to make the additional candles. If one of her friends orders the same candle that is in stock, she can save time by just pulling the candle from out of the corner and giving it to her friend. The time saved by not having to make a custom candle goes to efficiencies of time. Since Mary can turn out an average candle in less time than she needs for the custom candles, she is working less time in the evenings. Finally, word gets out that Mary has candles readily available, so you don't have to wait to get a custom candle. Now more and more people are showing up at her door wanting a regular candle instead of a custom candle. Mary's candle business is booming. The business is morphing from a pull supply chain to a push supply chain.

What happened to Mary's business?

- Custom to standard: People were willing to accept a tradeoff for availability.
- Speed of delivery: There was an unrealized market for Mary's standard candles.
- Inventory costs: The efficiencies of making and storing a standard candle made having the candle as a finished good instead of raw materials less expensive.
- Known demand was shifting to predictable demand.

Anyone who had been around the distribution supply chain business in the 1990s can remember where they were when someone said "just-in-time inventory." It was like Mary's husband, George, was the distribution manager sitting in some meeting in every company across the globe and blurting out, "just-in-time distribution!" Distribution supply chains could become super-efficient if the rules found in JIT production could be morphed to the distribution system. The question was, what needed to be morphed? Production could already handle a make-to-stock situation, and most of the cost of inventory was understood. Therefore, two key ingredients to a JIT distribution system were (1) reaction time or speed of delivery and (2) making predictable demand known. This is the point where the lines between a push and pull supply chain not only got blurred, they got obliterated. At the time when JIT distribution became a vogue methodology, the push system was suddenly "bad" and the pull system was "good."

The key driver of this morphing is not customization, speed, or costs. The actual driver is the definition of demand. When Mary and George were sitting down in their version of a sales and operations planning (S&OP) meeting, they were talking about the tradeoffs between building to order and building to stock. They realized they had a market for standardized candles that people would buy because they needed them rather than wanting something specific. They needed the candle quickly, so speed of delivery was important. The third, but not final, aspect of the process was the tradeoff between holding inventory in a raw-material state versus a finished-goods state. In this case, Mary and George saw very little cost penalty if there was the ability to get close on their estimate on what was needed to cover the build-to-stock finished candles. This leaves us with the final aspect—demand.

When a company is confident about the demand, planning becomes much easier. There literally is no planning in a make-to-order pull system. All you have to do is manage the finished goods delivery expectation and order raw materials to complete the production process. The rub is when a company uses a push methodology and there is a lack of confidence about the demand. We will see, in future chapters, the complexities organizations will go through to forecast demand so that there is confidence in the demand numbers. In turn, entire processes are set in place to help individuals collaborate to sharpen those statistical estimates with expert knowledge or intuition. In the case of Mary and George, they were relying on guesstimates from Mary's experiences with her friends over the past few months. In a way, this was no different from the methods used by JIT Kanban production companies: Use actual sales as a baseline planning estimate and keep constant focus on the amount of inventory consumption to see if you were trending up or down to the previous year's consumption.

THE JIT PRODUCTION SUPPLY CHAIN WEAKNESSES BECOME AMPLIFIED IN THE DISTRIBUTION CHAIN

The biggest weakness in the JIT production supply chain was the ability for suppliers to quickly react to unexpected needs of the production line. The Kanban system would alert everyone to the consumption, but if there was a larger than normal pull on parts compared to last year, the supplier had to react. If the supplier didn't react, the result was a slowdown or stoppage of production. As we saw, the natural reaction of suppliers in a JIT system was to carry extra stock to buffer themselves from this problem. In turn, those that knew about the JIT situation would build into their supplier estimates a 5 percent increase in costs due to the pushing of those costs from the customer to the supplier inventories and logistics. The JIT production system is very good at optimizing the inventory costs and production costs at the single facility. The weakness is that it just pushes inventory costs onto other participants in the supply chain.

SOME DISTRIBUTION ISSUES

Now let's move the horizon so we are not looking at a production facility and backward into suppliers. Let's move the visibility to the distribution system within a company. We are now positioned between production and the final customer who is consuming products. In the JIT production system, the suppliers were the buffer to variations in consumption at the production level. They had to react quickly or the production system would suffer. The JIT production system was practicing pull methodologies, and the cost savings were very good. In the late 1980s and early 1990s, management was hearing about this new efficiency process and how it could work in the distribution channel. You can imagine the concern on the face of the distribution managers—could their own production system react like the upstream suppliers, and where would those predictable demand numbers come from?

As stated before, if you know what the demand is, planning can be quite simple. The problem for the distribution chain is to figure out where the demand is coming from and how far ahead of time it is really known. Distribution managers must position product to react to demand, in most cases anticipated demand, not known demand. If this was a true pull methodology chain, they would simply move it to where people ordered it from. However, in the newly developed pull distribution chain, the organization's "production" becomes the "JIT supplier," and now the end customer expects uninterrupted supply chain service. Something tells the passive observer in this little story that an organization is not going to give up all of these newfound efficiencies just because distribution can't tell how much product needs to be ordered.

THE CUSTOMER PUSHES BACK

The ever-more-demanding customer expects to have an uninterrupted supply of goods just like the JIT-focused production environment. However, in the distribution system the organization is in a tough situation. It can't push the costs to another part of the chain without pushing it onto itself.

> Increasingly, retailers have pushed working capital back in the supply chain to suppliers and suppliers have done the same, pushing working capital to their suppliers, increasing the total cost of the supply chain.[7]

Even before JIT methodologies began to filter into the supply chain, retailers practiced one major aspect of the process. By relying on dependable and compliant suppliers, the retailer could push inventory costs back up the chain and squeeze more efficiencies into their systems. Retailing lives on the ability to quickly react to ever-shifting customer demand patterns. If the retailer can get the supplier to react quickly to the changing demand in a reliable way, the required inventory the retailer must carry can be shrunk. In the past the retailer would extract cost efficiencies by way of promo buy picking, forward buy options, or taking advertising monies. However, now retailers see the ability to push long-term efficiencies by trading on the same JIT processes found at Toyota or Dell. By negotiating with a vendor on replenishment efficiencies, the retailer can push the costs back into the vendor's supply chain. A two-day reduction of days of supply from a vendor can have a massive return in freed-up capital over time. This reaction time negotiation creates a dilemma with the vendor. Now, with a need to quickly react to a retailer's service level demands and a faster turnaround in replenishment, inventories need to be pushed closer to the retailer. Given that there are more regional warehouses than plant warehouses at the end of the vendor chain, the inventory gets multiplied.

Even more of an issue is the problem of known versus expected demand from the retailers. The mantra of the pull-based JIT system is the dependency on known demand to create the efficiencies. If the retailer(s) don't share demand information in enough time for a vendor to react, the vendor is forced to place inventory in "anticipation" of the demand, whether it is known or not. With the inability to effectively see end-user demand, and the need to provide high service levels in a shorter period of time, the required distribution inventory needed will have to rise regardless of how efficient your production system is.

THE SQUEEZE IS ON

The distribution supply chain is being squeezed at both ends. The JIT/production processes are in place so that there will be enough inventory on hand to execute long production runs. Given the reliance on organizational needs to be efficient in operations, the company will continue to focus on keeping the JIT/production in place and only make tactical changes when the need arises. In turn, the end customer is demanding ever-increasing efficiencies in service level and replenishment speed without the benefit of known demand. The distribution chain has become the barometer of internal efficiencies in the organization. If the system is in harmony, there will be just enough inventory available to satisfy the end customer with the agreed-upon service level. If it is not in harmony, the organization can be caught in a bullwhip of overstock and understock inventories and/or obsolete products. The inefficiencies of a distribution chain can show up in just about every line in a company balance sheet or operating income statement. It used to be that executives thought of a supply chain as a black hole where product simply moved through the company. Now, it has become apparent that not only can an efficient distribution system save money, it can define the company itself as well.

CREATING AN EFFICIENT SUPPLY CHAIN USING JIT FUNCTIONALITY

For a moment, let's go back to our candle analogy to see how companies have reacted to this squeeze of JIT methodologies. Mary's initial business was built on known demand. Customers were willing to wait for delivery of a custom-product built specifically for them. It was found that more and more customers were in need of a standard candle and would purchase it at the time of need. In most businesses, Mary's standard candle would become the staple of the company. In Mary's case, she is dealing with a single product at a single location. What happens if Mary expands her business?

Her three friends become distributers for Mary's candles. Immediately, Mary runs into a problem. Her friends don't know about custom candles and that different colors are customization. They just want the standard candle, but they want the standard candle in different colors. To make matters worse, her friends have no idea what the demand is for the various candles—they just need a lot of them. Mary starts making a lot of standard candles in different colors and sending them to her friends. Over time, the feedback is that some colors sell better than others, and the sales of the various colors also have some kind of dependency on the time of year.

The brown candles sell well in the fall, the red candles sell well in the winter, and everything slows down in the summer. Mary is starting to see the benefits of forecasting and seasonality. While it is not known demand, she is getting better at anticipating the customer demand. There is something else she is noticing. The cost of coloring the candles increases the cost of materials and the cost of labor, and makes it very difficult to put together a good assortment of candles for a shipment to her friends.

What if she only makes white candles and provides colored wax to her friends so they can dip the candles in front of the customer when they want a specific color?

In production circles, this is called *postponement*. By postponing the final steps of production until the right moment, the company takes advantage of several key aspects of the production and distribution model. In the end, it is breaking down the process and creating a JIT methodology where it makes sense to hold product in postponement production (pull) or move forward with a full production to supply (push):

- Keeping inventory positioned as raw materials instead of finished goods, you can keep costs lower. Mary was able to shift raw materials costs to her friends, but the cost was less than it would have been for finished candles.

■ By delaying the final steps of production, you have a better idea of the correct demand for the item and can reduce variability. Since Mary's friends were dipping candles right in front of the customer, they only had to come up with an aggregate demand for white candles and make the change at the last minute.

In our little analogy, we see how companies use JIT mythologies to assign processes to specific products. This process of figuring what products should be included in a push or pull methodology is focused on the tipping point. At some point along the production/distribution cycle, there is a point where it is more advantageous to maintain ready inventory in a raw material form and build to a need compared to building to a specific demand number with a single version of the product. The problem with this kind of decision making is in the complexity. In Mary's situation, she has, basically, one product and a few color variations. The complexity arises with many products, especially when production runs are introduced. Since you might have thousands of products in different sizes, colors, and flavors, it is a very difficult process to figure out the tipping point for each product. In the end, most companies try to lump similar items together in an effort to reduce this complexity, but any time you have aggregations or lumping you take the average, and to a large extent it is almost impossible to get the push/pull correct. It is just too complicated, and the splitting of the tipping is based on so many factors that inefficiencies get amplified.

PUSH-PULL TIPPING POINTS

Finding the tipping point of products or the known tradeoff between holding materials in a work-in-progress cycle as shown in Figure 2.2, so that there is a completion of production, was the perfect way to marry the push and pull mythologies from an internal position. If the product was more customized in nature, the production could wait for an order to create a Kanban-type reaction. If the product was customizable at a later date, a postponement method could be assigned to help in the

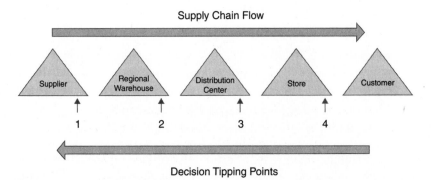

Figure 2.2 Inventory Decision Points
Source: Adapted from Vivek Sehgal, "Push or Pull?" Supply Chain Musings, October 7, 2009.

differentiation. Finally, if a product was standard enough that large lots of product could be produced, it could be positioned when needed.

IN SEARCH OF TRUE DEMAND

Companies found that the principles of JIT inventories created problems in the distribution chain. There was only a small supply of compliant, understanding participants on whom costs could be offloaded at either end of the chain. The result was an expanding safety valve of inventory accumulating in the distribution system. Tipping points worked well inside the organization, but once the distribution chain was touched, the majority of products had to be positioned or placed at various tipping points in the distribution chain to overcome response times of the end customer. Pull supply chains require customers to be compliant to time so they get the custom product they ordered. Just as Mary found, if a product is deemed to be standard, the speed of delivery overcomes the pull process and a different form of demand must be acceptable aside from orders.

> While there are many advantages to the pull approach—
> higher service levels, lower carrying costs, decreased
> inventory levels and fewer markdowns—there are some
> drawbacks. Chiefly, companies that rely solely on pull
> replenishment are susceptible to forecast inaccuracies if

inventory planning is done incorrectly. A forecast is simply a guess since consumer-buying behaviors are not always predictable. Basing a forecast entirely on what products sell or are invoiced for may result in a self-fulfilling prophecy in which the company only plans and replenishes based on past performance. In order for pull planning to be successful, *it must be based on true demand.* That alone can present a major challenge for today's companies. By pulling inventory into its network, retailers and suppliers can only carry inventory based on what they believe their consumers will want to purchase.[8] (Italics added.)

A pull supply chain has always been based on true or actually known demand, but this is where the vision gets a bit murky. What does true demand mean, and when, if ever, does it become the actual demand that powers a pull supply chain?

- Is the demand the result of consumption at customer-facing locations such as stores?
- Is the demand upstream the result of the downstream consumer demand or the downstream warehouse demand?
- How long is it before a forecast becomes true demand?
- Does the demand signal become true just because you believe it to be better?
- Do you have enough time to react to the true demand when it finally becomes known?

The search for true demand as a driver of the supply chain in the 1990s created a morphing of the push and pull methodologies into something that is literally run by all organizations today: the push-pull hybrid. This hybrid model is based on the premise that you push produce and pull distribute. The focus of the push-produce side of the equation is on costs, while the pull-distribute side is focused on service level. Therefore, there needs to be a synergy between production planning and sales so that the true demand can be communicated and acted upon in the most cost-effective manner and with the highest customer service levels.

However, one of the biggest problems found in this hybrid model is that the true demand signal morphs as it travels through the organization. It comes in as a granular point-of-sale input based on individual products and individual locations and then aggregates up into the organization. Once inside the organization, true demand transitions from a service-level key performance indicator (KPI) found in distribution and moves into a cost KPI in production. This inward, organizational focus creates an amplification of all of the JIT issues found in the production process. Each step in the organization is trying to optimize itself against the potential gap in supply. As we found in the JIT environment at Toyota, Dell, and others, there was a tendency to push costs onto the upstream location/supplier. However, in organizations practicing a push-pull hybrid methodology, each step in the supply chain is sending amplified signals to each upstream location. This is not just the aggregated "true" demand (actually, just predicted demand); it is sending along all of the baggage of the forecast, like aggregated forecast variance and aggregated average service levels.

As previously stated in "From Push to Pull—Perfecting the Means," suppliers who had experience with JIT processes understood that there was a 5 percent cost shift if a contract was accepted with a JIT customer. Remember, this is just a one-link-in-the-chain separation between a supplier of raw materials and a production site. If you take all of the links in an organizational supply chain and extrapolate the pushing and pulling of costs, it is not surprising to get the following result:

> AMR's study found that some companies in this hybrid mode have incurred up to a 5 percent higher supply chain operations cost with up to 30 percent higher inventory and significantly lower customer service.[9]

Conventional wisdom led many operations managers to focus primarily on operating their businesses as efficiently as possible. They believed they could be most successful if they strived for high product volume, high product standardization, and a continuous process. However, turbulent and misunderstood demand left them with excess inventory.

In the early 2000s, the introduction of inventory optimization was heralded as a perfect platform to reduce inventories and increase service levels. Early adopters were getting tremendous returns, but for the most part, the solutions were being ignored or had morphed into replenishment models.

Over the next few years, several large-scale adopters of inventory optimization began to realize huge savings in their inventory positions and reached almost unheard-of service levels depending on their need. It was during this time that I, as a product manager, began to notice how our inventory optimization users were gaining efficiencies.

In almost every case where an inventory optimization installation was successful, the user was shifting away from forecasting demand at every level of its supply chain hierarchy to communicating the leaf node or customer-facing demand signals up through the hierarchy. This shift of focus coupled with linking the supply chain together via *arc data* facilitated a synchronized supply chain that zeroed in on supplying to customer demand. It was an epiphany. Forward-thinking companies were using inventory optimization to make their push-pull supply chains work the way they were designed to work.

Up until inventory optimization was introduced, companies had to rely on alerts and reports to overcome their inherent transactional system shortcomings. With inventory optimization, the corrected inputs are positioned so that the system can react to predicted demand in an optimized and logical fashion. I was finally able to see inventory optimization for what it was—the last step in creating a supply chain that leans toward customer satisfaction but maintains the lowest cost inventory. In essence, inventory optimization becomes the hyphen in the push-pull supply chain.

NOTES

1. D. Simchi-Levi, P. Kaminsky, and E. Simchi-Levi, *Designing and Managing the Supply Chain: Concepts, Strategies, and Case Studies* (Boston: Irwin/McGraw-Hill, 2003).
2. Shigeo Shingo and Andrew P. Dillon, *A Study of the Toyota Production System* (New York: Productivity Press, 1989), 187.
3. Erik Kruse, "From Push to Pull—Perfecting the Means," Supply Chain Resource Cooperative, September 4, 2003, http://scm.ncsu.edu/scm-articles/article/from-pushtopull-perfecting-the-means.
4. Annual Gartner Supply Chain Study Highlights, *Supply Chain Digest*, June 18, 2010.

5. Lora Cecere and Abby Meyer, "What Drives Supply Chain Excellence?" *Supply Chain Insights*, February 15, 2013.

6. Ibid.

7. Ibid.

8. Greg Marmulak, "Supply Chain Comment: Balancing Push and Pull Strategies," *Supply Chain Digest*, March 31, 2011.

9. Kruse, "From Push to Pull—Perfecting the Means."

CHAPTER **3**

Just-in-Time and Enterprise Resource Planning Rise Together

Throughout the 1990s, organizations were upgrading their internal computer systems to embrace enterprise resource planning (ERP) systems from companies like SAP and Oracle. These systems were designed to facilitate all of the transactional activities that would occur and provide aggregated and hierarchical reporting. Given that a supply chain is like a river running through an organization, it was only natural for the ERP system to be used for inventory control and replenishment planning. It is interesting that the just-in-time (JIT) and ERP movements intersected as both were rising at the same time and, because of their respective shortcomings, quite naturally dovetailed together.

This dovetailing is due to the single site or facility concentration of JIT and ERP. As you remember from the previous chapter, the JIT production methodology focuses the cost improvements on production and moves the inventory risk back onto the supplier. The ERP system, due to its underlying data structures, makes assumptions about upstream and downstream inputs so that it can focus on the costs at the single location. The focus of a methodology and a technology toward single-echelon efficiencies allowed a lot of JIT methodologies to transition into the ERP calculations that are still in inventory management processes to this day.

DENORMALIZED TABLES

The transactional nature of ERP systems requires them to operate in near–real time using normalized tables—large tables that have been converted into a number of smaller tables to eliminate as much information redundancy as possible (see Figure 3.1). The small tables, called star schemas, are arranged so that the user can extract the information needed from other tables. Each table can quickly make the correct connections to other table combinations to retrieve necessary information. For instance, as the result of star schemas extracting data from various tables, a call center agent who needs some, but not all, customer information would see the name, address, cell phone number, cell phone model, and previous notes when responding to a technical problem.

When the user needs online analytical processing (OLAP) denormalization, data are extracted, transformed, and loaded (ETL) from

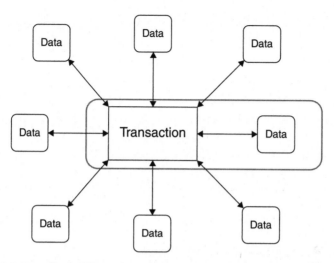

Figure 3.1 Normalized Tables Grab Small Bits of Data to Complete a Transaction

normalized tables into a format that can be analyzed (instead of simply being displayed). This array of table information for OLAP is called a snowflake schema and is designed to quickly pull data into usable OLAP cubes that can be viewed from several different perspectives. For example, OLAP data could be viewed as combinations of information over time; OLAP cubes are the basis for analytical review of transactional activities.

Denormalized tables create problems when users attempt to perform higher-level analytics or optimization with them. Analytics and optimization require calculations using variables—lots of variables. While most normalized tables and schemas adhere to a three-normal-forms (3NF) design, the number of variables required for optimization creates extremely large numbers of denormalized tables. The difficulty comes in when arranging the denormalized tables into logical snowflake patterns, because in fast-moving transactional systems, computing performance can and will erode quickly. In response, ERP developers created shortcuts to circumvent the problems caused by variables. The concerns then become ones of confidence: whether the information has value, is deficient, or is misleading because of some miscalculation or because of a misalignment of table data (see Figure 3.2).

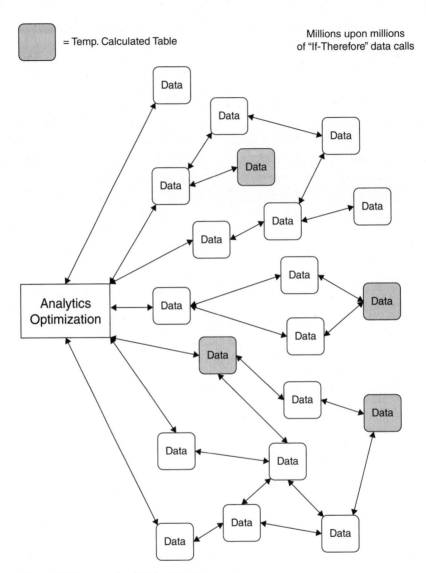

Figure 3.2 Denormalized Tables Process

The opportunities for miscalculated or misleading information are nearly infinite. Consider, for example, the complexity of a simple product like shampoo. Where did its raw materials come from? How many warehouses stored the materials? Where did the raw materials get combined, processed, and manufactured? The complexity grows exponentially when considering the millions of product combinations produced by consumer packaged goods, electronics, food and beverages, health-care products, pharmaceuticals, and industrial and durable goods companies.

Because of the enormity of the data requirements, high-powered analytics and optimization processes normally run as weekend batch jobs, to extract, transform, and load data from disparate, diverse sources into an optimization run. The objective is to pull this information together so that the system can attempt to understand the complex networks of inventory flow.

ERP systems have a limited ability to create denormalized tables. The requirement is to have large-scale batch runs outside of the transactions so that optimization can occur with high levels of confidence without degrading performance. Since batch run optimization is not inherent to ERP systems a shortcut process is introduced to create islands of efficiency, where it views a location or node as a single entity and then attempts to compile data specific for that location to produce projected best practice rules for the item-location pairings.

Manufacturers and retailers know that efficient management of their supply chain can be a competitive differentiator, but they struggle with customers' ever-increasing demands on overtaxed transactional and operational systems.

Industry executives increasingly acknowledge that moving from a push environment, where suppliers have relative control over their inventories, to today's pull environment, where customers dictate inventory, adds extra volatility to their ERP and supply chain management (SCM) systems. As a result, manufacturing companies are hedging their bets by acquiring and maintaining safety stocks to counteract the potential disruptive forces of unanticipated customer demand. From an SCM systems perspective, companies are using workarounds or special alert systems developed on an ad-hoc, reactive basis. The companies have still failed to achieve an optimized, balanced, or efficient state of inventory due to the inherent structure of ERP systems that creates problems for those trying to reduce safety stocks with analytics and optimization. What holds ERP systems back from conducting their own advanced optimization activities?

SEQUENTIAL OPTIMIZATION

The ERP processing of single, node-based denormalized tables is called *single stage calculations* or sequential optimization, where (as shown in Figure 3.3) the islands of efficiency links in the chain are optimized, and the system goes to the next link up the chain to continue optimization in sequence. The ERP process is locked into this sequential optimization format; there are few or no arc connections between the link locations, a limitation that reduces the number of variables that can be used, essentially creating a de facto optimization process of its own, with little flexibility or agility. *Arc* information is the introduction of unique relationships between inventory locations and the products being housed. For instance, actual service level requirements and actual lead time variability from upstream and downstream locations are considered to be arc information. Arc information creates the ability to see changes in such things as demand more quickly or anticipate shifts in inventory needs due to changes in variability.

While sequentially optimized islands of efficiency do generate some benefits, they also will amplify demand variations and literally make supply variability invisible. This occurs because they operate without knowledge of or visibility to communications within the chain, making it nearly impossible to maintain optimized inventories. The bullwhip effect can then throw everything else out of alignment when companies are attempting to use transactional ERP or SCM systems to develop optimized supply chain planning.

The following sections examine these activities and why they create problems in a transactional ERP or SCM system.

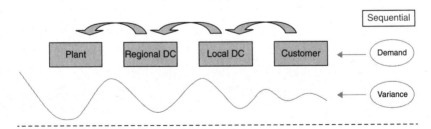

Figure 3.3 Sequential Optimization Process

UPSTREAM SERVICE LEVELS

Figure 3.4 depicts how the ERP or SCM system tries to optimize the customer-facing storefront (POS_1) with a 95 percent service level. Because the shortcut process in the transactional system is to optimize the island of efficiency, it is not going to cross over any variables from the upstream location (WH_1). The system's business rule or assumption is to provide a 100 percent service level at WH_1 to the downstream customer-facing location (POS_1).

Because there is no assumed uncertainty in the supply of inventory, the downstream POS_1 has an artificially low safety stock position. The demand variable has been factored in, but the supply variable has been withdrawn from the equation, and the buyer would become understandably panicked, possibly rushing stock from an internal warehouse or outside vendor because of unforeseen supply issues. The buyer suffers the consequences of removing the supply variability factor from the inventory calculations.

Supply variance can be a much more disruptive occurrence than demand variance. A demand variance is a small factor compared to

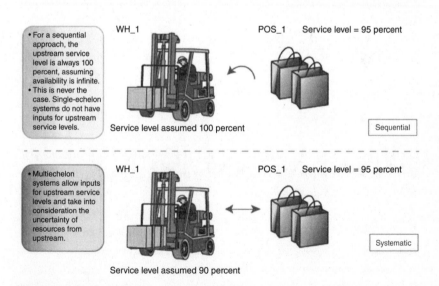

Figure 3.4 Upstream Service Level Assumption
Sequential optimization assumes the upstream service level will always be 100 percent, whereas systematic optimization recognizes that upstream service level varies.

the total demand. The overall demand is forecasted and the variance is factored in as a safety stock risk. This is a problem constrained to a specific product and can be seen in advance. A supply disruption or delay can be devastating. First, it is not known until it occurs and it can span many products. Suddenly, products that should have been delivered are days or weeks away from being in the inventory flow. The problem is amplified because there was not variance positioned for a safety stock. The out-of-stock is broad based and across many products or a single one in a potential promotion. It is no wonder that buyers fear the infamous supply disruption!

One immediate remedy is to reduce the expected service level to 90 or 95 percent. This would require the system to develop large numbers of denormalized tables to account for each service level combination, adding enormous complexity to the transactional systems' attempts to optimize the data.

In these circumstances, most organizations will try to circumvent the problem by either artificially increasing the safety stock on key items at customer locations or trying to create an early-warning system for potential shortages and increasing stock at the upstream location. Both workarounds create additional inventory. In fact, the second workaround actually amplifies the next problem occurring in sequential optimization—accounting for accumulated demand variance.

ACCUMULATED DEMAND VARIANCE

Accumulated demand variances create the need for additional short-cuts and have the effect of producing more inefficiency. Figure 3.5 depicts customer-facing locations having service level requirements based on the upstream location always having stock and each of the POC nodes having a 95 percent service level based on a demand projection with a built-in demand variance. Islands of efficiencies exist in every downstream location because each passes on its accumulated demand variances back to WH_1. This dramatically increases the inventory in WH_1 to overcome the assumed 100 percent service level required and prompts the first wave of the bullwhip effect.

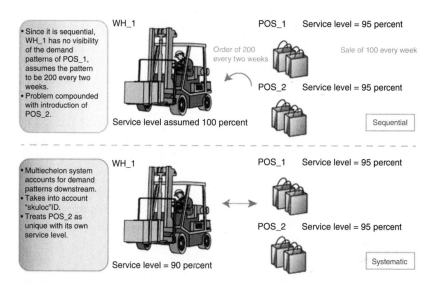

Figure 3.5 Demand Variance Assumption
The accumulated demand variance is pushed upstream with sequential optimization, but systematic optimization treats each downstream location as a separate, nonaggregated demand signal.

When distance and time increase from the initial demand signal, the systems produce notifications that more accumulated inventory is needed to offset the demand amplification. Termed *redundant inventory,* this escalating stock-up is in reaction to the accumulated demand variance repeated over and over. Upstream parts suppliers in the automotive industry have been rendered insolvent after being stuck with massive, obsolete inventories due to this kind of bullwhip effect.

MULTIPLE HIERARCHIES OF SERVICE LEVEL REQUIREMENTS

When ERP systems see accumulated demand working its way up the chain, they view that demand as an aggregated total and do not provide any additional insights into the different service level requirements necessary to meet that demand, either by site or by stock keeping unit (SKU). This causes the organization to protect itself with even more safety stock add-ons than it would have done in the previous two examples of assumed upstream service levels and demand variance. In the first example, based on the assumption of upstream service levels being 100 percent, the downstream buyer knows this not to be true and will automatically hedge against running out of stock by creating a rule-of-thumb days or weeks of supply requirement. In most instances the response is to overcompensate so that there is a reduction of alerts to potential out-of-stocks. The second example, based on aggregated demand variance, is a lot like a person driving down the road making small adjustments in steering instead of massive swings back and forth. The aggregated variance makes the buyer swing wildly between high and low inventories trying to adjust to the amplified swings in demand. In an effort to smooth the fluctuation, the buyer will try to overcompensate by having more and more safety stock on hand, thus raising inventories.

The usual workaround for adjusting inventories to accumulated demand is the installation of simple ABC classifications. In an ABC classification process, the A items will have an importance placed on them via cost, profitability, or customer need. The B and C items will have less importance. This classification process allows users to focus on the important products first. However, the ERP system struggles with millions upon millions of product and location pairings in a complex supply chain (see Figure 3.6). Whether it's a downtime service level agreement with huge penalties, or ensuring that enough cases of cola are at a featured event in a company's mountain and beach stores, incorrect service levels will create problems. The second part of the workaround is to assign review time with alerts for analysts to examine the A items that are beyond established tolerances.

THE EFFECTS OF ERP SHORTCOMINGS

Figures 3.4, 3.5, and 3.6 are just three examples of what happens when the shortcomings of the ERP system create islands of efficiency. Once each step or island of efficiency has been streamlined, they are linked together in a sequential line or links in the supply chain. That, coupled with the JIT methodologies of internally focused efficiencies, creates an increasing burden on the upstream facilities to support downstream demand. Indeed, each downstream location acts like a Toyota Kanban

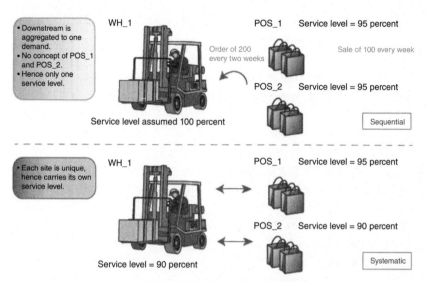

Figure 3.6 Unique Downstream Service Level Process
Sequential optimization cannot recognize different service levels, but systematic optimization allows for downstream location-product combinations to have unique service level requirements.

production location trying to push its inventory needs upstream in an effort to make itself more efficient. The offloading of inventory to upstream locations does not create more economical or efficient supply chains. The ERP "driven" supply chain pushes inventory inefficiencies upstream. Given that by nature supply chains tend to hold lots of inventory in the end, pushing inventory upstream would seem the right thing to do. The problem occurs when the upstream locations cannot react to demand changes in the customer-facing inventory locations. An upward shift in demand creates a slow reaction, and a downward shift creates the potential of massive obsolescences.

The Result of Performing High-Powered Analytics and Optimization with Normalized Tables

I was involved in a project around 2005 to measure the effects of analytics and optimization on a system using normalized tables where no shortcuts were in place to sidestep the calculation problems. The company I was working with wanted to develop a transaction-based optimization model. The idea was to make an ERP system do optimization.

Efficient normalized tables were developed so that just about every information requirement could be surfaced in a manufacturing or distribution environment. From those tables, data could be ETL'ed into usable forms for calculations. Once the data were ready, the pathway was cleared for if/therefore calculated tables for the optimization to progress.

Everything was fine until the system topped out at about 500 items in a single-echelon model. At that point, model performance started to slow down considerably. Indeed, if a second echelon was introduced, the system literally toppled over. If the number of SKUs was increased, even in a single-echelon model, the performance slowed to a crawl and toppled over at 1,000 SKUs.

I wish I had kept those performance charts. It became obvious that complete optimization without shortcuts in the calculations in a transactional system had little scalability.

Following is an example of JIT burdens being pushed upstream in a world-class organization.

SHIFTING COSTS ON A BALANCE SHEET

As discussed, single-service-level inventory management creates problems for large manufacturers through no fault of their own in seeking various remedies. One leading consumer goods company attempted working with its vendor-managed inventory (VMI) system to categorize all products and load all its important customers into a massive Excel spreadsheet and then updated the results on a monthly basis. The results allowed it to assign service levels to the major customers, major products, and the collective advertising budgets. From this information, the company was able to update upstream inventory locations with spreadsheet-assigned inventory projections. For a while, it seemed to work: The company was winning industry awards for its ability to perform VMI functions. However, in its efforts to support VMI, the company had simply transferred the inventory burden up the chain. In order to maintain the service levels required by the customers, the organization was spending massive amounts of money on expedited orders from its internal warehouses. The realized inventory savings were quickly consumed by cost of goods sold. No doubt the organization had a good idea, but its execution using the technology in place prevented a real solution.

MOVING THE FOCUS AWAY FROM INVENTORY TO REPLENISHMENT

As we will see later, the outgrowth of the ERP shortcomings was not to correct the normalized table problem because it was a baseline component of the way a transactional system worked. The shortcomings of ERP systems pushed development to an easier solution to overcome inventory issues. The focus shifted to replenishment. The way to handle out-of-balance inventories was to create a massive *check-and-balance* inventory management system based on replenishment. If you've ever noticed, inventory management is all about segmentation, monitoring, and reacting. Replenishment becomes, in essence, the great equalizer for out-of-balance inventories.

Segmentation

Companies have unlimited ways to segment products into manageable buckets. The concept is to limit the number of products that have to be reviewed and acted on so that the buyer/planner's time is most efficiently used. In most cases, the basic segmentation is called ABC. About 10 to 15 percent of all products are considered to be A items in a buyer/planner's portfolio. These items are the most important to the company by way of profitability or customer need. Often A items will have higher service level requirements by way of special customer considerations and must be watched carefully due to the ERP service level shortcomings. The B and C items have lower importance and, usually, have far fewer restrictions on service level or speed of replenishment.

In many cases, companies that have more in-depth contracts for replenishment and/or service levels will install a second tier of segmentation called strategic/nonstrategic products. A good example of this type of segmentation would focus on a product defining a company's reputation. For instance, General Electric might have an important part that is critical for running a hydroelectric generator. If that part were to fail and not be replaced quickly, it would cause a tremendous cost burden on a power company. General Electric would have that part designated as an A/Strategic product.

While not the only other segmentation methodology, there is one called forecast/lead-time analysis that is gaining ground in the supply chain industry for its ability to divide products out by the ability to react to demand signals in a timely fashion. Products are looked at with a focus on the product's replenishment lead time versus (1) the ability to know the demand and (2) the ability to understand the demand variance. Therefore, products whose lead time outstrips the ability to order to the anticipated or known demand must be monitored much more closely than those that can simply be ordered before there is a demand spike.

Oddly, there is a point of diminishing returns. How many different ways can a company segment out important products and fashion different ways to monitor and manipulate them? In some cases, buyer/planners have taken a 10 to 15 percent A item bucket and expanded it out to 30 to 50 percent of their product portfolio and quadrupled their workload without any reduction in inventory.

Monitoring

Oh, what would the life of a buyer be without monitoring problem products? Everyone has horror stories of buyers poring over reports trying to get a clearer picture of replenishment trends. I did it back in the 1980s! The first action is to segment the products into manageable buckets that will allow the buyer to reduce the overall workload. However, as with everything it still boils down to the infamous 80/20 rule: 20 percent of your products cause 80 percent of the headaches.

I visited a company that was globally recognized as a leader in collaborative planning, forecasting, and replenishment (CPFR). Their planners had extremely close relationships with their retail partners, and yet they had to deal with close to 20 different reports that matched inventory management, replenishment, and demand plans with different key performance indicators (KPIs). It was like watching a chess game being played on 10 different boards at the same time. With the CPFR vendor/retailer relationship so focused on on-time deliveries and service level, the reporting and monitoring took on a life of its own. The vendor staff was being graded from two directions: (1) maintaining a 98 to 99 percent service level with the same level of on-time deliveries and (2) recouping the extra cost of participating in the CPFR program by having lower, more responsive inventories.

The problem the CPFR practitioner had, and most other companies have, is that replenishment is a tactical activity attempting to control a strategic plan. The buyer is constantly fine-tuning the tactical activities to overcome the errors in the strategic plan. A good example of this would be when there are unforeseen increases in demand on a product being held to an artificially low safety stock. We have all seen this with working with ERP systems. The old-fashioned way to cut fat out of the inventory at the end of the quarter or fiscal year is to ratchet down days of supply. With fewer days of supply, any deviation from demand or supply targets will create an alert and/or a report anomaly. If the product is an A-type classification, the buyer will take action to manipulate the replenishment plan.

Reacting

Invariably, the buyer is left with the ol' equalizer to inventory problems—manipulating orders. While expediting or speeding up of orders is the most costly option, buyers have to deal with the full range of options as products slip and slide between being understocked or overstocked. The difficulty most buyers have in dealing with reacting to replenishment is the decision lead time. In other words, how do you know there is a problem? This last segment of the replenishment opens up all kinds of problems because of the explosion of products in vendor and retailer portfolios. Due to the slower volume of many products and the sparse or intermittent demand, it is way too late to react to inventory problems with replenishment activities. You have too much inventory before you even realize it.

This last issue is one of the key reasons ERP systems that comply with island-of-efficiency methodologies push inefficient inventory strategies into the supply chain: the long tail problem.

THE LONG TAIL

If you align all of the stock-keeping units (SKUs) produced by a company by sales volume from highest to lowest, the result would be a curve somewhat like that represented in Figure 3.7. The inflection point of the curve is at 50 percent. The head of the curve would be the SKUs doing 50 percent of the high volume, and the tail would represent the lower 50 percent of the slower-moving items. The graph in Figure 3.7 is fairly typical with about 30 to 35 percent of the products doing 50 percent of the high volume and 65 to 70 percent of the products doing the rest of the volume.

An interesting observation I have experienced over the years is the executive versus operational viewpoint of the 50 percent inflection point. Invariably, executives tend to have a much higher estimation of the SKUs representing the head of the graph compared to operation personnel. Oftentimes the estimation is in a 40 percent range. This could be due to the higher-level executive view of product families instead of the individual SKU level visibility. In turn, operational personnel tend to give much more emphasis to the tail products. I have heard operation personnel give a rating of 80 to 85 percent tail products when the real number was 60 to 65 percent. Given the problems tail products provide to buyers and planners, it is easy to see why this might happen, as we will see later.

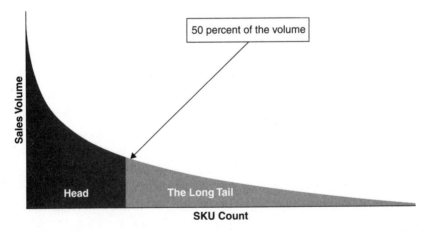

Figure 3.7 The Long Tail Visualized

The SKU distribution is often pushed by the industry or silo the company is in. For instance, smaller companies with laser focus will have a much more even distribution of products along the curve. On the other end of the extreme, spare parts and/or retail organizations can swing from 2 to 8 percent of the products in the portfolio doing 50 percent of the sales volume. While it would be wonderful to strip away items from the product portfolio, those companies in the service-type industries have to maintain those SKUs to fix machines and cater to broad consumer tastes. While there is a winnowing of products in all portfolios, the long tail will always be a problem.

What is wrong with the tail?

Products with high volume are pretty easy to manage. Their overall performance might have seasonal swings or be affected by consumer loyalties, but by and large, the sales volume stays within an expected performance parameter. Forecasts have a strong likelihood of being accurate. The demand by geo is known, so companies can position inventory where the demand is most likely to occur. At the other end of the scale are products in the tail of the sales volume. In the tail, products tend to have much slower or almost nonexistent volume. The demand might even be intermittent, sporadic, lumpy, or just plain sparse. Moreover, there may be little if any information to tell the company where the demand might occur. Now a company has little to go on to position inventory to cater to the limited demand.

The first issue with long tail products has to do with the sheer number of them. As companies introduce line extensions of products, the proliferations of SKUs multiply. Most companies have the intention of sun-setting items as new products are introduced, but due to a variety of reasons these SKUs continue on. This is usually due to service level commitments or regional acceptance of an item over other regions. In most cases, the goal is to have another company's items be discontinued so that the limited-volume item in the portfolio will carry on where the competitor's item didn't. Conversely, a service parts company makes a commitment to hold replacement parts for a product into the future. This is usually for a 10- to 15-year life of a washing machine or car. At the end-of-life process, around 10 years, the chances are dwindling that the part might be used, but it still has to be held—just in case. Love it or hate it, this carrying on of dead-man-walking products might increase shelf presences, market share, or just-in-case needs, but it wreaks havoc on the supply chain management system, income statement, and balance sheet.

The second issue with long tail products has to do with the disaggregation of products further and further down into the distribution system. This is known as end-of-chain explosion. Oftentimes companies will strive to maintain a 95 to 98 percent service level across the board on their portfolio of items. It is easy to do with those head products. However, tail products create ever-increasing inventory loads. The forecasts at this granular level tend to have wide variances or confidence levels. This leads to high levels of safety stocks on items that might sell only a little, if any, in a month. As you multiply the number of locations at the end of a supply chain, you can see the amplification of the extra "unneeded" safety stocks. The first thing that comes to mind of every supply chain manager is to pool the slower-moving items at an upstream location. The product occurs when lead times for the customer are factored in. The customer does not want to wait, so the product gets pushed out to the final resting place and inventory builds. Obviously, regional distribution can alleviate some of the problem—an item that just doesn't sell in the Southwest does not need to be stocked in the Southwest, but with the global economy it is difficult to anticipate the geo-requirements of products. Companies are left to create all kinds of business rules to help them cover the sparse or sporadic demand on these slower-moving, hard-to-forecast items in the tail.

The last and biggest problem facing the tail products is the demand variance amplification as the demand aggregation moves up the chain. Tail products have a much higher bullwhip effect than the head products. Demand variance of tail products wallops the organization with a double whammy. The high demand variance of slow-moving items is a much higher percentage of the total inventory needed. Intermittent or sparse-demand products have a naturally higher variance. With lower demand, the resulting safety stock will be higher than what is needed for high-volume, easy-to-forecast products in the portfolio. As this variance is aggregated and passed up the chain, the resulting safety stock gets higher and higher. It is not out of the ordinary to have so-called safety stocks at the central distribution center higher than the total yearly volume of a sparse-demand tail product.

This led a leading supply chain analyst, Lora Cecere, to exclaim, "In this scenario, traditional inventory techniques—safety stock logic based on normal demand distribution—just doesn't work!"[1] The premise of her assertion is that the classic, production modeling, deterministic demand systems housed in present-day transactional ERP or supply chain management systems don't have the ability to correctly position inventories in the distribution chain. Production inventory modeling, based on the old Kanban systems, relies on deterministic demand, but distribution systems act in a more stochastic or random manner.

As we have discussed previously, the curtailing of denormalized tables in the ERP/SCM-transactional systems has created a lack of visibility, so that each node or link in the chain does not have the knowledge to act as a cohesive unit. The deterministic chain does two things: (1) It creates an under-reaction to potentially random signals, in the deterministic chain, it discounts a random trend until it is considered to be a long-term trend, and the chain will ramp up or down depending on the direction; and (2) the sequential process of creating an efficient node or link before moving up the chain creates a lag in the response time.

Consider the natural reaction to these two actions. If there is a downturn in sales of automobiles at the customer level due to economic pessimism, the demand signals may be delayed for upwards of a month or two, depending on the overall aggregation of demand signals. The consumer pessimism has not been factored into the forecasted demand models, and there is a lag in getting the proper forecasts calculated. Upstream at the corporate headquarters there is visibility to a *trend*, but it is not recognized as a general downturn yet. Since there is now a slightly higher than normal inventory on cars, a dealer incentive is placed on high-inventory cars to move them through the system. The incentive helps move some cars, but production has not been slowed as management saw the trend as a temporary problem. After several months, production levels have pushed too many cars into the system, and the incentives are not moving the expected volume. Production is curtailed by 30 to 40 percent to help move the inventory glut through the system. We are now about three to four months into the consumer pessimism, but the demand signals are just getting back to the production vendors. The production vendors have been following demand signals from the auto production facilities and have just realized a 30 to 40 percent reduction in demand. Their inventories are now out of balance to the point that they have backloads of inventory that will take them a year to draw down. Those vendors are in a cash crunch—huge amounts of capital are tied up in potentially obsolete inventory, and they are tied to an auto production system that has stopped. They have no place to go to unload excess inventory. This is an example of a devastating bullwhip effect across companies, but it can happen within a company's supply chain, too.

MAKING MISTAKES FASTER

At the time of development, the combination of ERP functionality with JIT methods did not create obvious mistakes or problems. Indeed, the formalization of activities provided rigor to supply chain management that had not been in place before. Once the electronic communications were established between internal operations and out into the vendor community, orders could be processed using electronic data integration (EDI); technological advancements led to better and faster replenishment activities. However, just as I had found holes in my buying wisdom during my time as a pseudo-VMI practitioner, other, much more advanced practitioners were witnessing problems put forth by both Kruse and AMR studies—the conflicting methodologies of push and pull supply chains were promoting larger and larger inventories when all of these technological advancements were being put in place.

While I was working on orders with a calculator and a pencil, the development of the transactional ERP system pushed speed and precision into the replenishment mix. These new replenishment procedures were based on something called economic order quantities (EOQs).

WORKING WITH ONE HAND TIED BEHIND YOUR BACK

The idea behind an EOQ is the balancing of the overall cost of order compared to the cost of holding the inventory. The result is the lowest possible cost of an order to maintain the proper inventory levels.

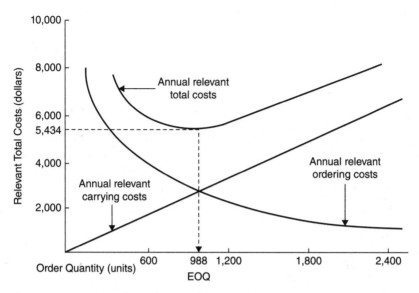

Figure 3.8 Economic Order Quantity Decision Model

As you will see, once again, a production scheduling activity has been morphed from one side of the supply chain and into the distribution chain, with dubious results.

Economic order quantity is the order quantity that minimizes total inventory holding costs and ordering costs as shown in Figure 3.8. It is one of the oldest classical production scheduling models. The framework used to determine this order quantity is also known as the Barabas EOQ model or Barabas formula. The reasoning behind the EOQ model was to create a quantity threshold where the cost of ordering and the cost of inventory were factored into the overall replenishment process so that the right amount of inventory was purchased for the demand in an efficient manner. Up until noted production engineer Ford W. Harris's work, inventory purchasing was all art and very little science. The model was developed by Harris in 1913, but R. H. Wilson, a consultant who applied it extensively, is given credit for his in-depth analysis.

However, the EOQ applies only when demand for a product is constant over the year and each new order is delivered in full when inventory reaches zero. There is a fixed cost for each order placed, regardless of the number of units ordered. There is also a cost for each unit held in storage, sometimes expressed as a percentage of the purchase cost of the item.

The required parameters to the solution are the total demand for the year, the purchase cost for each item, the fixed cost to place the order, and the storage cost for each item per year. Note that the number of times an order is placed will also affect the total cost, though this number can be determined from the other parameters.

Six underlying assumptions must be made in order for the EOQ formula to work:

1. The ordering cost is constant.
2. The rate of demand is known and spread evenly throughout the year.
3. The lead time is fixed.
4. The purchase price of the item is constant (i.e., no discount is available).
5. The replenishment is made instantaneously; the whole batch is delivered at once.
6. Only one product is involved.

EOQ is the quantity to order, so that Ordering Cost + Carrying Cost finds its minimum.

So, why would I say that using the EOQ process might create a situation where the practitioner is working with one hand tied behind her back? The issue is that the same limiting factors found in transitioning deterministic production modeling (Kanban and JIT methodologies) into the random activities of distribution can be found in the economic order quantities process.

At issue are the topline limitations shown above, such as constant ordering costs, known demand spread evenly over the year, fixed lead times, and no discounting. At the heart of the drawbacks are these more nebulous factors that tend to create problems:

- **EOQ cannot calculate batch sizing based on costs.** If the costs of ordering shifts from single product, a layer of product, a pallet of product, or a full truck of product, the EOQ formula will not take that consideration into the equation. Most ordering is done in a batch process. A minimum is derived, and multiples of those minimums are the order points. Therefore, we often see products with a layer of a pallet minimum order, and the order is multiplied by the layer up to a total on a pallet. There might be price breaks if thresholds in the batch sizing are reached. This might be a truckload discount or an end-of-quarter quantity discount.

■ **EOQ does not account for backorders.** If an account delays the acceptance of a shorted order with a backorder, the EOQ will cast a blind eye to the backorder and create a later overstock situation. The backorder dilemma is often seen within ERP systems, and a business rule is put in place to recognize the backorder as a segmentation of a new order being generated down the road. If there are financial ramifications to the backorder such as a discount or cost break, the system will be hit with deductions and accounts payable slowdowns, not to mention receiving issues.

■ **EOQ cannot optimize service levels based on costs.** EOQ has a reliance on days of supply or days of inventory. The rule-of-thumb basis of days of supply sets up a broad net to all activities around that point of inventory level. If the criterion is set on "35 days of supply," the ordering on all products will be based on the same flow for the inventory level and the same replenishment plan. However, in the real world, only a small percentage of items actually are driven by those specific days-of-supply numbers. Most products are either above or below that rule-of-thumb "35 days" or whatever is chosen as a baseline. What actually happens is the products with too much inventory days of supply get set up on a pathway to constantly be overstocked and those with too few days of supply get set up to constantly be understocked.

SO, HERE WE ARE

Organizations have heard the siren call of efficient pull supply chains and have been working to implement them so that they can be responsive and nimble. Over the past 20 to 25 years, work has been done to bring order to the inventory and replenishment processes by developing ERP and supply chain management systems so they cater to this need for a more efficient supply chain. However, as we have seen, the development has been based on the old Kanban/JIT production processes that push costs around—not eliminate them. The developments of islands of efficiencies in the supply chain have just made the inefficiencies more accurate and faster. As Kruse explained, the underlying premise of shifting supply chain costs made the push-pull hybrid supply chain increase the overall costs by 5 percent at best and much more if any incorrect assumptions are made along the way.[2]

We have supply chains built on a premise that a certain rule-of-thumb days-of-supply key performance indicator will allow for demand and supply variation and a replenishment process that creates delays in response times. Each link in the chain is vying with links both up and down the chain to hold the least amount of inventory needed. Just like the old Kanban systems, they are built on the premise to shift costs up the chain and shorten the replenishment cycle to circumvent the shortage of inventory when the rules called for too little stock. The delay in demand signals and the inability to see demand changes beyond the next level below creates the dreaded bullwhip effect. Given that each link in the chain is attempting to be as efficient as possible without regard for the total network, the result will be redundant safety stocks, incorrect replenishment, and out-of-stocks on key high-volume products. In a way, after billions of dollars have been spent to improve supply chains over the past 20 to 25 years, the underlying structure has made them no different from the one I was trying to improve on as a pseudo-VMI person way back in the 1980s.

The old inventory management techniques just don't work.[3]

NOTES

1. Lora Cecere, "Of Long Tails and Supply Chains," AMR Research Report, January 2008.
2. Erik Kruse, "From Push to Pull—Perfecting the Means," Supply Chain Resource Cooperative, September 4, 2003, http://scm.ncsu.edu/scm-articles/article/from-pushtopull-perfecting-the-means.
3. Cecere, "Of Long Tails and Supply Chains."

CHAPTER 4

How Does Days of Supply Wreak Havoc on the Supply Chain?

have been surprised at the number of times "days or weeks of supply" comes up during a discussion about supply chain efficiencies. Going all the way back to my first attempt at getting an order correct I was instructed to keep in mind "the weeks of supply" rule of thumb. One of the most enjoyable experiences (read *funny*) was listening to an inventory control manager talk about how he would "ratchet down days of supply" at the end of the year to make the balance sheet and income statement more acceptable. This executive talked about the fine line he walked between lost sales and reduced inventory. Anyone who has worked in supply chain management has been in those shoes. In order to meet organizational performance indicators, an inventory control manager has to face crippling customer service issues over the short term to get inventory under control for a finite period and then let it bounce back to "normal." The result is a temporary fix to make things appear acceptable, but the underlying problem continues to limp along.

That problem is inventory placement based on rules that are good for only about 10 percent of the products.

As we saw in the previous chapter, enterprise resource planning (ERP) and supply chain management (SCM) systems are built using shortcuts to overcome the absence of relationships between links in the supply chain. There are assumptions put in place, like always having 100 percent service level from the upstream location. These types of assumptions pervade the system. The use of days or weeks of supply is a classic rule-of-thumb key performance indicator (KPI) for inventory health. The computation of days or weeks of supply provides the system with an inventory range to keep the inventory levels within by placing a high and low tolerance and coupling the order lead time and ordering costs to allow for an economic order quantity. Together they make up the logic in the ERP system to run in harmony.

RULE-OF-THUMB DAYS/WEEKS OF SUPPLY EXPOSED

So, here we are with inventory control managers around the globe practicing short-term "ratcheting down days or weeks of supply" to get inventories in line just long enough to get the numbers in and release the pressure and ERP systems that are built along the same lines of

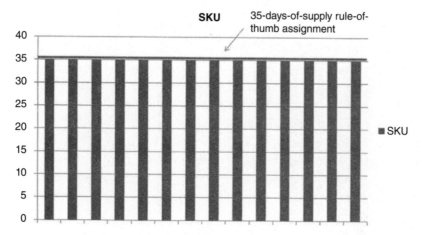

Figure 4.1 Rule-of-Thumb Inventory Levels

rule-of-thumb days or weeks of supplies. What could possibly happen to cause problems in a supply chain?

Let's take a look at the classic days-of-supply problem shown in Figure 4.1.

Within this figure, the inventory control manager has set all of the stock-keeping units (SKUs) at a 35 days inventory KPI. This one-size-fits-all rule of thumb is used in inventory management and is the backbone of ERP system control. Literally, everywhere I have gone in my travels to review and improve supply chain techniques I run into the problem of buyers and analysts recognizing the infamous 10 percent problem. Our teams started doing tests of the data to try to figure out whether this 10 percent rule happened more often than we thought. We found that it did and we called the 10 percent the *Goldilocks products* (see Figure 4.2).

Everyone remembers "Goldilocks and the Three Bears." In that story, Goldilocks tries out the three bowls of porridge and finds one too hot, one too cold, and one just right. The same can be said for products in a rule-of-thumb days-of-supply situation. In our reviews of various companies, we found that, on average, about 10 percent of all products fell into a situation where the rule-of-thumb days-of-supply inventory was "just right." On either side of that 10 percent sweet spot,

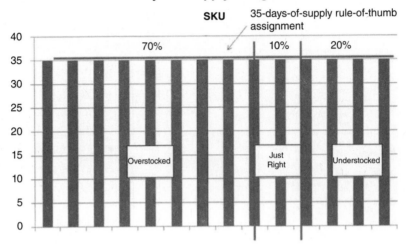

Figure 4.2 The Goldilocks Effect

the products tended to fall into a 70/20 split of overstocks and under-stocks. In most cases, 65 to 75 percent of the products in question had way too much stock on hand to cover the expected service level. On the flipside, 15 to 25 percent of the products did not have enough stock on hand to cover the expected service level. If you are a buyer, you know all about the amount of time you spend in your portfolio trying to handle the problems—the infamous 80/20 rule—you spend all your time tracking and covering the 20 percent of those products that are chronically understocked.

Here is where things can get a bit sticky as inventory management meets reality. Let's suppose that you want to increase customer satis-faction and increase service levels. By increasing days of supply, you fix the problems for a few of the 20 percent products. However, given that ERP systems cannot differentiate service levels of products the whole portfolio has to go up (see Figure 4.3).

As you drag the inventory of the portfolio along, the 20 percent products begin to be part of that "just right" 10 percent. Starting with the products closest to the left of the 20 percent, they start to be enveloped by the 10 percent. Let's say, for argument's sake, you move the portfolio by 5 percent. You now have 15 percent of your products

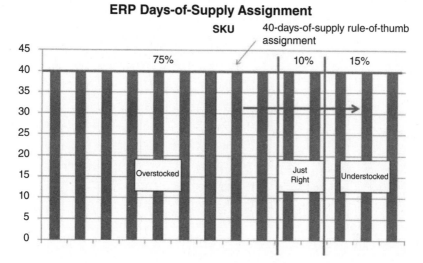

Figure 4.3 Increasing Service Level by Raising Days of Supply

in the understocked category, but you have increased the overstock category to a 75 percent range. Your inventory just skyrocketed for a very nominal increase in customer satisfaction due to increased service levels. We have often seen inventories increase by 15 percent to get as little as a 2 percent gain in service levels because you are dragging along already overstocked items that represent 70 to 75 percent of your portfolio.

The last process is the one that gets everyone in trouble. Indeed, whenever I am out in the field talking about being more efficient and reducing inventories I can see in the eyes of the listeners the number of times they have fallen into this trap. In this case, either at the end of the year or when some executive has decided to be more efficient, the decision is made to ratchet down days of supply (see Figure 4.4).

When you shift the product portfolio to run leaner, you don't have the heavy overstock problem to help you soften the blow. The inefficiencies of the understocked products are amplified and they are, usually, the most important products to both the organization and the customer. The products in the understocked 20 percent most affected are not the ones closest to the "just right" 10 percent. They are at the right side of the graph and have the biggest out-of-stock potential.

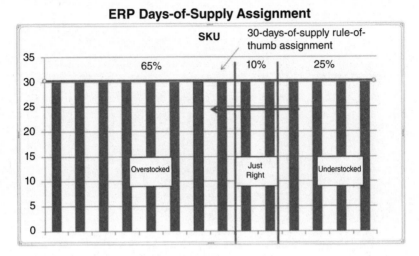

Figure 4.4 Reducing Inventory by Lowering Days of Supply

As you push the portfolio to fewer days of supplies, this amplification gets huge. First, there is little benefit of the move of the "just right" 10 percent down into the overstocked products. In this situation, if the portfolio moved 5 percent, that means just a very small portion of the overstocked 70 percent had any significant improvement. Second, the overstocked 70 percent got very little benefit in inventory reduction across the board. The sheer number of items will affect the inventory. Last, the propensity of the top-level 20 percent to go out of stock rises far faster than the overall reduction in stock. You might get a 15 percent increase in stock to a 2 percent gain in service level; for trying to increase stocks for better service levels/customer satisfaction you get a massive whiplash to stock reductions. In many cases, organizations can see a 5 to 7 percent service level decline to 10 percent stock reductions over a long period of time.

This is the perilous position buyers and analysts get into when they have to ratchet down days of supply. Anyone can do it for a short period of time, but a company can risk customer satisfaction and company image if there is an attempt to hold it down over the long term.

Over the years, I have found this definition of inventory optimization (that you can lower inventories) has stopped more engagements than just about any other reason. The company has a problem with inventory—too much cash is being eaten up in obsolete inventories, there are huge out-of-stocks, and customer service is at all-time lows—but the minute executives hear "lower inventories," they remember trying to do that at the end of quarters and the end of the year only to have to raise inventories after seeing short-term gains. If they are at the lower end of the supply chain, they think of their buyers trying to expedite shipments while inventories are held artificially low. This lowering of inventories in a Goldilocks environment of days of supply is a no-win situation.

INEFFICIENCIES OF RULE-OF-THUMB DAYS OF SUPPLY

As you can see in Figure 4.5, rule-of-thumb days of supply works pretty well when there are low expectations of service level. The overall costs stay fairly low. However, when service levels start to climb into the 90-plus range, the costs begin to climb exponentially. Why is this so?

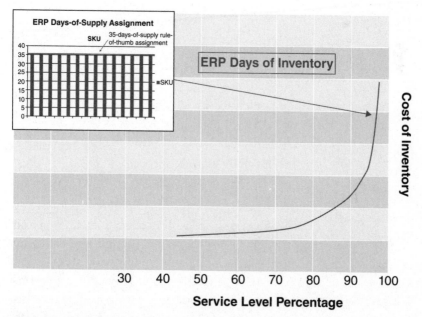

Figure 4.5 Cost of Inventory against Service Level Based on Rule-of-Thumb Days

Lora Cecere says, bluntly, but oh, so well: "In this scenario, traditional inventory techniques—safety stock logic based on normal distribution—just doesn't work."[1]

The inefficiencies of the rule-of-thumb days-of-supply problem go everywhere in the supply chain. Think of all of the various outlier reports produced to help buyers catch part of the infamous 20 percent understocked problem or the efforts of some to artificially increase or decrease inventories like I did 25 years ago in my efforts to make myself more efficient. Another problem rule-of-thumb days of supply creates is the aggregation issue. With the proliferation of products and the push to having replenishment locations closer to the customer, the multiplication of the days of supply creates a massive bullwhip effect when the rule and the resulting "redundant safety stock rolls up the chain."

This last issue, of rolling up aggregated inventory based on a rule, shows up as different problems in different companies. However, there seems to be two kinds of issues. The first is the *rolling amplification*, where stock gets larger and larger the further you go up the supply chain. The second is the *echelon reaction* that occurs at each step up the chain.

The rolling amplification contributes to the bullwhip effect (see Figure 4.6). The bullwhip effect is driven by a delay in demand signals being processed up the chain. Unless there is an immediate signal of a demand change to all participants in the chain, the signal gets muddled.

There is an old game called Telephone that illustrates this point. In the game people sit in a circle. A message is whispered into the ear of the first person. Once the message has been heard that person leans to the next and whispers it until the message goes all the way around the

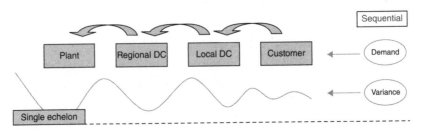

Figure 4.6 Sequential Optimization/Bullwhip Effect

circle. The message cannot be repeated if it is not heard the first time. Each person has to repeat the message the best he or she can. There are very few times the message actually gets all the way around the circle intact. Indeed, even single-word messages get morphed into just about anything.

The point of the game brings to bear the problem of passing demand signals from one island (link in the supply chain) to the next. Oftentimes, an organization will forecast for each distribution center, plant, or store. By doing this, the demand signal goes through its own Telephone-like process. First is the delay, and second is the amplification. If each island is being forecasted as a separate entity, the granular aspect starting in the stores creates a larger than needed statistical variance due to sporadic or intermittent demand. This creates a need for additional safety stocks since there is lack of confidence in the forecasted number. The cumulative number from this aggregation with significant variance is now taken on by the upstream distribution center. The distribution center can't see the customer-facing demand. It has to rely on the cumulative number moving up the chain. The separate forecast now being generated for the distribution center is now creating its own bias byproduct. This continues on and on up the chain to produce the dreaded bullwhip effect. This bullwhip goes both ways. The high-up part of the chain gets the brunt of this action. At best, it cannot react to demand above expectation and the result could be periodic shortages. However, it can be catastrophic if the opposite happens. What if there is a massive slowdown in demand over a long period of time? The auto industry is a perfect example of this situation. Automotive parts suppliers to auto manufacturing assembly lines can be wiped out if their inventory suddenly becomes obsolete and they are left with massive amounts of capital tied up in useless inventory.

Most everyone has heard of the bullwhip effect and how it can cause havoc in the supply chain. A great teaching example of this can be found at www.beergame.org.[2] The game can be played online and allows participants to work together in solving distribution issues around the delivery of beer to thirsty college students.

After this rolling amplification or bullwhip effect has taken place there is a much more silent killer of supply chain efficiencies. Creating a rule-of-thumb days or weeks of supply number creates a false sense of security at the mid-range warehouses. This is what I call "echelon leveling." In this situation, the effects of the 70/10/20 rule distribution against products can cause problems at distribution centers.

The best way to explain this phenomenon would be to take the example of a major North American fast-moving consumer products company (see Figure 4.7). The organization had developed and implemented a vendor management inventory (VMI) division to handle the inventory control and replenishment of the largest retail customers in their portfolio. Over the course of several years, its VMI program was winning awards in supply chain excellence. Its efforts were being touted by trade groups, vendors, and retailers as the model for the future. I went to this organization to get inputs on how it managed this successful process from a software and process perspective. Over a two-day period I was simply awestruck at how efficient its VMI personnel were and the constant interactions between vendor and retailer. It was amazing and a testimony to how the organization could outperform its competitors in both speed of delivery and order fill rates. The organization was great at its job and customers loved it.

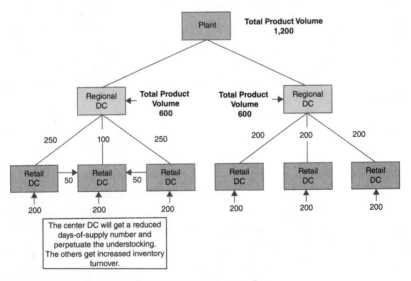

Figure 4.7 False Demand Signals Due to Echelon Leveling

When I was there, one of the VMI people suggested I go talk to "her boyfriend." While she was responsible for the distribution center to customer logistics or outbound deliveries, her boyfriend was one of the many "internal logistics" managers at the company. He was not directly tied to the VMI operations, but he had to deal with both their activities and the movement of products with normal distribution. He was a delightful young man who, you could tell within minutes, was under a tremendous amount of strain.

He explained to me that in order to have the high fill rates and delivery speed expected from the key retailers, he and the rest of the internal operations team had to constantly reposition distribution center inventories. The days-of-supply threshold was too narrow to react to upticks in demand on the most visible and volatile products. Therefore, he constantly had to shift product from one peer warehouse to another because the upstream plant warehouse did not have the time to replenish correctly.

The poor boyfriend was dealing with echelon leveling. The plant warehouse above the distribution centers was restricted on the amount of inventory that could be placed by the production scheduling. The stores were unable to hold stock due to capacity issues. The retailer wanted to hold a limited amount of stock because it is in a VMI environment and that was what it signed up for. The resulting pressure was the same thing that happens in the JIT/Kanban world: The pressure gets shifted to the vendor distribution center. However, the biggest effect is on the infamous 20 percent of the products that don't have enough stock due to the limits from the days-of-supply rule of thumb. Instead of increasing days of supply in the distribution centers (DCs), the DCs are getting good reviews for staying within the days-of-supply threshold and for fast inventory turnover—on paper, they're doing great.

The problem is the leveling. The shifting or leveling of inventory between warehouses creates two streams of supply, but only one recognized stream of demand. This can happen just about anywhere in the chain, but the biggest problem seems to come into play at vendor warehouses close to the point of ownership transfer. The demand forecast is flowing up from the downstream location and the days-of-supply number is played on that expectation. For argument's sake let's say that the expectation is for having 200 cases to account for 14 days of supply and you want to have your inventory turns at 12 to 14 times.

What happens when you introduce a second, hidden stream of demand? When a product gets transferred around, it is covering the initial demand, but that demand stream is moving up the chain, not sideways. What if we add an unexpected demand of 100 cases funneling through that warehouse out to a retailer from sister warehouses? The upstream plant did not see the demand come from a single location—it is being both shared and hidden as a total from the lower echelon. The upstream plant will see the 100 cases, but the leveling of product did not allow for the true demand to come from the proper location. What it sees is a lowering of the volume at the inflow warehouse and an increase in the other two warehouses that supplied the lateral transfer. What ends up happening is the affected distribution centers continue on with the noted days of supply and their cumulative inventory turns get better, but there is not a realignment of days of supply to compensate for the increase in business. In the end, the tightly held days-of-supply sharing artificially lowers down the actual service level attainment because inventory levels needed are shared and flowing to two streams of demand and being graded against a single stream of demand. The better those VMI people got at dealing with the customer, the more our poor boyfriend felt like he was getting hit from all sides.

TURNING DAYS OF SUPPLY ON ITS HEAD

The past 20-plus years of supply chain processes have been based on production rules from the initial development of JIT/Kanban. As the ERP systems were built out they took the learnings of the production processes and made them their own. This marriage of siloed JIT/Kanban rules and ERP was made in heaven. The normalized tables in the ERP systems found their match in the siloed models. With each siloed link in the chain being optimized the process mimicked production optimization as defined by JIT/Kanban principles. The outgrowth of that system—days of supply—has created inefficiencies where any attempt to move toward lesser inventory or greater customer satisfaction is met with spiraling costs or lost sales.

What if we turn days of supply on its head? Instead of making days of supply the result of the equation, what if we make it the result of a requested service level that the days of supply would adhere to? What if we linked the siloed links in the chain? What if we could create individualized days of supply that were integrated throughout a network so that they acted more efficiently? (See Figure 4.8.)

Over the past 10 years, inventory optimization has entered into the discussion surrounding supply chain efficiencies. The concept of inventory optimization is to create individualized inventory policies so that each product/location combination is uniquely fashioned to keep the costs as low as possible while attaining an optimized service level. The policies create individualized inventory ranges for products based on a service level to balance the costs against the demand and lead-time variations.

For simplicity's sake let's suggest that you wanted to make all of the products attain a 90 percent service level at the customer-facing locations. This process would take the rule of thumb out of the mix and replace it with individualized days-of-supply computations. Therefore,

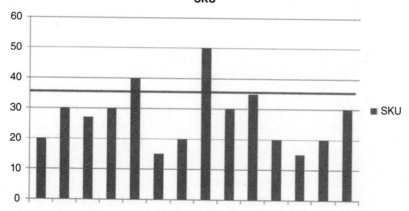

Figure 4.8 Uniquely Optimized Inventory Levels Based on a Balance of Service Level and Costs

Creating uniquely optimized inventory policies for every product/location combination makes each assignment of days of supply a perfect Goldilocks result. All inventories are "just right."

instead of having everything at 35 days of supply the result would be each product having its own days of supply focused on a 90 percent service level. Now, when you want to make a change in the service level or days of supply, you aren't saddled with the inefficiencies when dealing with the 70 percent of the overstocked items or the 20 percent of the understocked items. This individual assignment process actually provides even more benefits. When dealing with individual computations for service level, you can provide (1) individualized safety stocks, (2) individualized order-up-to levels, and (3) order point thresholds so the replenishment process links to the inventory levels correctly.

When you link individualized service levels to products, you are going beyond what the ERP system can do, and you have the ability to make that ERP system run better. Remember, ERP systems are built on the island-of-efficiency premise and the linkages are limited. In ERP systems, upstream locations are always at 100 percent service level, and the upstream location can't recognize multiple service levels from locations below it; hence, rules-of-thumb days of supply. The ability to open up the ERP system to multiple service level computations provides three distinct advantages. The first is the ability to create individualized days-of-supply numbers. The second is to adjust the service level and not have to deal with moving already inefficient days-of-supply inventories. The last is having the ability to adjust service levels individually:

- **Individualized days of supply.** Within this computation there is an optimized balance between the cost of the inventory and the service level required. This can tell you where your inventory is relative to where it needs to be, instead of having arbitrary days-of-supply numbers placed upon it. This means there is no longer a Goldilocks assignment where limited numbers are just right; you have a map of what it takes to make sure all of the products are just right. As you can see, in the chart shown in Figure 4.9 the individualized days-of-supply numbers are dramatically different from a simple 35-days-of-supply rule of thumb. As we will see later, this optimal-versus rule can have a dramatic effect on how you manage the inventory.

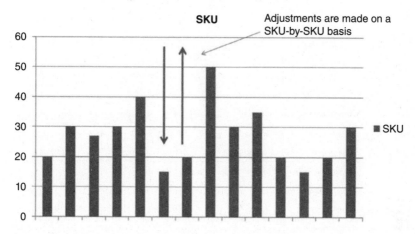

Figure 4.9 Adjustment of Inventory by SKU/Location Granularity

- **Adjustments of individual inventories (vertical arrows).**
  This is one of the hardest actions to take in an ERP system.
  An ERP system will not allow you to adjust the service level
  requirement of individual products or small groups of products.
  This falls outside the range of days-of-supply rule-of-thumb
  assignments. A valued customer comes to you and wants
  to sign a service level agreement where you will provide a
  98 percent service level on a group of products at a specific
  warehouse. In the rule-of-thumb days-of-supply environment you can't take specific products and adjust them to a
  specific service level. You are bound by the days-of-supply
  restriction.

- **Individually assigned location/product inventory policies.** When you have individually assigned location/product
  inventory policies instead of broad-based rule-of-thumb
  days-of-supply assignments, the adjustments of those policies
  become much easier. In the previous example in which the
  customer wanted to have a 98 service level placed on a few
  products at a single location, a simple adjustment could have
  been made to the 98 percent service level and the optimized
  system would adapt to the new requirements.

CREATING THE EFFICIENCY ENVELOPE

The ability to close some of the shortcuts in the ERP systems allows the product portfolios to have a much more dynamic way of reacting to changes in strategy. As you can see in the graph in Figure 4.10, the two methodologies hover close together at the lower ends of the service level thresholds. However, as the service level gets to the 85 to 90 percent level, the difference widens. Once it hits the 95 to 97 percent range, the days-of-supply methodology takes off exponentially, whereas the optimized service level methodology continues on to the 98 to 99 percent level at a far lower cost.

The efficiency envelope is created when the rule-of-thumb days of supply are measured against the optimized inventory policies that generate inventories based on a service level outcome at the lowest possible cost and assigned to individual products. The envelope is designated the difference between the lowest acceptable service level and the highest service level reasonably attainable. In this diagram we have chosen 90 percent at the low end and 99 percent at the high end.

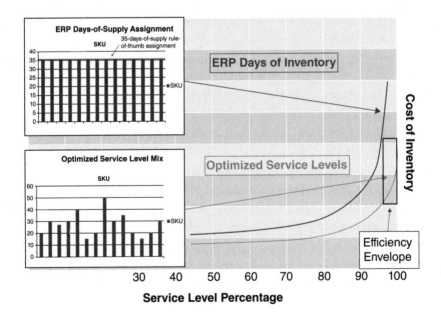

Figure 4.10 The Efficiency Envelope

In a simplistic fashion the practitioner could choose to keep the service level at 90 percent and enjoy the new lower inventory levels. This strategy would enable the company to free up cash from inventory and be a much more nimble organization. Companies that do this kind of strategy are those that might have a problem with obsolescence and/or bullwhip problems. On the other end of the spectrum the practitioner might want to embrace the 99 percent service level and gain additional market share by way of reduced lost sales and increased customer satisfaction. Indeed, the possibilities are endless with ways the efficiency envelope can be used to examine strategy. More important, the ability to measure the difference between individual products and their present-versus-optimal inventory position can help develop unique portfolio strategies to maximize both inventory efficiencies and revenue expansion.

In most cases, when an organization looks at reevaluating its rule-of-thumb ERP strategy and moves toward an optimized state, it is motivated by a potential reduction of inventory. This is logical. Inventory efficiencies are rarely thought of for increasing revenue, but this is a perfect example of taking advantage of revenue and costs. The 70 percent (or more) of the products in the portfolio that are thought of as overstocked compared to their actual inventory need to reach a 95 percent service level. Over time, these products will bleed off inventory and fall in line with the optimized level. As shown in Figure 4.11, this is going to have a tremendous effect on the balance sheet with regard to decreased working capital invested in inventory and cost of goods sold.

The inventory reduction is a huge opportunity, but in most cases, it does not get the C-level executive excited because reduced working capital is usually looked at from the perspective of increased opportunity costs and efficiency. The key to the real benefits of changing your strategy away from rules and moving to optimization is found in the operating income statement. As the products in the lower half increase their inventory positions and come into line with the required stock to attain the 95 percent service level, multiple lines on an income statement are affected. First, the supply chain costs will stabilize due to a marked reduction in the number of expedited shipments. Second, the reduced inventory and focused inventory level reduces the cost of

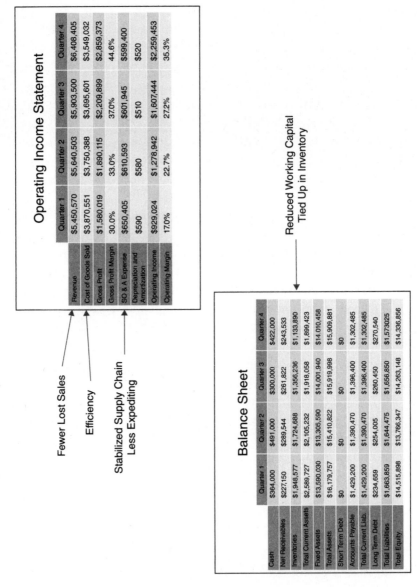

Operating Income Statement

Fewer Lost Sales

Efficiency

Stabilized Supply Chain
Less Expediting

	Quarter 1	Quarter 2	Quarter 3	Quarter 4
Revenue	$5,450,570	$5,640,503	$5,903,500	$6,408,405
Cost of Goods Sold	$3,870,551	$3,750,388	$3,695,601	$3,549,032
Gross Profit	$1,580,019	$1,890,115	$2,209,899	$2,859,373
Gross Profit Margin	30.0%	33.0%	37.0%	44.6%
SO & A Expense	$650,405	$610,593	$601,945	$599,400
Depreciation and Amortization	$590	$580	$510	$520
Operating Income	$929,024	$1,278,942	$1,607,444	$2,259,453
Operating Margin	17.0%	22.7%	27.2%	35.3%

Balance Sheet

Reduced Working Capital
Tied Up in Inventory

	Quarter 1	Quarter 2	Quarter 3	Quarter 4
Cash	$364,000	$491,000	$300,000	$422,000
Net Receivables	$227,150	$289,544	$261,822	$243,533
Inventories	$1,948,577	$1,724,688	$1,356,236	$1,133,890
Total Current Assets	$2,589,727	$2,105,232	$1,918,058	$1,899,423
Fixed Assets	$13,590,030	$13,305,590	$14,001,940	$14,010,458
Total Assets	$16,179,757	$15,410,822	$15,919,998	$15,909,881
Short Term Debt	$0	$0	$0	$0
Accounts Payable	$1,429,200	$1,390,470	$1,396,400	$1,302,485
Total Current Liab.	$1,429,200	$1,390,470	$1,396,400	$1,302,485
Long Term Debt	$234,659	$254,005	$260,450	$270,540
Total Liabilities	$1,663,859	$1,644,475	$1,656,850	$1,573,025
Total Equity	$14,515,898	$13,766,347	$14,263,148	$14,336,856

Figure 4.11 Effects of Optimized Inventories on the Balance Sheet and Income Statement

goods and speeds up inventory turns. However, the biggest benefit will be when the revenue number goes up as "in-stock" products allow for less out-of-stocks and overall increased sales and revenue.

THE JOURNEY, SO FAR

In the past 30 years, the supply chain has been asked to take on a leading role as a facilitator for the proposed pull methodology needed to be more responsive to demands of the customer. This new and reactive supply chain would enable practitioners to quickly act on demand signals and get product to the customer "just in time." The model to be used was being practiced throughout the production segment of the business and should easily be transitioned into the distribution stream. Learned best practices could be easily moved from one side of the business to the other.

The problem that almost immediately cropped up was that a pull methodology did not align to all product strategies due to the required customization needed for pull process to work. A pull system had always required the customization to be considered acceptable to the consumer; otherwise, the delay to get non-customized product was too long and unacceptable.

From this situation, the supply chain developed the hybrid push-pull model to mimic all of the required actions needed to deliver both standard products and custom products. This hybrid push-pull methodology is in place in just about every organization and provides the backbone to supply chain management to this day. At issue is that the methodology mimics the same problems the JIT/Kanban systems developed in production: It does not reduce costs so much as push the costs around. In the production model, the costs moved back to the vendor with such things as speed of delivery and increased inventory to anticipate unforeseen demand. The result was a 5 to 10 percent increase in the cost of doing business with a production JIT/Kanban system. In turn, the internal supply chain of a company did not have the capability of sloughing off costs to a vendor and simply moved costs around to different links in the chain.

At the same time these actions were taking place in the supply chain, organizations were in the process of installing ERP systems.

The effect was to marry the two projects and they were willing participants that allowed for siloed efficiencies. The JIT/Kanban system wanted to create single locations of efficiencies and the ERP's internal table system catered to the separation of locations for best results. This marriage of methodology and process developed the island-of-efficiency system where arc data are lacking to overcome the problems of normalized tables, but more important, mimicked the JIT/Kanban methods.

This ERP-based JIT/Kanban process is now in place just about everywhere, but inventories continue to climb. Inventories are out of balance, responsiveness is slow, and any attempt to solve the problem either increases out-of-stocks on important products or creates more inventory than what was in place already. In short, costs are up and customer service is down. Even more at risk are seemingly well-structured supply chains being pushed to the limit by internal transfers and expedited shipments to create the illusion of efficiencies.

In the end, the systems are being pushed to the brink by the reliance on archaic rules and the inability to view demand and cost across the network so that the network acts in concert. We have seen how the system can be modernized by simply changing the way weeks of supply is validated to deliver a service level and how assigning unique "policies" to individual product and location combinations can take away huge inefficiencies and lead companies to finding both reduced inventories and increased revenues.

This journey has led us to a crossroads: Continue on with the ways of the past or embrace how optimization can transform the organization so it can finally be both responsive and efficient. We've seen where we've been; now let's see where we're going.

NOTES

1. Lora Cecere, "Of Long Tails and Supply Chains," AMR Research Report, January 2008.
2. Kai Riemer, "The Beergame Portal." University of Sydney and University of Münster—Department of Information Systems (IOS work group), 2007–2012, www .beergame.org.

CHAPTER **5**

What Will You Accomplish with Inventory Optimization?

have had the great fortune of working with three gentlemen who have influenced me when it comes to all things inventory optimization. Tugrul Sanli, Jinxin Yi, and Xinmin Wu have, literally, taught me inventory optimization over the past 12 years. As I started to write this chapter, I looked for the best way to share information about the inner workings of inventory optimization without going overboard on technical jargon. The more I looked around, the more I kept coming back to the same information. Drs. Tugrul Sanli, Jinxin Yi, and Xinmin Wu have been the authors of the *SAS Inventory Optimization User Guide* since it started publication back in the early 2000s. Over the years, it has been upgraded with new information as it became available and included in the solution. I spoke with each of them about the use of their information in this book, and I am particularly thankful that they gave me the opportunity to pass on a lot of the information found in the *SAS Inventory Optimization User Guide* for reference material. While I have added verbiage here and there, the technical information comes directly from the user guide at SAS.

HOW DOES INVENTORY OPTIMIZATION IMPROVE THE ERP SYSTEMS?

So, what does inventory optimization do to counteract the short-comings found in present-day enterprise resource planning (ERP) and supply chain management (SCM) systems? In a nutshell, it turns days of supply on its head so that each and every product/location combination has a unique inventory policy assignment so that the days of supply become a result of inventory constraints and costs are applied to a service level need. More importantly, though, it opens up the linkages between the supply chain locations so there are no longer rule-of-thumb assumptions and the information flows as a single voice.

A good way of understanding the effects of inventory optimization on a supply chain system is to take a look at the information flow from inputs to outputs (see Figure 5.1). As stated before, this is not a book written for the PhD, looking to validate the inner workings of a stochastic algorithm. It is a book written for the businessperson thinking of using inventory optimization properties to advance his or

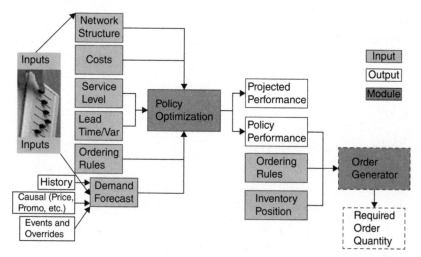

Figure 5.1 Input and Output Flows of Inventory and Replenishment Optimization

her supply chain requirements. As such, the view of the inputs and outputs will be at a high level, focused on how the information flows.

DEVELOPMENT OF THE INVENTORY POLICIES AND REPLENISHMENT PLANS

The inputs to the inventory policy calculations span across the structure of the supply chain, the unique cost interactions of the product and the locations, the variations of demand and supply, and the demand patterns of the product. These interactions are, then, focused on keeping the lowest possible cost equated to a service level requirement. Where the product rests in the chain will dictate the projected service level. The most important component of the calculation is the required service level at the final customer-facing location.

THE NETWORK STRUCTURE

The network structure is important for the system to understand. Given that the final customer-facing location is supreme in the development of the policies, all other upstream locations are set up to support that leaf node or final resting place service level. For instance, the customer-facing location has a requirement of a 98 percent service level. This does not mean that every step in the upstream locations will have to have 98 percent service level to keep the customer-facing location in stock for a 98 percent service level. As we will find out later, given such constraint inputs as lead time, order frequency, and demand confidence, the upstream locations could get by with much lower service levels.

The inventory costs at the various locations where the product is stored are the costs the system is looking to minimize. The assumptions about the cost structures are important. There are three types of costs that are taken into consideration as constraints:

1. Ordering costs are the costs incurred every time a replenishment order is placed. This fixed cost includes the expense associated with processing the order and is usually independent of the size of the order.

2. Holding costs are the costs of carrying inventory and might include the opportunity cost of money invested, the expenses incurred in running a warehouse, handling and counting costs, the costs of special storage requirements, deterioration of stock, damage, theft, obsolescence, insurance, and taxes. The most common convention is to specify holding cost (per-period per unit) as a fixed percentage of the unit cost of the item. This cost is then applied to the average inventory.

3. Penalty (backordering or shortage) costs are the costs incurred when a stockout occurs. This cost might include the cost of emergency shipments, cost of substitution of a less profitable item, or cost of lost goodwill. For instance, will the customer ever return? Will the customer's colleagues be told of the poor service? The most common convention is to specify penalty cost as per-period per-unit and then apply it to the average number of backorders.

In practice, it is often difficult to estimate the ordering (replenishment) cost and the penalty cost. As a result, practitioners often put restrictions on the ordering frequency rather than estimate the cost of ordering. Likewise, specific target levels for service measures can be substituted for the penalty cost.

THE SERVICE LEVEL

Service-level measures are often used to evaluate the effectiveness of an inventory replenishment policy. You can influence policy calculations by imposing desired service-level requirements. Inventory optimization usually supports the use of three different service constraints:

1. *Fill rate* is the fraction of demand satisfied directly from on-hand inventory. Fill rate is one of the most frequently used service measures in practice. You can set a minimum fill rate as a service constraint.

2. *Ready rate* is the probability of no stockout in a review period. You can set a minimum ready rate as a service constraint.

3. *Backorder ratio* is equal to the average number of backorders divided by the average demand. You can set a maximum backorder ratio as a service constraint.

These service constraints provide different ways of penalizing backorders. When fill rate is used as a service measure, the focus is only on the number of backorders, whereas with back-order ratio as a service measure, the focus is on both the amount and length of backorders. When ready rate is used as a service measure, the focus is not on the number or length of backorders, but on whether a stockout occurs.

Setting a high target service level might result in high inventory levels, which can be very costly if demand is intermittent (slow moving). In these cases, estimating penalty costs and performing a cost optimization might be preferred.

Oftentimes, there are other inventory optimization measures to evaluate the performance of a policy, as follows:

- Average ordering frequency is the number of replenishment orders placed per review period. You can set a limit on the average ordering frequency.

- Average inventory is the average on-hand inventory at the end of a review period.

- Average backorder is the average amount of outstanding backordered demand in a review period.

- Inventory ratio is the average inventory divided by the average demand.

- Turnover is the average demand divided by the average inventory.
- Average cost is the average cost of holding and replenishment.
- Incurred per period is if the backorder penalty costs are present, these are included as well.

THE LEAD TIME AND LEAD-TIME VARIANCE

There are three aspects of lead time that are important to the inputs of inventory optimization. The first is the actual or mean lead time. This lead time is a function of the time it takes to order plus the time it takes for the inventory to arrive at the new location. Inventory optimization tends to use a mean average of the lead time to account for slight variances. Let's say that the order time is one day between the inventory position being evaluated and an order being placed. Once the order is placed, it takes the time to pull the order, put it on a truck, and transport it to the new location as six days. This makes the total mean lead time of seven days. The second part of the lead-time input is the variance away from the mean for orders. In this case, is the vendor or upstream location consistent in taking seven days total from the time of order evaluation to delivery? This variation, if not taken into account, can be a real problem for the replenishment system and one of the key points lacking in ERP systems. It is an easy input to pull from warehouse management systems (WMS) by pulling the actual delivery versus predicted delivery. Once this has been included in the computations, a much more accurate safety stock number is developed. Last is the lead time/demand input for recognition of fluctuation in demand beyond the ordering lead time. If there is a nonstationary demand with a lead time longer than the review period, a replenishment system will lag behind or be ahead of the true demand number. To overcome that, it will take an average of the demand and position it within the lead time to help raise or lower the amount within the lead-time period when required.

ORDERING RULES

It is important to bring up, at this point, an outgrowth of the lead-time situation that leads into ordering rules. Oftentimes, replenishment systems will be set up to review an inventory position periodically. In a majority of cases an inventory might be reviewed weekly. This periodic review places an artificial lead time that might lead to holding excess stock. Given the cost and demand, there are times when a much shorter review period is required. This change from periodic is called *continuous review*. In most cases, the term *continuous* is a misnomer. The review is still periodic, but the time horizon is greatly reduced to twice a day or daily. The key to this being an advantage against periodic review is the cost of ordering. If the cost of ordering is extremely low and low quantities can be ordered, the continuous review can reduce the lead time and, therefore, reduce the inventory carrying costs.

Therefore, the important aspects of ordering rules center on the ordering lots, ordering minimums, and the ordering frequency. Inventory optimization takes the process of economic order quantities (EOQ) and adds into it the constraints normally found in replenishment activities. A good example of this would be that an EOQ might come out as 3 on a slow moving item. However, the optimization system will understand that the lot size minimum of the product is a layer on a pallet equal to 12. This means the order will have to be increased or delayed until there is enough demand to equate to an order of 12. Conversely, the order is increased by a multiple of 12 for each layer on the pallet. On the final point the frequency of the orders is taken into consideration. The 12 order would be much easier to attain in a weekly periodic review than in a continuous review done daily.

DEMAND

This topic causes the most understanding of what the input is, but the most misunderstanding of what the input does. On the subject of demand or demand forecasting, the increase or decrease will have a serious effect on the replenishment side of the fence. The effect on the inventory policy side is much different. Interestingly, this topic is the one that causes the most confusion to executives when they are looking at inventory optimization as a contributor to their activities.

The effect of the demand velocity will certainly have an influence on the amount of inventory required. However, the confidence level or variance of the demand is far more important to the inventory policy than the actual demand number. The confusion factor comes down to how executives view replenishment versus inventory. Replenishment, again, is all about reaction, whereas inventory policy is all about holding inventories at a point where replenishment can act within effective tolerances and not react to wild swings of purchasing.

This means that the important aspect of demand for the inventory policy is the size of the demand variance against the expected size of the inventory requirement. This is important on both sides of the demand spectrum. For instance, even if there might be 1,000 widgets a week being forecasted, if the demand variance is only 1 to 2 percent, that means there only needs to be a safety stock of 10 to 20 widgets on hand to satisfy the extremely high confidence level. On the flipside, an intermittent demand product might only sell 1 widget every other week, but the forecast confidence is low at 20 percent. This would mean a high number of low-volume widgets on hand to counter the low demand/high variance dilemma.

DEVELOPING POLICY OUTPUTS

Inventory optimization calculates four types of replenishment policies, based on the specified policy type:

1. $SS = (s, S)$ policy: When the inventory position falls to or below the reorder level, s, an order is placed so as to raise the inventory position to the order-up-to level, S. In other words, if the inventory position is y and y is less than s, then an order of size $S - y$ is placed. The (s, S) policy is sometimes referred to as the min-max policy. Note that the size of the replenishment order is always greater than or equal to $S - s$.

2. $BS = (s, S)$ policy when $S = s + 1$ (base-stock policy): When the inventory position falls to or below the reorder level, s, an order is placed so as to raise the inventory position to the order-up-to level, S. When $S = s + 1$, the (s, S) policy is called a base-stock policy. (A base-stock policy is also called an order-up-to policy, one-to-one replenishment policy, or installation stock policy.)

3. $NQ = (s, nQ)$ policy when you have a fixed ordering cost for each lot ordered: You incur a fixed ordering cost for each lot ordered.

When the inventory position falls to or below the reorder level, s, an order is placed to bring the inventory position just above s. The size of this order is a multiple of the base lot size, Q. In other words, if the inventory position is y and y is less than s, then an order of size nQ is placed, where n is the smallest integer such that $y + nQ$ is greater than s. In this case, both s and Q are decision variables; you can use the LOTSIZE = option if Q is to be a previously specified value rather than a decision variable. When $Q = 1$, the (s, nQ) policy becomes a base-stock policy.

4. $RQ = (s, nQ)$ policy when you incur a single fixed ordering cost: You incur a single fixed ordering cost independent of the number of lots ordered. When the inventory position falls to or below the reorder level, s, an order is placed to bring the inventory position just above s. The size of this order is a multiple of the base lot size, Q.

Now that we have a basic understanding of the various inputs that go into the calculations of inventory optimization policies, let's take a look at the various ways the output can be produced. It is important to understand that outputs can be different, depending on whether you are looking at a single-echelon, two-echelon, or multiechelon output with replenishment. Therefore, let's take a look at each combination.

The Single Echelon

The single-echelon problem is the most simplistic and, in most cases, mimics what happens in ERP systems due to the overall lack of arc data flowing from one location to the next. The key differential is that the optimization results will allow for individualized policies, whereas the ERP system will run on the rule-of-thumb days or weeks of supply. However, it is good to see the effects of the single echelon before advancing to more complex models in dual- and multiechelon models.

A single-echelon model follows the concept of a single warehouse, group of warehouses, or stores that do not ship to each other. They occupy a single level in the hierarchy. As such, the input table is simplistic and would look something like the one shown in Figure 5.2. The main inputs are holding cost, fixed costs, mean or average lead time,

				Input Data Set			
Obs	sku	holding Cost	fixed Cost	LTmean	RTDmean	RTDvar	service Level
1	A	0.35	90	1	125.1	2170.8	0.95
2	B	0.05	50	2	140.3	1667.7	0.95
3	C	0.12	50	3	116.0	3213.4	0.95
4	D	0.10	75	1	291.8	5212.4	0.95
5	E	0.45	75	2	134.5	1980.5	0.95

Figure 5.2 Single-Echelon Input Data

mean or average demand, demand variance, and the required service level. From these inputs, the inventory optimization procedures are going to produce an output that will be consumed by the ERP system to optimize the inventory positioning away from rule-of-thumb days or weeks of supply to a unique inventory policy specific to the cost and demand inputs (see Figure 5.3).

At this point, it may be advisable to refer back to Figure 5.1. The output of the policy data set fulfills two functions: policy and reporting.

The first part of the results will be the "output." Referring to Figure 5.3, the required output for inventory optimization would be

				Policy Data Set				
Obs	sku	reorder Level	order UpTo Level	avg Inventory	avg Backorder	avg Order Freq	avgCost	inventory Ratio
1	A	211	463	133.739	6.0735	0.43646	86.0905	1.06906
2	B	335	842	229.279	6.8941	0.29107	26.0175	1.63420
3	C	470	792	216.028	6.0123	0.34361	43.1037	1.86231
4	D	432	1074	282.873	14.4130	0.42098	59.8611	0.96941
5	E	382	597	131.757	6.6193	0.50730	97.3379	0.97961

Obs	backorder Ratio	turnover	fill Rate	ready Rate	_algorithm_	_status_
1	0.048550	0.93540	0.95155	0.87037	FR-SS-NO	SUCCESSFUL
2	0.049138	0.61192	0.95139	0.88256	FR-SS-NO	SUCCESSFUL
3	0.051830	0.53697	0.95122	0.90925	FR-SS-NO	SUCCESSFUL
4	0.049393	1.03156	0.95062	0.85239	FR-SS-NO	SUCCESSFUL
5	0.049214	1.02082	0.95109	0.86866	FR-SS-NO	SUCCESSFUL

Figure 5.3 Single-Echelon Data Output

the "order-up-to level" and the "reorder level." As you can see from the "Obs" or five "SKUs," each has been assigned a specific policy output instead of a rule-based days or weeks of supply.

- **Reorder level:** The reorder level is the inventory level at which a replenishment order should be placed.
- **Order-up-to level:** This specifies the order-up-to level, S, for (s, S) policies or the sum of the reorder level and the base lot size, $s + Q$, for (s, nQ) policies.

Each of these policy parameters is assigned to the product/location combination and moved to the ERP system for execution. Each of these assignments overcomes the 20/10/70 problem of rule-of-thumb assignments. These policies give the product/location combinations the ability to be right-sized and, if needed, moved individually or in mass if a different service level is required. To illustrate this point, stock-keeping units (SKUs) C and E had mean demand numbers of 116 and 134.5, respectively. In a rule-of-thumb scenario, they would most likely have had similar inventories. However, due to (1) different holding and fixed costs and (2) different demand variances, the inventory positioning is dramatically different in the optimization mode. Indeed, the slower-moving SKU C has a higher policy requirement due to lower costs and a higher demand variance. In the rule-of-thumb assignment mode, SKU C would have been in the 20 percent understock category.

The rest of the output from the inventory policy optimization has to do with reporting. Each of the reporting key performance indicators (KPIs) in Figure 5.3 can be used for review and alerting to potential problems. Those KPIs are as follows:

- **Average inventory:** Average inventory is the average on-hand inventory at the end of a review period.
- **Average backorder:** Average backorders is the average amount of cumulative backorders in a review period.
- **Average order frequency:** Average ordering frequency is the average number of replenishment orders placed per review period.

- **Average cost:** Average cost is the average cost (including holding, ordering, and backorder penalty costs) incurred per review period.

- **Inventory ratio:** Inventory ratio is equal to the average inventory divided by the average demand.

- **Backorder ratio:** Backorder ratio is equal to average number of backorders divided by the average demand.

- **Turnover:** Turnover is equal to the average demand divided by the average inventory. The value of this variable is set to missing if the estimated average inventory is 0.

- **Fill rate:** Fill rate is the fraction of demand that is satisfied from on-hand inventory.

- **Ready rate:** Ready rate is the probability of no stockout in a review time period.

- **Algorithm:** The value of the _ALGORITHM_ variable is in the form of XX-YY-ZZ, where XX indicates the type of optimization used, YY indicates type of policy calculated, and ZZ indicates the approximation used for both lead-time demand and (Lead Time + Review Time) – Demand distributions.

An example of algorithm variables is shown in Figure 5.4.

Possible Values of the _ALGORITHM_ Variable

String	Value	Description
XX	PC	Penalty cost
	FR	Fill rate
	RR	Ready rate
	BR	Backorder ratio
YY	BS	$(S-1, S)$ base-stock policy
	SS	(s, S) policy (or (s, nQ, S) policy if a base lot size Q is specified)
	NQ	(s, nQ) policy, fixed ordering cost for each lot ordered
	RQ	(s, nQ) policy, single fixed ordering cost independent of the number of lots ordered
ZZ	NO	Normal distribution
	GA	Gamma distribution

Figure 5.4 Possible Algorithm Variables

The Two-Echelon Distributions

A two-echelon-distribution inventory system consists of a single warehouse and multiple retail locations.

The retail locations do not incur a fixed cost when ordering from the warehouse; therefore, the retail locations usually follow a base-stock policy. However, the warehouse incurs a fixed cost when ordering from an outside supplier; the warehouse can therefore follow an (s, S) or (s, nQ) policy. Inventory optimization can find nearly optimal policies for two-echelon-distribution inventory systems with different service constraints on the retail locations.

As you can see in Figure 5.5, the two-echelon input looks similar to the single-echelon except there is the introduction of a location hierarchy and the assignment of the respective needs of fixed ordering costs at the warehouse and the service level requirements at the customer-facing stores.

At this point, it is extremely important to examine the output data from a reporting perspective (see Figure 5.6). The report and order-up-to levels have been assigned for the warehouses and the

Obs	sku	warehouse	location	holding Cost
1	A	Raleigh, NC		0.35
2	A	Raleigh, NC	Atlanta, GA	0.70
3	A	Raleigh, NC	Baltimore, MD	0.70
4	A	Raleigh, NC	Charleston, SC	0.70
5	B	Greensboro, NC		0.05
6	B	Greensboro, NC	Atlanta, GA	0.10
7	B	Greensboro, NC	Charleston, SC	0.10

Obs	fixed Cost	LTmean	RTDmean	RTDvar	service Level
1	90	1	125.1	2170.8	.
2	.	2	32.6	460.2	0.95
3	.	2	61.8	1133.5	0.95
4	.	1	30.7	577.1	0.95
5	50	2	140.3	1667.7	.
6	.	2	68.4	907.3	0.95
7	.	1	71.9	760.4	0.95

Figure 5.5 Dual or Two-Echelon Input Data

Obs	sku	warehouse	location	reorder Level	order UpTo Level	avg Inventory
1	A	Raleigh, NC		124	376	67.550
2	A	Raleigh, NC	Atlanta, GA	168	169	66.030
3	A	Raleigh, NC	Baltimore, MD	293	294	98.618
4	A	Raleigh, NC	Charleston, SC	132	133	66.694
5	B	Greensboro, NC		238	745	151.103
6	B	Greensboro, NC	Atlanta, GA	296	297	83.004
7	B	Greensboro, NC	Charleston, SC	217	218	64.683

Obs	avg Backorder	avg Order Freq	avgCost	inventory Ratio	backorder Ratio	turnover
1	26.8844	0.43646	224.864	0.53997	0.21490	1.85197
2	1.9299	0.99984	46.221	2.02547	0.05920	0.49371
3	3.4774	1.00000	69.033	1.59577	0.05627	0.62666
4	1.7799	0.99820	46.686	2.17244	0.05798	0.46031
5	25.7180	0.29107	36.877	1.07700	0.18331	0.92851
6	3.7423	1.00000	8.300	1.21351	0.05471	0.82406
7	3.6626	1.00000	6.468	0.89962	0.05094	1.11158

Obs	fill Rate	ready Rate	_algorithm_	_status_
1	0.79626	0.64136	__-SS-GA	SUCCESSFUL
2	0.94991	0.92813	FR-BS-GA	SUCCESSFUL
3	0.95002	0.91638	FR-BS-GA	SUCCESSFUL
4	0.95101	0.93722	FR-BS-GA	SUCCESSFUL
5	0.83310	0.72480	__-SS-GA	SUCCESSFUL
6	0.94927	0.89959	FR-BS-GA	SUCCESSFUL
7	0.95155	0.88633	FR-BS-GA	SUCCESSFUL

Figure 5.6 Dual or Two-Echelon Output Data

stores. That information will be sent off to the ERP system for execution. The majority of the reporting data will be the same between that of the single-echelon and the two-echelon system. However, now we are entering into the true benefits of inventory optimization. The Raleigh and Greensboro, North Carolina, stores have been optimized with near 95 percent service levels at customer-facing locations. The optimization process examined the inputs of the fill rate service level at the stores and computed the proper upstream service levels at the warehouse to support the 95 percent store requirements. Given the lead-times, costs, and demand/supply variances, the warehouses only need a 79 to 83 percent fill rate service level to insure the stores are at 95 percent. This creates two key advantages of inventory optimization: (1) Upstream locations do not need to mirror downstream service levels to get high SLs at the stores, and (2) the demand and supply variances do not amplify as they aggregate and move upstream. This stops the redundant inventory problem found in bullwhip situations.

The Multiechelon Distribution with Replenishment

The multiechelon system is where we move into the true benefits of optimization. The key to that next step is the understanding and rational response to the upstream locations having finite quantities of inventory to deliver across large numbers of downstream locations.

When replenishment is added to the mix, the arc information traveling back and forth between nodes resonates. At this point, the penalties of too much stock are measured against the downside of out-of-stocks. Now the system has to consider the following three questions:

1. Where should inventory be stocked?
2. When should the inventory be stocked?
3. How much of the inventory should be stocked?

In the situation where multiechelon is positioned, there is more than one way for the product to flow (networks) and how the flow is manipulated (multiple service levels). This complexity is further complicated by the way replenishment acts.

In the beginning of this book, I made a comment about the perception of *what inventory optimization is* by where you sit in the supply chain. The premise was that the closer you were to the customer the more optimization was replenishment. Here is the tipping point of that misconception. When it comes to replenishment, nothing is more pure than continuous replenishment. Earlier in this chapter, we talked about periodic versus continuous replenishment. In actuality, we are not talking about replenishment as much as we are talking about the period of review of the inventory to best place an order. In continuous review, the concept is just like Kanban: one consumed/one ordered. To a person involved in replenishment, if a product could be continuously reviewed and have a very short lead time and known demand, there would be very little reason to hold inventory.

Continuous review can and does work in a very limited window of products. However, most products have constraints placed on them to help the economics of positioning inventory and the logistics of moving stock from one place to another. Continuous replenishment would have millions of little packages being carried on a million UPS trucks,

FedEx trucks, or mail carriers. In actuality, replenishment orders need to be accumulated into mixed orders from the same location or vendor and shipped under agreed-on minimum and maximum weights and cubes. For that to occur, the concept of periodic replenishment was introduced. Periodic review mimics the daily or weekly base period between orders.

When the lag in review is introduced, the rest of the constraints can fall into place. The key to this rolling together of the various constraints to a periodic review is the introduction of a unique safety stock calculated for each location as it interacts with the rest of the network. The safety stock number is not so much a real number as a segment of the low end of the inventory levels set up so that there is the allowance of variability to demand and supply.

For instance, let's take a look at a single-echelon situation through the calculation process of multiechelon optimization.

The first step is to see the simplistic output of the policies shown in Figure 5.7.

As you can see, there really isn't much difference between single-echelon optimization and single-location network flows and a time period. Given that the input demand was consistent, as was the demand variance, the reorder levels, order-up-to levels, and the safety stock policies are going to stay consistent for the next five periods.

The second step is to see the order generation produced at the network level shown in Figure 5.8.

Again, you can see a pretty consistent view to the way single-echelon optimization works. The network order is generated for the warehouse location "W" for the current period. There is no need to

Obs	Network ID	Sku Loc	Description	Echelon	Period	Reorder Level	Order UpTo Level	Safety Stock	_STATUS_
1	S1	W	WAREHOUSE	1	1	234	235	55	SUCCESSFUL
2	S1	W	WAREHOUSE	1	2	234	235	55	SUCCESSFUL
3	S1	W	WAREHOUSE	1	3	234	235	55	SUCCESSFUL
4	S1	W	WAREHOUSE	1	4	234	235	55	SUCCESSFUL
5	S1	W	WAREHOUSE	1	5	234	235	55	SUCCESSFUL

Figure 5.7 Single-Echelon Inventory Policies

Obs	Network ID	Sku Loc	Description	Echelon	Period	Order Quantity	Allocated Quantity	_STATUS_
1	S1	W	WAREHOUSE	1	1	139	139	SUCCESSFUL

Figure 5.8 Single-Echelon Order Suggestion

produce orders out into the future unless different lead times were required.

The real benefit of multiechelon optimization is the weighing of the various KPIs of inventory costs and ordering costs against the expected demand and supply variances (backlog). Once the threshold has been crossed, the order is generated. Keep in mind that this is a single-echelon environment. In larger and more complex networks, the orders would be weighed against the cost of the total network to insure harmony between upstream and downstream locations.

In this example shown in Figure 5.9, the warehouse has a very stable demand stream at 90 units per week. The on-hand average/mean

Obs	Network ID	Sku Loc	Description	Echelon	Period	External Demand Mean	External Demand Var	Internal Demand Mean	Internal Demand Var
1	S1	W	WAREHOUSE	1	1	90	900	0	0
2	S1	W	WAREHOUSE	1	2	90	900	0	0
3	S1	W	WAREHOUSE	1	3	90	900	0	0
4	S1	W	WAREHOUSE	1	4	90	900	0	0
5	S1	W	WAREHOUSE	1	5	90	900	0	0

Obs	Order Mean	Order Var	Planned Receipt Mean	Planned Receipt Var	Pipeline Mean	Pipeline Var	OnHand Mean	OnHand Var	Backlog Mean
1	0.0000	0.000	96.000	0.000	139.000	0.000	15.0955	395.38	9.43364
2	90.3378	917.582	139.000	0.000	90.338	917.582	56.6423	1544.42	1.94400
3	89.9639	925.177	90.338	917.582	89.964	925.177	57.4567	1591.12	1.76038
4	89.3397	891.304	89.964	925.177	89.340	891.304	57.3119	1547.10	1.77337
5	90.1216	917.221	89.340	891.304	90.122	917.221	57.1314	1548.43	2.00373

Obs	Backlog Var	Shortfall Mean	Shortfall Var	Ready Rate	Fill Rate	Backorder Ratio	_STATUS_
1	237.270	0	0	0.56231	0.89557	0.10443	SUCCESSFUL
2	61.301	0	0	0.89954	0.97839	0.02161	SUCCESSFUL
3	53.870	0	0	0.90489	0.98030	0.01970	SUCCESSFUL
4	57.150	0	0	0.90547	0.98032	0.01968	SUCCESSFUL
5	64.418	0	0	0.90002	0.97767	0.02233	SUCCESSFUL

Figure 5.9 Single-Echelon Reporting

for the week is 15, so an order is generated. However, a closer look sees the additional computations that will come into play later in more complex networks. The backlog mean jumps up to show the expected potential of not being able to cover demand, and the variance also jumps. As a result, the fill rate continues for the period at just under 90 percent and, given the steady demand, the fill rate will rise to 97 to 98 percent going forward. This ability to anticipate ordering during a periodic review across networks gives power to inventory optimization.

When are different policy types required?

The Min-Max Policy

The min-max policy is recommended when the fixed ordering cost is significantly higher than the inventory holding cost. In this case, a large amount of inventory should be ordered to make replenishment less frequent. The order-up-to level in this policy is greater than the reorder level by at least one.

We often see this type of policy in place at a distribution center compared to that of a store situation. In a distribution center, the constraints placed on ordering dictate that more than just one unit is required to complete an order. In many cases, fairly large minimums can be in place, and those minimums must be further constrained to fill a complete truckload quantity so that added ordering and transportation costs are not levied. The result of the min-max policy is to create a natural periodic review that coordinates the total ordering of like items from a vendor or upstream location. Oftentimes this might be set up so that ordering from a specific vendor and vendor location is to be done on a weekly basis on a consistent day. This further allows for the consistent delivery on a projected day a week or more out depending on the lead time negotiated.

The min-max process will drive a lot size multiple order so that it goes from the order point threshold and up to the order-up-to point or slightly beyond. In a single-echelon environment, there are few or no penalties placed upon the timing of the order. However, in the multiechelon system the timing of the order goes beyond just the crossing of the order point threshold. The constraints on backlog, backorder penalty costs, and lost sales are taken into consideration as further measurements to the total network orders in the chain are synchronized.

- ■ **Backlog:** The backlog is the amount of demand that is not satisfied by the on-hand inventory at a SKU-location. The backlog is carried over to future periods until it is satisfied.

- ■ **Backorder penalty costs:** Penalty (backordering or shortage) cost is the cost incurred when a stockout occurs. This cost might include the cost of emergency shipments, cost of substitution of a less profitable item, or cost of lost goodwill. For instance, will the customer ever return? Will the customer's colleagues be told of the poor service? The most common convention is to specify penalty cost as per-period per-unit and then apply it to the average number of backorders.

- ■ **Lost-sales option:** A lost-sales inventory system enables unsatisfied demand to be lost rather than backordered. For an (s, S) policy, this system can be approximated by using the fill rate service measure with some slight modifications.

The Base-Stock Policy

The base-stock policy is recommended when the fixed costs of ordering are lower compared to the inventory holding costs. This creates an ordering environment where very small quantities are replenished. Indeed, in most cases the order is 1. Often we see this type of behavior in a retail store situation where orders are placed by the 1s and 2s and banded together at the upstream warehouse for delivery over a short time horizon. The lengths of the order period and lead time are much shorter than one would experience in a min-max process.

While important in a base-stock inventory model, the backlog, backorder penalty costs, and lost-sales options are not as critical to the order threshold timing. Orders are placed when there has been a reduction in stock. In many ways, the base-stock policy is the method of ordering for any Kanban-style system. The JIT/Kanban system was built on low ordering costs to the cost of the inventory. As such, and one can see why a Kanban-style environment would create problems for a min-max world, there is one-for-one replacement of stock just as there would be on the production floor. With min-max, there is too much time taken up overcoming the ordering cost constraints. This was a most serious flaw in the ERP ordering systems and led to what we previously showed as rule-of-thumb days-of-supply requirements. The rules were an attempt to overcome the min-max constraint problems.

Let's take a look at an example of what a siloed or sequential optimization process looks like compared to multiechelon optimization. One can see how constraints of upstream and downstream locations can have an effect on the inventory.

In the optimization run in Figure 5.10, you can see several things happening:

- Each of the components or retailers in the other example has almost identical reorder levels and order-up-to levels. There is no distinction from one to another; they all have the days-of-supply metric of 97 or 98.

Obs	Network ID	SKU Loc	Description	Echelon	Period	Reorder Level	Order-Up-To Level	Safety Stock
1	N2	FC	Retailer 1	1	1	97	98	2
2	N2	FC	Retailer 1	1	2	97	98	2
3	N2	FC	Retailer 1	1	3	97	98	2
4	N2	FC	Retailer 1	1	4	97	98	2
5	N2	FC	Retailer 1	1	5	97	98	2
6	N2	FC	Retailer 1	1	6	97	98	2
7	N2	FC	Retailer 1	1	7	97	98	2
8	N2	FC	Retailer 1	1	8	97	98	2
9	N2	FD	Retailer 2	1	1	96	97	1
10	N2	FD	Retailer 2	1	2	96	97	1
11	N2	FD	Retailer 2	1	3	96	97	1
12	N2	FD	Retailer 2	1	4	96	97	1
13	N2	FD	Retailer 2	1	5	96	97	1
14	N2	FD	Retailer 2	1	6	96	97	1
15	N2	FD	Retailer 2	1	7	96	97	1
16	N2	FD	Retailer 2	1	8	96	97	1
17	N2	FW	Warehouse	2	1	84	85	21
18	N2	FW	Warehouse	2	2	84	85	21
19	N2	FW	Warehouse	2	3	84	85	21
20	N2	FW	Warehouse	2	4	84	85	21
21	N2	FW	Warehouse	2	5	84	85	21
22	N2	FW	Warehouse	2	6	84	85	21
23	N2	FW	Warehouse	2	7	84	85	21
24	N2	FW	Warehouse	2	8	84	85	21

Figure 5.10 Sequential Optimization Based on Hierarchies Being Optimized without Visibility Upstream or Downstream: Islands of Efficiency

- Given the base-stock policy at the stores and the always-assumed 100 percent service level from the upstream location, the safety stock will be extremely low.
- While the upstream warehouse category "finished goods" has a low total inventory, the safety stock is pretty much an accumulation of the store safety stock.

Every buyer who has ever done any replenishment in a store/warehouse chain knows the problem this methodology just set up. The downstream locations are set up with a baseline inventory with no variation. Just like the 20/10/70 split shown before, we have stores that are either overstocked, understocked, or just right, but the safety stock has no bearing on the real variations of demand placed on the store. Given the random readiness of the downstream stores to support the demand, the upstream warehouse is not in a position to support any variation in demand from those stores. Just like in the Toyota Kanban situation, the stores have off-loaded their inventory risk upstream to the warehouse. By having low inventory and low safety stocks, the stores have put the warehouse in a precarious position. The warehouse is expecting consistent demand due to the low inventory levels and low safety stock requirements in the stores. Similar to the Toyota Kanban environment, an unexpected uptick in store demand will create a supply disruption and a recipe for disaster.

Now we shift to a true multiechelon optimization process in Figure 5.11:

- Each of the retailer locations is positioned as the main point of the demand stream. Therefore, each location is assigned its own inventory policy to fit the costs and the variation of demand.
- Stock levels are uniquely positioned, going from a low of 61 to a high of 100.
- Safety stocks are correctly placed to react to the appropriate supply and demand variations.
- The correct upstream inventory positions have been set so they recognize the true downstream variations.

Obs	Network ID	SKU Loc	Description	Echelon	Period	Reorder Level	Order-Up-To Level	Safety Stock
1	N2	FC	Retailer 1	1	1	66	67	12
2	N2	FC	Retailer 1	1	2	60	61	11
3	N2	FC	Retailer 1	1	3	60	61	11
4	N2	FC	Retailer 1	1	4	72	73	13
5	N2	FC	Retailer 1	1	5	83	84	14
6	N2	FC	Retailer 1	1	6	89	90	15
7	N2	FC	Retailer 1	1	7	95	96	16
8	N2	FC	Retailer 1	1	8	95	96	16
9	N2	FD	Retailer 2	1	1	81	82	12
10	N2	FD	Retailer 2	1	2	93	94	14
11	N2	FD	Retailer 2	1	3	99	100	15
12	N2	FD	Retailer 2	1	4	99	100	15
13	N2	FD	Retailer 2	1	5	99	100	15
14	N2	FD	Retailer 2	1	6	93	94	14
15	N2	FD	Retailer 2	1	7	87	88	13
16	N2	FD	Retailer 2	1	8	87	88	13
17	N2	FW	Warehouse	2	1	113	114	8
18	N2	FW	Warehouse	2	2	140	141	9
19	N2	FW	Warehouse	2	3	146	147	8
20	N2	FW	Warehouse	2	4	151	152	9
21	N2	FW	Warehouse	2	5	150	151	10
22	N2	FW	Warehouse	2	6	150	151	11
23	N2	FW	Warehouse	2	7	149	150	11
24	N2	FW	Warehouse	2	8	149	150	12

Figure 5.11 Multiechelon or Systematic/Network Optimization Where the Entire Network Optimizes as One Entity

■ Rather than be an accumulated number for the safety stock at the warehouse, the correct safety stock is in place because of far less randomness from the downstream locations.

The buyer in this situation will be doing far fewer tactical replenishment activities to overcome mis-positioned inventory at the stores and warehouse and will be able to let the optimization system do the heavy lifting, thereby saving time and money.

CHAPTER 6

Shifting the Focus from an Algorithm Discussion to a Business Discussion

A s discussed earlier, the math behind inventory optimization had its start in Operations Research and came to fruition in the late 1990s and early 2000s. Professors at various universities, both domestic and international, developed processes that would enable the calming of the bullwhip effect and assign inventories in the best possible positions for the highest service levels at the lowest costs. At first, this PhD "mumbo-jumbo" was viewed as cutting-edge functionality and the realm of the innovator-adapters in various industries. Every new technology idea has the infamous hype cycle.

All business technologies go through an adoption process that has five phases. The length of the adoption rate corresponds to a secondary process called the hype cycle. The hype cycle represents developers of the technology pushing or hyping itself. In Figure 6.1 you can see how the typical adoption process goes through innovation and early adopter phases. During the early adopter phase the hype outpaces the adoption. In essence, the technology almost becomes too good to be true. It is during this period that a technology can solve all business problems during the day and have enough time to fix dinner and put

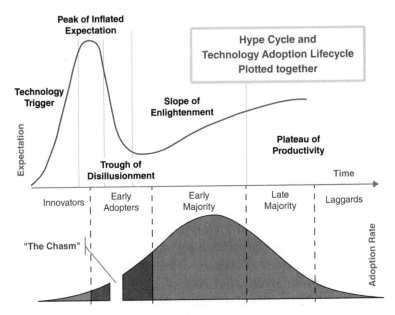

Figure 6.1 Hype Cycle and Acceptance Rates

the kids to bed! Most technologies hit what is known as the *chasm* at this point and, if they are lucky, go through a *trough of disillusionment*. Many technologies don't and stall out before there is a major adoption process.

Inventory optimization hit the chasm in 2010. There was massive evidence of business success produced by the innovators and early adopters, but inventory optimization expansion slowed. There are several ideas about why this happened, but most fall into two areas. First, the global recession starting in 2008 dramatically slowed the adoption of inventory optimization techniques. This is especially true in inventory areas where company performance was difficult to pin to the inventory in question. For instance, the service parts inventory optimization segment dried up as companies decided to put emphasis on other areas for cost control. Indeed, at a time when inventory cost control should have been at the forefront of executive focus during a recessionary period, the vision shifted to market share protection and revenues. Second, there was a view that inventory optimization required a room full of workers with PhDs to continue the success found in the innovator and early-adopter projects. During my time working in the industry, I saw this second chasm maker as a bigger problem than the shift in executive focus!

Inventory optimization experts would assemble at the install site and begin to talk about the proprietary algorithms or the fancy fine tuning that only "this particular technology provider" could do. I can imagine the thought process the organization in question would have when the "experts" left the install site. Instead of making inventory optimization easier to use, technology providers were making the solution seem extremely difficult to use and even more difficult to understand. No wonder there was so much pushback from planners, buyers, and analysts when it came to the adoption of inventory optimization. They were being told that technology was going to help them, but it was too "technical" for them to understand.

This, in my humble opinion, is where the inventory optimization adoption chasm has opened up. It keeps inventory optimization from being widely adopted and used. In order for the technology to be accepted, it has to pass the usability test. Up until this time, the usability test has been focused on the person who develops and maintains the optimization data model and not the typical business user who might interact with the decision support provided by inventory optimization. Think of it this way: The usability has been focused on how you build and fix the car, and not how it drives.

Building and maintaining models is not the only facet of inventory optimization. Certainly model integrity is important to the results, but inventory optimization can be used to measure the impact of optimization from a business perspective. How does your supply chain react to demand changes? Service-level changes? Lead-time changes? In a way, IO should be thought of as a *cost-reaction* business repository for your distribution supply chain.

Instead of being a reactionary, execution system just feeding optimal inventory policies to the ERP system, inventory optimization can help the supply side be a collaborative partner in demand planning and be a forward-looking inventory planner. In essence, it can be a productivity tool for business users. For instance, inventory optimization should be able to use either the statistical forecast or the consensus forecast for best results. Having the ability to loop a weighted consensus forecast and use the same disaggregation process allows for inventory optimization to be an active participant in the S&OP process—not just an outgrowth of the operations silo.

Allowing the user interface of inventory optimization to cater to the business user enables the functionality to spill over into real business processes and business decision making. There needs to be a place for the inner fine tuning of models and that should not be overlooked, but the true benefits of inventory optimization only come through when the "doers" of the supply chain can participate in its use.

PUTTING THE ALGORITHMS INTO THE HANDS OF THE BUSINESS USERS FOR BEST RESULTS

Okay, how do I adjust the lead-time variance of x product and y location?

This question comes up all the time during an install of inventory optimization. I find it amusing because prior to learning about inventory optimization, the person in question never heard of lead-time variation. Inventory optimization suddenly opens up all kinds of options to fine tune models, and many analysts feel like a kid in a candy story with so many choices. Inputs can be shifted to allow for dampening of demand variance. Outputs can be overridden to bring down inventory when *tribal knowledge* trumps the computations. The options are almost unlimited.

However, in the hands of many buyer/planners with individual goals, an optimized inventory model can be rendered inoperable in a very short time. Some may disagree with me, but I have found there are two distinct users of inventory optimization: business users and analyst users. It is best to let the business users work on the business decisions and let the analysts deal with the data integrity. Let me explain why. A client who had purchased inventory optimization was dealing with high levels of seasonality and expensive, intermittent demand products. In this case, *intermittent* meant that they were sporadic and lumpy. The orders would come in not as 1, but 5 to 10 after many periods of no demand. The business users were extremely concerned about any deviation of the inventory and wanted to have close tolerances placed on all inventory levels. The company wanted business users to have control of the inputs and outputs of their portfolio. Within weeks, the results were out of control and the inventory was at an all-time high, and out-of-stocks were increasing. One look at the information quickly showed that the business users were putting tight thresholds on the outputs and overriding the optimization with their own business-rule-generated outcome. In other words, if *a* happens, do *b*, *c*, *d*, or *e*, depending on the product classification.

If it wasn't so expensive, it might have been pretty comical. The business users were doing what they have always done. They were gaming the system to make themselves look good. They were chasing numbers and overriding the results whenever the output did not meet with their knowledge. As I pointed out in the reference to the MIT Beer Game 2, individuals will overreact to a change in demand. This inward view of the supply chain will optimize the individual node but push suboptimized inventory onto other nodes in the chain. Giving technical and advanced functionality to untrained business users can and will have an adverse effect on inventory optimization.

In essence, fine tuning of models is the realm of the analysts. They need to be able to deal with the models in a more detached manner and have a network view, not a node view. They need to work in the data with data integration tools, not in an inventory optimization user interface. That inventory optimization interface to get beyond the chasm must be built for the business user!

So how do we put the algorithms into the hands of business users?

WORKING IN A BUSINESS USER ENVIRONMENT

Let's take a look at the interaction of a business user dealing with inventory optimization in a strategic manner. I am going to use SAS Inventory Optimization Workbench and its supporting technology, Data Integration Studio, to demonstrate how business users and analysts might deal with various inventory optimization situations. From the perspective of a business user we will enter into the SAS Inventory Optimization Workspace/Scenario Development Area. The idea is to use the optimization what-if process to understand the implications of strategic business decisions. We are going to take a look at three types of strategic business decisions:

- Service-level changes
- The effect of a business constraint on best-case optimization
- Lead-time changes

In the first instance of service-level changes, we have all experienced situations where a downstream customer wants to have a higher service-level attainment or a service-level agreement is in play for a service parts environment. In these situations, the business user is faced with the limitations of the single-stage calculation problem or sequential optimization found in ERP and SCM solutions. The system simply cannot recognize individual service-level requirements. Therefore, groups of products are given average service-level requirements based on segmentation. Given this situation, this requires an analyst to pull out the products in question and compute a simulation at a higher service level. A single-echelon problem is not too difficult, but adding echelons onto the problem expands the problem exponentially.

I was onsite with a customer who was trying to tackle this from a two-echelon problem perspective. I asked how long would it take for them to compile the simulation and get results. The best guess was two weeks, but there might be some fine tuning and go out to a month. To say the least, I was *gob-smacked*, to use a term I have picked up from my friends in England. I had been using the SAS Inventory Optimization Workbench to do this and was able to get results in minutes.

Changing the Service Level of a Group of Products at a Customer-Facing Location

Using the scenario development workspace, I set up my inputs. I am interested in looking at nine products in RDC7 to understand the inventory requirements in my supply chain to attain a 99 percent service level. Not all of the products in question have one service level so I will be required to bring them from a 92 to 96 percent up to 99 percent. As shown in Figure 6.2, I have named my scenario "SL99_at_RDC7." It is not required, but for many users it is a good idea to create a description so anyone in an approval process will have a good understanding of what is being analyzed.

As far as setting up the inputs, the products, locations, and network flows are created. These inputs can be pulled using various filters like "17 oz. Dee Products with an A classification" in "Customer Facing Locations in the Southeastern United States." It is important to align the network flows so you have the correct directions products are getting to the final destination. For instance, we could see the inclusions of regular and omnichannel directions would help expose the proper results when required.

You could set up multiple options in the same scenario. In this instance, I am only going to look at the results of hitting a 99 percent service level. However, by setting up multiple-service levels one could easily set up a sensitivity analysis and potential diminishing returns at extremely high service levels.

Once the scenario has been set up, the user can also be alerted to KPIs that go out of tolerance and set the thresholds by a percentage. It is interesting how supply chain practitioners will push back on inventory optimization, because they will have *black-box results* shoved at them. The threshold alert process enables the scenario developer the option of communicating major changes to help practitioners

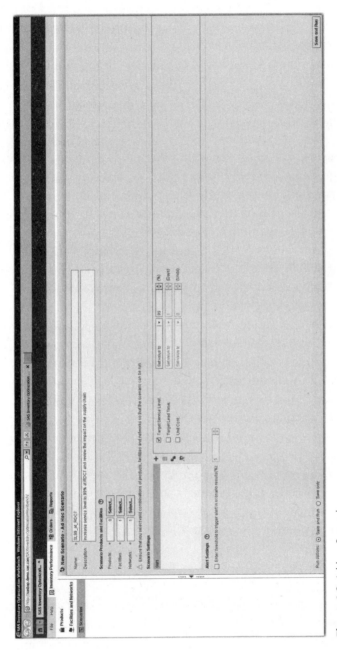

Figure 6.2 Ad-hoc Scenario

understand the results. I am now ready to run the scenario and see the results.

When scenarios are run, the overall results will be the default view. This is extremely important with broad-based strategic changes, but when it comes to spot scenarios on a small set of data, it is best to drill to the specific products and locations to observe the change. In Figure 6.3, I have the RDC7 open, and it will show its position in the network. From the location view, you can see that the service level will go to 99 percent from an average of 95.111 percent. The lead time and demand will be assumed to stay the same in this scenario. If, for instance, demand might change when the service level hits 99 percent, it would be a simple step for the inventory analyst to seamlessly work with the forecast analyst to come up with a new forecast and import the data.

As you can see in Figure 6.3, the required inventory will increase on the portfolio of 17 oz. Dee products at RDC7 to attain the 99 percent service level need. The total cost increase will go from $1,053 to $1,524. The largest cost increase will, obviously, be the *on-hand* inventory costs.

In Figure 6.4, I have shifted the view to the actual products in the scenario. Given the previous service level requirement and inventory cost, the shift in inventory between the current level and the new "Set1" will be computed. As part of the process flow, we often find that analysts are required to get approval before approving any updates. In the SAS Inventory Optimization Workbench, there is an approval/audit trail process in place. As part of this scenario, let's assume that my manager has approved the change to 99 percent service level. What happens next?

In Figure 6.5, I can simply ask for the Set1 scenario to be promoted to the master data. It is simply a click of the "OK" button and the scenario is promoted. An email to the administrator will allow for the update to be ready in the next batch run.

Placing a Budget Constraint on Customer-Facing Locations

Oftentimes, a budget constraint is placed on a product or group of products so that attaining an unlimited service level is not an option. In that case, it is a stepped process of understanding the current service

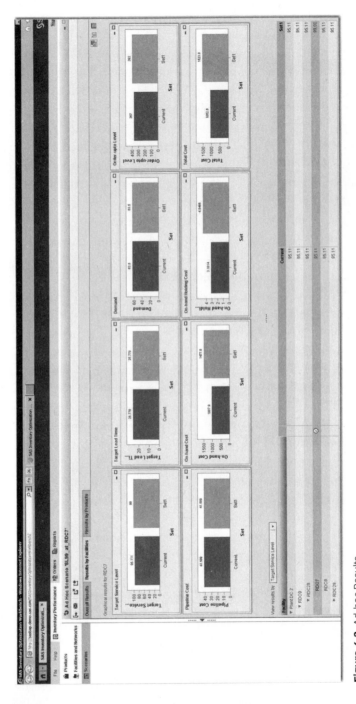

Figure 6.3 Ad-hoc Results

118

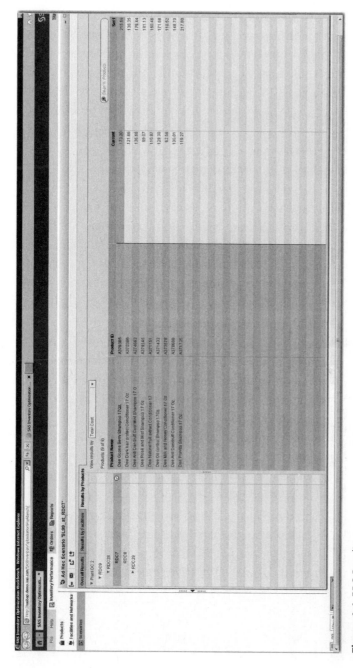

Figure 6.4 RDC Results

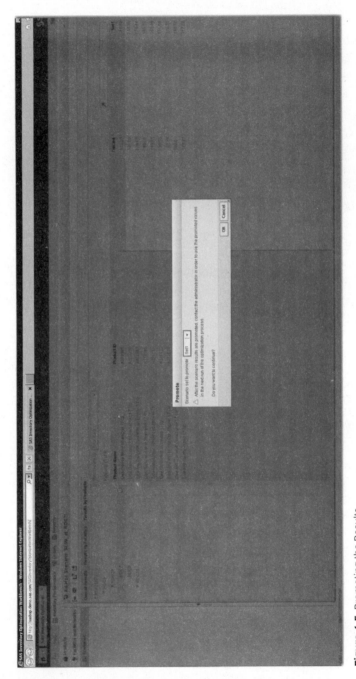

Figure 6.5 Promoting the Results

level, the optimal service level, and the constrained service level at the budget in question.

In Figure 6.6, we are going to go back to RDC7. I have taken all of the facilities and the 15 products in question and run an optimization scenario. I find the stepped process of "current," "optimal," and "constrained" results helps paint a picture for decision makers in this scenario. The current service level in RDC7 is a 95.33 percent average. However, the optimal service level is an average of 96.98 percent.

This is a common occurrence in inventory optimization. Usually, service levels have been set via some kind of business rule, like A items get a 98 percent, B items get a 95 percent, and C items get a 92 percent designation. However, the optimization gives a different view where the cost of holding the inventory allows for a better mix. It can still be adjusted for the A, B, C designation, but it gives a much better assortment projection to keep the unconstrained optimization.

You now have two projections: current and optimized. What is the budget-constrained option?

In Figure 6.7, management has indicated that we cannot go above $9,000. We place that as the maximum inventory and reoptimize the scenario.

Figure 6.8 shows us the results. In the budget-constrained situation, the average service level will come in around 90.5 percent, with the product portfolio based on costs ranging from 89.64 to 92.89 percent. The user can override the optimization to suboptimize to a management prerogative, but it can be documented as being done in the audit trail and communications.

Just as before, in Figure 6.9 the user can quickly and easily promote the results so that the inputs can be changed before the next batch run. When I spoke with a customer about how long it would take to do this process with spreadsheets or single-stage calculations, the answer was three to five weeks. That kind of time makes decision making around budgets or customers to get the best service level extremely unwieldy. This can now be done in minutes!

Changing the Lead Time at a Location

Lead-time changes can be one of the most interesting adjustments because you know you will have a shift in inventory—but just how

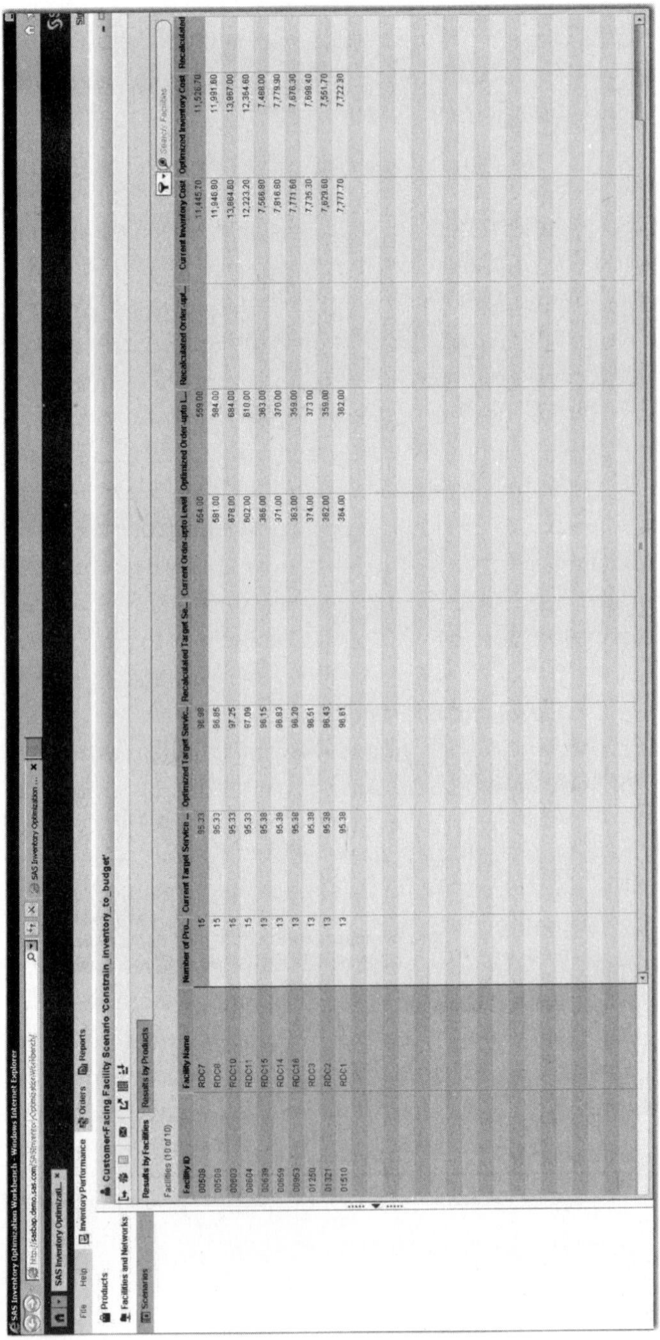

Figure 6.6 Customer-Facing Scenario

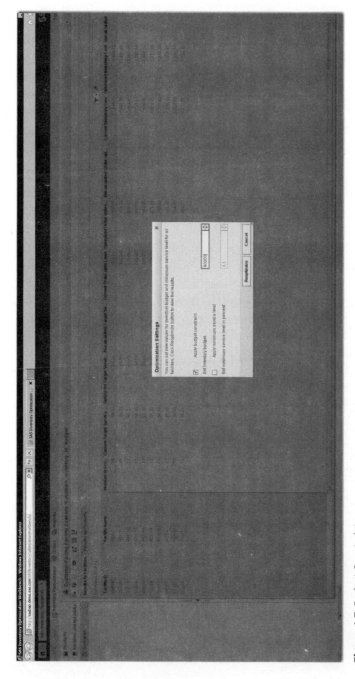

Figure 6.7 Budget Constraint

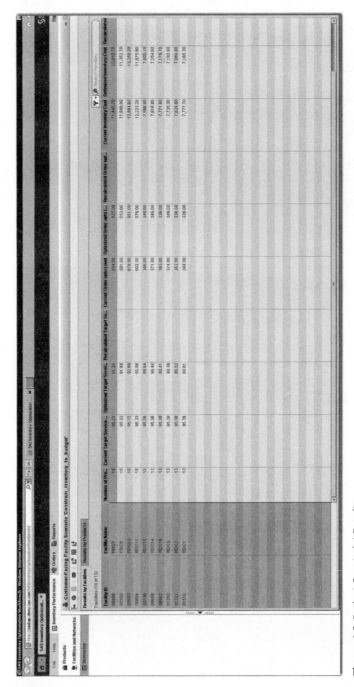

Figure 6.8 Budget Constraint Results

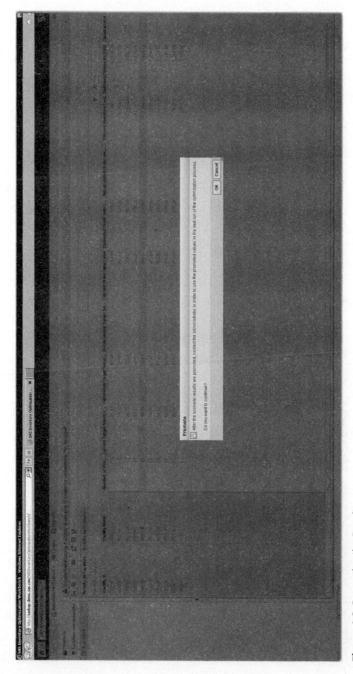

Figure 6.9 Promoting the Results

much, and why? In the majority of cases I have seen in the *spreadsheet management process* of inventory control, the shift would be to raise or lower the lead time and adjust the inventory once the lead time becomes normalized. This would be extremely difficult, using a days-of-supply or coverage number at a single location, but it is next to impossible at a multiechelon situation. However, lead-time shifts do not have to be a problem for the business user. It is simply a process of developing the required order-up-to level, ordering threshold and safety stock for the products in question against the service level using the new lead-time variable.

Let's follow the process of a business user looking to understand the effect of dropping the Dee products lead time from 23 days to 10 days at RDC7. RDC7 is a customer-facing location. When a lead time drops for a single customer facing location it rarely has a huge effect on the upstream location supplying it.

In Figure 6.10, the business user sets up the lead time in Dee products at RDC7 to 10 days. Once the scenario has been set up, the system is run.

In Figure 6.11 the results of the scenario are shown. Obviously, the lead-time drops, but the key is the order-up-to level or max inventory required to attain the same service level. In the case of Dee products at RDC7, there is a 38 percent drop in inventory to 456 units. The pipeline dropped in half due to the shorter lead time. The inventory will be lower and inventory turns will dramatically increase, due to that shorter lead time and the same demand. Overall, the total cost will drop by about 28 percent. When it comes to inventory, lead time has a huge influence.

Let's dig a little deeper. By clicking on the results by product, the order-up-to level for each of the products is now shown (Figure 6.12). Now the results can be promoted by a simple click of the promote button to allow the new inputs to be positioned in the next batch run.

As indicated, it is pretty straightforward to predict a change at a single location. What happens when you make changes to upstream locations? Is there an optimized way the system generates downstream reactions?

To add to the complexity, let's add RDC28, the upstream location to RDC7 and RDC8. We already have RDC7 set at 10 days lead-time.

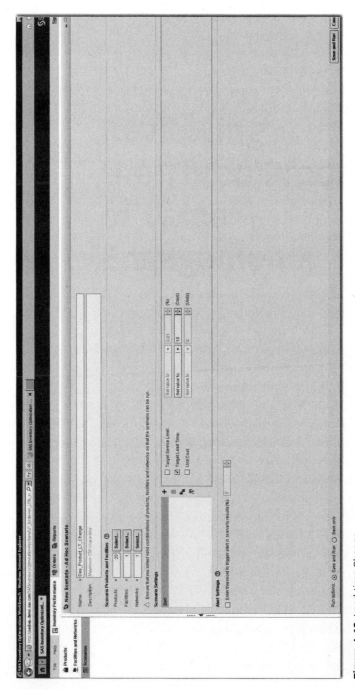

Figure 6.10 Lead-time Change

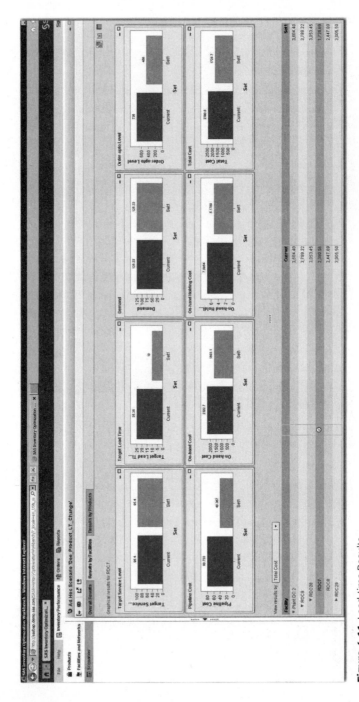

Figure 6.11 Lead-time Results

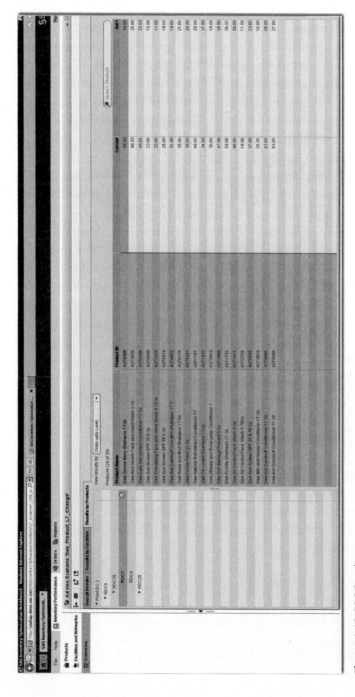

Figure 6.12 RDC Results

Let's keep RDC8 at the same lead-times as before, but lower RDC28 to 10 days lead-time. What is the effect?

The results in Figure 6.13 show that RDC7 will stay the same. RDC28 total cost of inventory dropped to 2145.60, or a reduction of almost 30 percent. Interestingly, there was a slight drop of inventory at RDC8. This is where it gets interesting. I often find inventory control will stop at the RDC28 level and paint the inventory as an aggregate and the underlying inventory will be spread out evenly. Not true! Even without touching RDC8 there will be an effect, but not an even *spread*.

This is where the single-stage calculations or sequential optimization found in most ERP systems fall short. The cutting of the arc data connections makes it so the upstream and downstream locations get proportionate spreads, but they aren't correctly spreading the inventory. In our previous example, you see RDC28 and RDC7 getting most of the benefits, but RDC8 gets a residual effect. Imagine the incorrect results that would have occurred if RDC8 got the same spread as RDC7. The out-of-stocks would have soared! However, if you look closely at Figure 6.14, there is only one product that was affected: Dee Dark Hair Conditioner. While all of the products have very slight shifts in inventory, the Dee Dark Hair Conditioner had a distinct lowering of inventory. In this case, RDC28's LT shift had a profound effect on one product—not on everything!

Most business users playing in the inventory space have been trained to think in a siloed environment. As we have discussed, given the opportunity they will push inventory outside of their silo and claim they are efficient. This is the squeezed-balloon problem. Most inventory, when attacked from a siloed basis, simply moves to another location and the costs remain the same or increase. Multiechelon inventory optimization what-if scenarios enable the business users to see the effects of their decisions.

Why do I bring this up?

There is a distinct difference between what a business user and a technical analyst would be after when dealing with multiechelon inventory optimization, and it is the crux of what I called the optimization *failure to leap* into daily corporate culture.

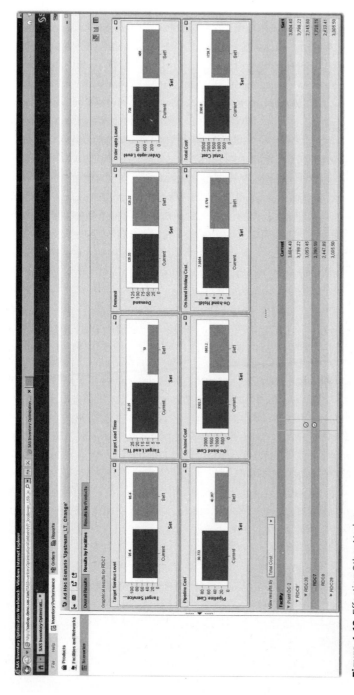

Figure 6.13 Effecting Other Nodes

131

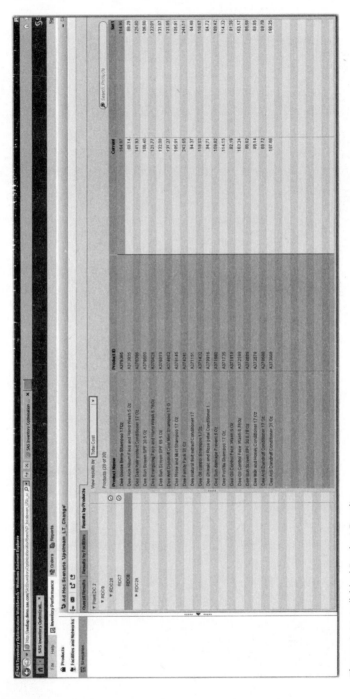

Figure 6.14 Individual Product Results

The Business User Solution

Give them the strength of multiechelon inventory optimization, but provide it with guidelines and fences around their capabilities. Teach them the benefits of cost elimination instead of cost shifting. The business user's job is not to fine tune the tactical inputs and outputs. If they did, they would be caught in a black hole of cause and effect. Since most business users do not have the full view of the supply chain they can't drive down to the minutia. The business user should be looking at the strategic activities in the supply chain and act with decision support from the solution. Measuring the cost implications of a potential service-level agreement is the realm of the business user—not the fine tuning of a coefficient of variation on an intermittent demand product.

The Technical Analyst Solution

I was, recently, at a major food manufacturing site and got the opportunity to sit down with the technical analysts assigned to work with multiechelon inventory optimization. This is a leading CPG company doing almost $20 billion in annual sales. It is a leader in inventory optimization. Guess how many technical analysts it has on staff? Two! This is one of the reasons I feel IO has had a tough time entering the consciousness of most supply chains. The optimization user interfaces are built for a finite technical user who fine-tunes the models.

However, let me be clear. The technical analysts are extremely important to multiechelon inventory optimization. You simply can't turn on optimization and get perfect numbers. There will be improvements, but the best practice is to review and update. Indeed, inventory optimization is a journey, not a final destination. While the business user needs to have boundaries, the technical analyst needs to have free reign.

WORKING IN THE TECHNICAL ANALYST ENVIRONMENT

Technical analysts tend to work on fine-tuning in inventory optimization. That is a bold statement, so let me clarify. I've visited scores of installations, and the majority of time I spend with technical analysts

I find they are working on either fixing bad inputs or adjusting various constraints to cover for an input problem. Therefore, the analyst seems to be put into a strange position of data entry via their user interface. It is no wonder that IO has not crossed the chasm into mainstream inventory management. How boring to spend the day adjusting minutia!

However, this is an important role, but it is not the sole focus role of a business-driven inventory optimization solution. Business users, if given the ability to open up all inputs, would do what they have always done—try to shift the inventory away from their portfolio. The role of the technical analyst is to provide the in-depth knowledge and network-wide influence so costs are pushed out of the chain, not just shifted around.

There are three basic tenets of adjustment when it comes to the internal workings of inventory optimization:

1. Shifting of the safety stock based on a finite inventory budget
2. Aligning a true service level to the importance of the product to the portfolio
3. Adjusting the lead-time variance to provide a true capturing of vendor performance

Shifting of the Safety Stock Based on a Finite Inventory Budget

Let's face it: All inventory is not created equal! The forecast is going to give a confidence level to the demand number and inventory optimization is going to give a projected policy parameter to keep the inventory at the level needed to attain the service level. However, the total inventory is expected to be x dollars. How can I ensure that the most profitable or most important products get the best performance? One way to do that is to fine-tune the coefficient of variation in the inventory optimization solution. You can cap the variance and limit the safety stock. This allows for the upward adjustment on other products to ensure best performance. We see this all the time with long-tail products. Given the high variance due to granular forecasts over time, the IO analyst can see the actual tolerance and adjust down the safety stock

Figure 6.15 FORECASTED_DEMAND_FACT Properties

to correctly cover the required demand. This opens up dollars to apply to other products that require a wider tolerance.

In the SAS Inventory Optimization Workbench, the technical analyst would go to the FORECASTED_DEMAND_FACT Properties, as shown in Figure 6.15, and adjust the variance of the demand for the product/location pairing.

Show in Figure 6.16, the technical analyst would adjust the CV by pairing or create an SAS Data Integration Studio "job" to create a mass change.

Aligning a True Service Level to the Importance of the Product to the Portfolio

Although service level can be adjusted in the business user interface via scenario analysis, the use of table adjustments can increase

Figure 6.16 The SERVICE_LEVEL Properties Table

the fine-tuning done by the technical analyst. The business user service-level adjustments are designed to measure the cost effects of service-level changes to products. This use case centers on something like a service level agreement (SLA) to a downstream location. The technical analysts are fine-tuning the service levels and the coefficient of variation to come up with a safety stock mix. Often, a C product has less need for a high service level. However, it may be more advantageous to tweak the service level and coefficient of variation to come up with a better inventory policy. For instance, the item may have a known constraint capability over time to lower the CV. This may allow for the increase of a service level, but keep the inventory lower than if it had simply been created using service level alone.

The technical analyst can go into the SERVICE_LEVEL Properties table shown in Figure 6.16 and adjust the service level and match it with any fine-tuning down for the CV.

Adjusting the Lead-Time Variance to Provide a True Capturing of Vendor Performance

The business user can adjust lead-time as a mean or average in the ad-hoc scenario. The technical analyst can use the tables to widen or tighten the upper and lower bounds. Vendor performance can have a huge effect on overall service level. A demand variance only affects the *single* product/location pairing. Since the supplier is shipping multiple items on an order the variance of lead-time can have an amplification effect on the entire portfolio. If a vendor has a delivery performance issue, many products can fall out of tolerance. Therefore, the technical analyst can open tables and adjust the upper and lower tolerances. This, effectively, can adjust the overall safety stock for a vendor or location.

In the ARC Properties shown in Figure 6.17, the technical analyst has the ability to adjust the tables for a single or multiple products, by

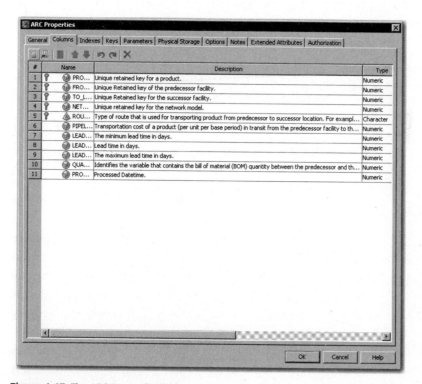

Figure 6.17 The ARC Properties Table

increasing or decreasing the min or max days in the lead-time over the mean or average.

THE BUSINESS AND ANALYST PERSONA CHASM

Since the exception of inventory optimization the goal of the user interface was to allow for the manipulation of the inputs and outputs of the data. This was, in most cases, the realm of the technical analyst. This fine-tuning or adjustments are still the realm of the technical analyst, but it holds back the ability of the business user to fully grasp the functionality of inventory optimization.

Business users need to understand and act within an inventory optimization solution and not just view the results. The key to the crossover to business use is the ability to show the siloed business users the ramifications of their adjustments. They need to understand the concept of cost reduction compared to cost shifting. Too often, the business users, if left to their own devices, will push costs to their trading partners. Multiechelon inventory optimization can show the business user the ripple effect of service-level changes, lead-time changes, and better forecasts. Above all, if the solution can put fences around the decision making and allow for audit trails, the system can be a great facilitator of inventory so that the entire portfolio of products can attain the highest customer satisfaction, lowest costs, and highest profits. That should allow for inventory optimization to leap the chasm and become part of the everyday life in the supply chain.

Power to the business user!

CHAPTER 7

Fitting Unlimited Optimization into a Constraining World

Positioning inventory correctly can save a lot of time and effort when it comes to making sure replenishment practices are in synch. So far we have examined how inventory optimization methodologies can dramatically improve the performance of enterprise resource planning (ERP) and transactional systems by correctly positioning the right inventory at the right place to satisfy customer demand. Indeed, the inventory optimization process turns days of supply on its head to create individualized inventory policies that overcome the inefficiencies of rule-of-thumb assignments. However, have you ever noticed when you walk into a buyer's office that the first thing you see on the desk is a very big report? Almost without exception it will be a report generated with Excel. It will be collated and either paper-clipped or stapled with the biggest fastener available. If you are in the office of a busy buyer, you will see multiple reports strewn all over the office.

THE CURRENT STATE OF AFFAIRS IN REPLENISHMENT PLANNING

During one of my visits to a national grocery warehousing company, I had the chance to interview various buyers in an effort to see how they were dealing with a recent installation of a competitor's inventory optimization system. The installation was a single-echelon environment (individual warehouses in various locations that were not linked) and had taken just a little over six months. It had been up and running for about four months. At the location where I was doing the interviews, approximately eight buyers were working with product portfolios supported by the inventory optimization solution.

By and large, the buyers were happy with the performance of the solution. Products that were considered to be basic volume contributors were performing well, but some of the highly promoted products were not doing as well, and some had large fluctuations between overstocks and out-of-stocks. During the interviews, I glanced around each of the offices, and I saw those classic reports everyone finds in a buyer's possession. I asked the buyer I was sitting with to share with me how the report was used.

What was shared was a classic time-phased on-hand and pipeline inventory report on key product categories that were deemed critical to the grocery chain. You could see the ebb and flow of the inventories. However, there was an obvious problem where there were sudden spikes of inventory after medium-size drops from the previous week. The buyer explained that the report offered him the ability to react to "unanticipated" advance demand for scheduled ads. Now, this kind of action of a buyer who was using "inventory optimization" caught me a bit by surprise. If the demand was actually sensed and anticipated, why was the grocery warehouse caught flat-footed when early orders came flooding in before ads?

If you remember back to the beginning of this book, you heard me comment that inventory optimization means different things to different people, depending on where they sit in the supply chain. The closer you get to the customer-facing location, the more optimization means replenishment. Quite honestly, even with inventory optimization, the last step of the supply chain tends to become a veritable cornucopia of exceptions and constraints. What this grocery buyer and many other types of buyers were experiencing was one of the shortcomings of some inventory optimization solutions—the inability to correctly mimic the constraints of replenishment.

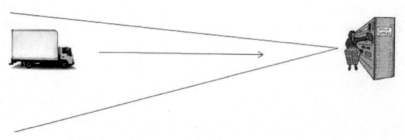

The end of the supply chain tends to restrict the inventory.

Due to the various constraints placed on inventories, as they get closer and closer to the end of the supply chain, the replenishment process takes on more and more influence. Inventories can still be optimized, but the constraint problems that are focused on reaction times, demand streams, short supplies, lead-time delays, and space make the last steps of the supply chain particularly hard for inventory optimization to interact with replenishment.

HOW ALERTS TAKE ON MORE SIGNIFICANCE WHEN CUSTOMER SERVICE IS PARAMOUNT

In our previous illustrations of the 20/10/70 inventory situation, we found that only 10 percent of the days-of-supply assignments were considered in the Goldilocks or just-right threshold. That meant that 90 percent of the inventory assignments were either overstocked or understocked. Obviously, the degree of variance could be small or large, but just the same, the assignments were out of compliance. When you move up the supply chain, the 20 percent understock problem continues to be problematic because even at the higher levels of the chain the response still is dependent on getting stock from another location. Meanwhile, the 70 percent overstock problem consumes vast amounts of working capital, but the stock can move from the present location without reliance on the upper inventory locations. The result of this in-stock/out-of-stock problem within the island of efficiency is that the buyer will spend the vast majority of time focused on the 20 percent understock problem and only shift focus onto the overstocks when she is forced to acknowledge the problem. Therefore, all through the supply chain, buyers zero in their focus on the 20 percent of the inventory where they feel they are most graded upon—those products that will reduce their customer satisfaction and/or service scores. When you move up the supply chain several things surface that allow for a bit of relaxation and that are not in place at the end of the chain: time, space, and the resulting order consistency.

TIME

The upper ends of the supply chain tend to be set up for understandable fluctuations. Whereas the last steps of the supply chain have lead times of one to two days from an upstream inventory location in the vicinity of 100 to 200 miles away, the plant and regional distribution centers are dealing with lead times in the weekly or monthly range. Indeed, some upper levels of the supply chain might have lead time in the months to accommodate inventory. This lead time creates both a larger inventory and a larger confidence buffer. In the ERP-type inventory and replenishment process, the steps to create this buffer would have been developed by using demand accumulation via location forecasts. A distribution center would take all of the forecasts from the downstream locations and aggregate them into a single forecast. Once the anticipated demand is understood, the appropriate inventory would be positioned given the lead time required for the downstream locations to produce their demand signals, turn orders into shipments, and have those shipments received.

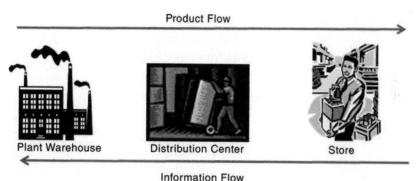

Product Flow

Plant Warehouse   Distribution Center   Store

Information Flow

"Any delay of information results in an inefficient flow of products."

The time it takes to develop those aggregated demand signals and position the inventory creates an increase in the overall inventory, but most important, it accumulates the demand variance. This does two things. It creates the bullwhip effect, but it also relaxes the replenishment demands. Inventory optimization is designed to alleviate the accumulated demand variance by using a single demand signal from the customer-facing locations and not trying to accumulate the demand. This overall reduction in the safety stock *redundancy* helps make inventory optimization so effective, but it comes at a price.

The price is that the time constraint in the supply chain becomes problematic the closer you get to the ending inventory position of customer-facing locations. Inventory optimization uses a predicted lead time and lead-time variance to position inventory. When there is consistent timing of replenishment, the inventory can be reduced to acceptable levels so that only the demand variance becomes problematic. The further up the chain you go, the more predictable the lead time. The problem most supply chains run into is that the last inventory points are restricted by space versus the variation of order size. The inventory demand filters down from truckload quantities to pallet quantities to case and/or each-type quantities. Correspondingly, the inventory space allocated to the quantities is being positioned the same way. This is all well and good until the demand spikes.

SPACE

Inventory optimization works great if there is no constraint on space. Imagine a world where inventory could fluctuate without regard to the space it required to hold it. Inventory optimization tends to look at inventory as a thing with no regard for the space it takes up or the financial commitment it consumes. Plant warehouses and regional distribution centers have large amounts of space to cater to the volume fluctuations, but as you get closer to the final resting spot of inventory for the customer-facing location, you get a slimming of space.

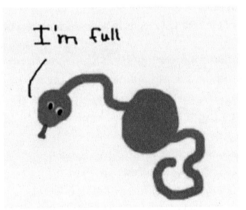

"Promotional volume quickly outstrips the allotted shelf space."

Most final destination inventory points have restrictions that only allow limited space for inventory positioning. The problem arises when an event occurs where there needs to be far more inventory to support the demand than the space allocated to the product. A good example of this problem is a grocery store trying to support a loss-leader, feature ad. This promotional volume will far outstrip the constrained shelf

FITTING UNLIMITED OPTIMIZATION INTO A CONSTRAINING WORLD ◀ **145**

space allocated to the product. In most cases, a product in this situation would have a shelf-holding power of 2 to 2.5 cases, but the potential demand will be in the 50- to 100-case ranges for the week. The result could go in two directions: 50 to 100 cases are ordered and held in the backroom so that the shelf is constantly filled when needed, or a display is built away from the shelf so that demand can be supported in two places. In each of these cases, the normal inventory constraint is violated at the store due to the massive increase of demand.

THE COMINGLING OF DEMAND

In almost all cases, inventory optimization looks at a single demand stream. It makes perfect sense to have the single demand stream when looking at upstream locations. There is a normal flow of information, a consistent lead time, and a lot of space for the fluctuations of inventory volume. However, when the leaf node or customer-facing locations have winnowed the expected volume and inventory space down to accommodate "normal" volume, you end up with anything but normal volume. The time and space constraints create the problem of turn versus promotional volume expectations and the problem of how to comingle the products once that expectation is met.

Most demand fluctuations can be accommodated in normal swings in volume. Turn volume is the amount of stock that flows through the system to account for the everyday demand swings. As I learned, way back when, to account for slight upticks in volume from temporary price reductions or subfeature ads, the turn volume would go up and down as the minimal promotion ran its course. The thing that throws the turn volume calculations out of control is when a huge promotion arrives (see Figure 7.1). Promotional volume has to be separated, and all of the normal demand and inventory control key performance indicators (KPIs) are suddenly irrelevant. Inventory optimization has a lot of trouble with this comingling of turn and promotional volume.

For instance, inventory optimization would look at the promotional volume and drive it using the normal lead time. First of all, this lack of foresight puts the user into an immediate expedite mode

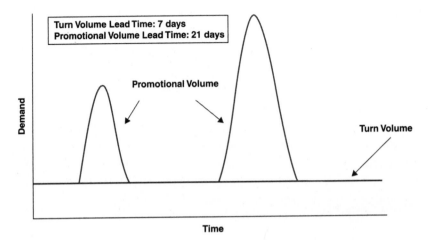

Figure 7.1 Turn and Promotional Volume Is Usually Treated Differently When Large Promotional Orders Are Placed

to get product out as fast as possible. Second, the lack of visibility into separate inventory metric needs will drive higher than needed inventory levels due to increased safety stock needs over the "known" turn volume requirements. Finally, the ending inventory, after the promotion, will undoubtedly have overstocks at the leaf node or customer-facing locations due to the lack of demand variance activity. This comingling of turn and promotional volume is a real bottleneck in inventory optimization. It tends to only crop up at the winnowed end of supply chain locations, but it can turn up just about anywhere.

THE SHORT SUPPLY OR ALLOCATED PRODUCT

Inventory optimization is known as the purveyor of socks in the world of high fashion. That means it tends to perform extremely well in a space where there are known, long-term demand signals and predictable supply. However, that kind of inventory control and replenishment is pretty standard and easy to deal with. The problem that occurs in a replenishment environment delivered by inventory optimization is what to do in a situation where supply is not known or is constrained by the inability to produce enough to support the demand. I use the phrase *high fashion* as it relates to socks, but the term could be used just about anywhere that a product is purchased in bulk, then doled out, or a limited supply is projected and a decision is made on where the product should go for best fit and coverage.

The concept of inventory optimization is to properly position the inventory and replenishment in such a way as to reduce the capital expenditure and maximize service level or customer satisfaction. In many cases, the product is constricted and cannot support the projected demand. In these cases, most replenishment processes institute an alerting mechanism so that buyers can push product to needed locations for best results or simply stop shipments to lower-volume stores. The ultimate shortcoming of inventory optimization is when a single purchase has been made in bulk, and a plan needs to be developed on how the product will be moved throughout the fashion season. This is in contrast to the flow of product needed in inventory optimization. The inventory optimization structure would look at the total required inventory need and project the inventory positions at each location and try to fulfill the demand as time goes forward. There is no logic as to what happens when there is no more product, and the result is that fast-moving stores get the majority of the product, and when the stock is exhausted, nobody gets any more.

When I visited a buyer's office, this short supply/allocation of products, along with understocked A-type items, was the basis of about 80 percent of all replenishment reports being reviewed on a daily basis. Even in the situation where short supplies were known, the buyer was working with alerts and manually adjusting the replenishment using tribal knowledge as to where the stock needed to go. This type of behavior amplified itself when the short supply products were also A-type products already understocked in the first place. In the majority of cases, buyers could deal with this kind of replenishment problem when their buying portfolios were relatively small or constricted by limited store/doors. The minute a portfolio was large or the geographical focus was extensive, the alert/manual override process was ineffective. It would seem that the inventory optimization system would be perfect to overcome these types of issues, but the majority of optimization systems do not take into effect the short supply problem and just pull in the alerting/manual override process already put in place. The result is a highly responsive system when there is a known demand

and unlimited supply, but it grinds to a halt the minute there is a limit on the replenishment.

The result of the present state of affairs in inventory optimization puts the winnowed-down, end-of-chain locations at a disadvantage. Limited space and wild variations in replenishment needs drive buyers crazy as they deal with the constraints. These constraints amplify the problem of understocking and overstocking of inventory. There is an old adage about the courage needed to walk on a narrow beam of wood. It is easy to summon the courage when it is only a few inches above the ground. This is what it is like to deal with upstream location inventory and replenishment needs. When you add in all of the constraints found at the end-of-chain locations, it is like raising that beam up to 100 feet in the air. It is much tougher to deal with "what might happen" if the wrong decision is made. At the end of the chain, the out-of-stock ramifications are much higher. Indeed, when a bad decision is made at this place in the supply chain, there are no second chances. The results are lost sales across broad swaths of the company and, potentially, lost market share as customers move to other points to get their demands met.

WHERE DOES "OPTIMIZED" REPLENISHMENT NEED TO GO IN ORDER TO ENCOMPASS THE ENTIRE DISTRIBUTION CHAIN?

In order for inventory optimization replenishment to properly move forward within inventory control, it needs to better mimic the real activities found in buying so that these issues are not ignored. Oftentimes, replenishment is left up to the already-installed purchasing system when inventory optimization is installed. When this happens, more and more replenishment activities are taken out of the optimization mix and then set up with exceptions. This, again, might work in a small portfolio or a single-echelon environment, but once complexities are added to the mix like multiechelon optimization or end-of-chain constraints, inventory optimization starts to disengage.

"Technology needs to be more than just alerts."

There seem to be three basic areas where optimized replenishment needs to go in order to fully integrate with overall inventory control, management, and optimization. The first area is in developing consistent upstream reactions. The second is to have replenishment functionality better mimic the constraints and actions found in end-of-supply-chain environments. Finally, there need to be better understandings of the constraints placed on both logical and physical inventories so that the solution set takes into account not only natural replenishment, but limited space and limited supply.

THE UPSTREAM REACTION

Inventory optimization, when built in a multiechelon environment, understands the concept of networks. A network is a specific path a product takes to get to a final customer. Products will take a multitude of pathways or networks to get to the customer. In inventory optimization, the pathway is normally defined at different locations and can be an internal step toward the customer-facing location, or it can actually be the customer-facing location for either certain products or a percentage of the total volume of a product running through the warehouse. When reacting as an internal warehouse, it is responding to the downstream customer-facing location demand. When it is acting as its own customer-facing location, it is reacting, specifically, to its own demand signal. These single or multiple demand signals constitute different networks in multiechelon optimization.

Another good example of networks can be seen when inventory pooling is put into place for slower-moving products. In this case, there is not enough justified demand at the majority of individual customer-facing locations. As a result, a decision would be made to pool product at an upstream location and distribute the product to a wider geographic region than would have been justified at the local warehouse. In constructing pooling locations, the organization sets up multiple networks to economically deliver product that would not justify having costly inventory in all locations.

Problems can occur in inventory optimization when multiple upstream sources or multiple delivery processes can be tapped into, depending on the replenishment need. Let's take a look at a few illustrations of upstream reaction issues.

Multiple sources mean that product could come from a broad array of upstream or sister/peer locations depending on the type of replenishment required or deemed most economical. In the majority of cases, the idea is to circumvent supply chain inefficiencies. Since inventory optimization is designed to make the supply chain run at an extremely efficient state, the multiple-source issue would seem to be irrelevant. However, the optimization should recognize these decision points because, given a change in costs, both the inventory policies and replenishment strategies change. Given this shift of cost, inventory optimization should work to integrate all facets of multiple source decisions so that the replenishment process mimics real decisions and does not simply palm them off as outside the realm of inventory optimization.

Multiple Sources

- **Bulk purchasing discounts:** Many times a vendor will provide some kind of incentive to purchase a bulk order from a manufacturing or plant facility. This might be a lump-sum truckload allowance or per-case allowance that makes it attractive to get a large order directly from the source location. This is usually done when it is recognized that the logistical cost of moving product down through the chain would be far greater than the allowance put in place for the customer to pick the product up at the source. It becomes a win-win proposition and is cost effective for both parties.

- **Multivendor products:** Oftentimes, a generic product will have many vendors. There comes a point where the vendor of choice does not have the product and a potential supply disruption is in place. In many cases, some kind of rule is put in place where the next vendor in line is evaluated and selected as the vendor of choice. However, the creation of multiple vendors in an inventory optimization leads to suboptimization by developing poor service-level metrics and lagging lead times due to constantly shifting vendor expectations.

- **Outside staging locations:** A new development in select supply chains is outside inventory locations used for staging promotions. Vendors will position products that have a history of promotional uplifts into a specified geographical location so that it services multiple downstream locations instead of having to move large quantities of product through normal channels. This new development is a cross between pooling and plant direct shipments. The vendor flows back and forth between a regular network and a promotional network. The difficulty is in trying to understand the trigger mechanism for shifting between the normal network and the promotional network.

- **Alternative sources inside the supply chain:** Oftentimes, an inventory position is deemed overstocked at one location and needs to be repositioned to other locations to cover demand. This type of inventory leveling is done as an ad-hoc process where inventory is identified on a scheduled basis. The overstock will be deemed as the amount above and beyond that which could cover the predicted demand over a period of time. This is not a rob-Peter-to-pay-Paul affair. The idea is not to hurt the inventory position of Peter. It is to spread the inventory to more useful places. Therefore, there might be times where inventory does not come from the recognized network, but it might come from just about any location. Moreover, in some supply chains the default replenishment process is to use internal inventories before going to an external source. This process is called *auto-leveling* and opens up all kinds of upstream and peer inventory sources. In most cases, this type of replenishment scheme requires some kind of rules based on the acceptable logistics cost that could be incurred so replenishment costs are kept in check.

Multiple deliveries mean that a product's replenishment plan is outstripping the limits of physical space or time at the inventory starting point or ending point. At the upper end of the supply chain system, full trucks of product move from one warehouse to the next or at least large orders of specific products. We have discussed how product quantities get winnowed down to smaller and smaller quantities. As you get closer to the end of the chain, there is also the propensity to have broad fluctuations in replenishment quantities due to customer demand. This creates the problem of replenishment spacing to overcome restrictions on where product can be positioned.

Multiple Deliveries

- **Multiple deliveries for one event:** Oftentimes, the landing point for a large group of orders does not have the delivery capacity or the space to accommodate the entire product for one event. This means deliveries are spaced over a period so that staged quantities can be moved through the location. There is a buildup of product right before the event, with multiple trucks arriving over a span of a week. These orders are usually manipulated in some manner to create the spacing.

- **Multiple deliveries over a period:** In this situation, a planned order has gotten some kind of incentive to commit to staging of orders over a period or season. This kind of order creates a multiple-lead-time assignment that is far different from the normal network lead time. We often see this type of behavior in quantity commitments between a vendor and a retailer.

- **Pushing the lead time out for an event:** When large quantities of product are committed to for a promotional event, there needs to be a process in place both to secure the large replenishment order from the vendor and to move it out the store/doors for merchandising. This will require an extended lead time over the normal order sequence. Most grocery product retailers work on this premise.

- **Pulling the lead time back for an event:** In some cases where product is seasonally oriented or holiday focused, the lead time needs to be expedited so the product can be placed into stores before the holiday volume increase occurs. We see this type of behavior in fashion style or clothing retailers.

Adaptable upstream reactions are paramount to inventory optimization if it is to be an integral part of replenishment planning. This is especially true as the product moves to the customer-facing locations. It is one of the key reasons inventory optimization tends to stay in the upper segments of supply chains instead of spanning the entire distribution chain. When inventory optimization can integrate these replenishment challenges to the equation, it becomes a much more dynamic planning tool compared to a simple, back-end policy optimizer.

MOVING UPSTREAM REACTIONS INTO REAL REPLENISHMENT

A key area where upstream reaction meets real replenishment is when demand splits into turn volume and promotional volume. Within most inventory optimization solutions, demand is simply demand. This is to say that inventory optimization will naturally recognize a spike in demand created by a promotional event and position inventory required to support the event at the predetermined service level. However, this was one problem I found at installations where inventory optimization had been running and promotions were in place. The demand would spike, but there was a lag in the reaction to the demand from the promotional event. The problem was stemming from the constant lead time focused on normal turn volume. The result was that buyers needed to create alerts and manually circumvent the optimization process by expediting orders or delaying orders depending on the event plan.

Turn Volume versus Promotional Volume

The first thing that needs to be done to help inventory optimization overcome the restrictive one-size-fits-all reaction to demand is to help it recognize the differences in turn and promotional volume (see Figure 7.2). This is sometimes more difficult than it sounds. However, in various leading-edge installations I have found a good template. The idea is to create a turn volume baseline. As you know, turn volume is the normal demand of a product over time. This could include everyday volume, seasonal volume, and even normal increases and decreases as minor shifts in consumer demand that are not attributed to a demand event. This would mean that turn volume could be an average four- to six-week period that tends to hold within a 10 to 15 percent range of demand. This turn volume forms the basis of inventory optimization.

Since multiechelon inventory optimization is based on using the demand at the customer-facing location, the upstream locations need to understand the different metrics of demand. The normal turn

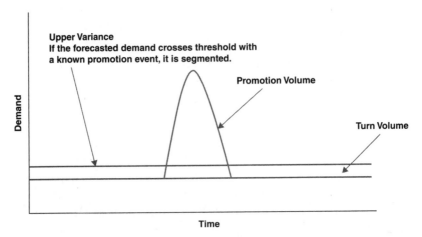

Figure 7.2 Using Turn Volume Variance to Recognize and Act on Promotional Orders

volume is based on a set of inventory parameters that are consistent. For instance, most ordering would be set up on a one-to-two-week lead-time period for product to get from one location to the next in support of a normal demand variance. However, due to the time and space constraints at the end of the supply chain, promotional demand needs to be treated differently. Therefore, the system needs to understand when promotional demand hits. A good way of identifying the promotional demand is to set the demand signal to recognize when the demand volume jumps a specific threshold over normal turn volume.

When that threshold is broken, the system needs to know what to do with the demand. Let's take a look at a couple of different scenarios that might occur.

The Single-Source/Single-Delivery/Short-Term Event

This is the most common of all promotional events. In this kind of situation, there is a definite increase in the demand signal over the normal turn volume baseline. Think of this kind of behavior that might happen if a loss-leader, feature ad was created in a grocery store. The demand signal will jump by 70 to 200 percent over the normal turn volume baseline. This kind of volume is not expected in the supply chain. In most cases, the upstream inventory locations will need some kind of advanced warning to accommodate this kind of demand signal jump.

There is no way the upstream locations can react if the event is not known. It is too far outside of the variance of demand for the normal turn volume. Therefore, the demand signal must be recognized early and communicated. This is a tough assignment for normal inventory optimization. Given that normal inventory optimization only looks at the "next period" to optimize, the system would only be looking out one period. In this situation, the forecasting models need to work in concert with inventory optimization. The promotional demand stream needs to be positioned to react in inventory optimization at a different lead time. When the uptick in demand occurs, there needs to be some kind of business rule in place to pull the demand away and apply it to a different lead-time metric. This means that a strong inventory optimization solution must view multiple demand streams to be effective;

otherwise, it will create a lag time in reacting to promotional demand. If you remember, this was one of the problems I found in that grocer vendor using inventory optimization—it had to override and quickly react even though it had optimization in place.

The Single-Source/Single-Delivery/Long-Term Event

This is the same as the above scenario with a twist. We see this in the retail industry when a holiday or seasonal upswing goes into effect. Instead of using the normal lead time, the larger-than-normal order needs to be shipped faster than the normal period so the stores can have the product staged and on display before the seasonal surge begins. We often see this type of behavior when the normal lead time is fairly long due to manufacturing constraints. The holiday volume is transmitted to the production schedule to produce more, and the volume is quickly pushed out. I have seen this in long-term fashion markets like pants or shirts that are staple products, compared to short-term fashion products.

The key influencer to the metrics is to expedite the production/shipment compared to looking out over the horizon and using a buildup of inventory to cover extremely large orders in a short period of time.

The Multisource/Multidelivery/Single Event

This situation is a nightmare to many inventory optimization solutions because the product flow mapping takes on extremely complicated inputs. Think of it this way—how expensive would it be to ship massive quantities of promotional volume through a vendor supply chain when the product could simply be picked up at the plant warehouse? What is the trigger point, and what is the savings to open up that plant warehouse for shipments to an outside entity? Indeed, the retailer could get a truckload allowance as a way of compensating for the supply chain savings. This is simple in theory, but extremely difficult to deal with in inventory optimization. In this situation, you have an upstream inventory location that is not customer facing. There is no direct demand coming from the customer—it is coming up through the system until it gets to the plant. However, if a large promotional quantity is recognized, it makes sense, from a supply chain perspective, to sidestep all of the regional and local warehouses and ship the product directly from the plant. This is a supply chain mapping nightmare, but doable.

To do this, the inventory optimization system needs to know that a specific demand volume threshold has been met. What is the threshold quantity that is best supplied from the plant warehouse? At that moment the plant warehouse needs to shift from an internal warehouse to a customer-facing warehouse for a specific quantity of product. The final step is that the plant warehouse needs to have specified quantity breaks for best fit, such as only truckload quantities and/or multiples that are allowed to ship out of the plant warehouse to qualify for the business rule exception.

Of all of the various mapping problems, the multisource promotional location shift brings the most value. Obviously, the pure-play promotional recognition process of pulling promotional demand volume into different delivery metrics has important contributions, but the shifting of warehouse supply can have a huge effect on supply chain cost savings. Having inventory optimization allow for the shifting of lead time to accommodate inventory production and/or positioning creates savings by way of reduced expediting, better production scheduling, faster response times to large-quantity orders, and, the thing that always jumps out as a surprise benefit no one seems to see until after the fact, buyer efficiencies.

REPLENISHMENT AS A MEANS TO INVENTORY OPTIMIZATION HARMONY

In literally every installation of inventory optimization ever undertaken, the affected buyers will have a skeptical view. As shown at the beginning of this chapter, it was apparent that the buyers at the national grocery warehouse company were already looking at ways to overcome perceived shortcomings so they could better anticipate demand outliers. It is human nature to have a skeptical view of technology as the answer to 30-plus years of tribal knowledge built up in the trenches. It is no wonder that those who work at the bitter end of the supply chain rely on replenishment to be the optimizer. There are so many constraints and constrictions to the chain that optimization is viewed as a hindrance and not a help. This does not have to be the case. The goal of inventory optimization should be to effectively mimic each point in the supply chain. Inventory optimization works extremely well at the upstream inventory locations because of consistent lead times and flexible space. The last links in the supply chain require flexibility in lead times and space to mimic how the replenishment cycles work.

This flexibility can be accomplished if the demand streams of turn volume and promotional volume can be recognized and dealt with separately, and then drawn back together after the promotion has been completed.

CHAPTER **8**

Reviewing the Three Proof of Value Engagements

Oftentimes, I am asked to demonstrate *inventory optimization*, and I get sucked into a vortex of various things a user might do to update or change to make sure the information being loaded is correct so that the outputs are optimal. The viewer of the demonstration is left with more questions than answers.

Things changed for the better when I decided to have a little fun with the demonstration and ask the rhetorical question, "How would you like to see a demonstration of a day in the life of an inventory optimization analyst?" When everyone indicated they thought that was a great idea, I shut off the screen and said, "Here it is."

You could see the light bulbs going off over the heads of people in that demonstration when they realized inventory optimization is not so much a demo of additional work as it is a backend process that allows for improvements in the overall enterprise resource planning (ERP) system and requires little, if any, major inputs on a daily or weekly basis. It is not there to create more work; it is there to reduce the workload.

When inventory optimization is working correctly, the time and effort placed on buyers to create and execute replenishment plans decreases dramatically. The day in the life of a buyer using inventory optimization shifts from 70 percent tactical to 70 percent strategic. Buyers can let inventory optimization do the heavy lifting of normal inventory control and normal replenishment so they can focus on what really matters, like long-term planning and increasing revenues.

PROVING THAT INVENTORY OPTIMIZATION IS A GOOD BUSINESS RATIONALE

The key to a successful inventory optimization implementation has more to do with the organizational goals than witnessing a nifty demo. I know that sounds glib, but as I said above, the proof of good inventory optimization has more to do with aligning a balance between inventory costs and attainable service levels than ways a user can manipulate the inputs and outputs. Obviously, manipulation is important, but it is critical to understand that 95 percent of the work accomplished by inventory optimization is done behind the scenes from a backend perspective, and the output makes inventory control and replenishment easier tasks. The focus should never be taken off the ultimate goal of having a broad-range improvement that can go toward either increased customer service (service level), increased revenue (decreasing lost sales from out-of-stocks), or reduced inventory costs (rightsizing inventory versus demand and supply variables).

I am forever amused with how inventory management is palmed off as inventory optimization. Building a replenishment system with all the bells and whistles centered on buyer activities that is driven by business rule alerts and calling it optimization just confuses the market space. However, that is what happens when an industry strategy becomes the vogue. The outcome of optimization takes away a lot of the buyer functions centered on taking action on problem orders due to unbalanced inventory. Many times these so-called inventory management systems selling themselves as optimization only really optimize about 10 to 20 percent of the items and then segment the rest of the items and apply business rules for best results. In the end, they will say that optimization is "too hard," and being "close enough" with business rules is good enough. These inventory management practitioners are missing the point just as the ERP systems missed the point by assigning blanket weeks-of-supply numbers. The buyers get overrun with out-of-tolerance inventory levels and have to quickly alter orders and increase their overall workload, which could have been avoided by the optimization routines.

However, there comes a point where technology ends and business practices and change management come into play. Inventory optimization is a gentle balance between technology and change. The goal should be to fully recognize the interplay for best results.

THE GOOD: WHEN PROOF OF VALUE ENGAGEMENTS WORK

Let's take a step back and look at a successful proof of value engagement focused on inventory optimization so we can see how aligning inventory can create the efficiency envelope. The premise of this proof of value engagement was to understand how inventory optimization could do the following activities:

- Increase service levels at least 2 percent from 96 to 98 percent.
- Keep inventory levels at the same levels they were at the beginning of the engagement.
- Reduce the amount of markdowns used to get rid of excess inventory.

Here are the basics of what this potential customer was dealing with:

- This is a large U.S. retailer doing business in a variety of household goods and clothing items. The focal point of the engagement was to review, with forecasting, inventory optimization, and replenishment, a group of items deemed to be "problem products" that fit into replenishment cycles and not products that were fashion oriented with single or multiple bulk purchases and allocation issues. The key points of this engagement were to take a representative sampling of products that spanned the spectrum from slow moving all the way to fast moving, seasonal issues, and markdown issues.
- This large U.S. retailer was using widely used ERP and supply chain management (SCM) systems designed to give it inventory control and replenishment recommendations. As indicated earlier in this book, both the ERP system and the SCM system used were giving the retailer a days and weeks of supply number needed to maintain. In the majority of cases, the inventory on hand was to be in the range of two to four weeks of stock on hand with an order point of either one or two weeks' supply.

Here are the problems that the buyers were having:

- The buyers had developed, over a period of time, a list of trouble products that had been produced using tribal knowledge. These items tended to be items with limited demand histories and longer than normal lead times.
- In the vast majority of cases, the items they were focused on were normally in short supply or in out-of-stock situations due to the reliance on limited demand histories.

- The buyers estimated that 60 to 70 percent of their time was spent reacting to problems with these products, and most of the cost was spent on expediting orders.

Here are the problems that management was having:

- Large numbers of items were slipping into overstock situations. The buyers were spending a lot of their time focused on the out of stocks, but the overstock items were taking up valuable capital and slowing down inventory turns.
- Markdown activities at the end of promotional periods or at the end of the season were cutting into the category profits of large segments of their retail business. In some cases, the overstock problem with markdowns negated earned profits during the season.
- Buyers needed to better understand the ramifications of overstocks as much as they did in dealing with out-of-stocks. Management needed a way to show buyers how to manage the total category instead of focusing almost totally on lost sales.

This engagement was a classic example of the Goldilocks problem. Only about 10 percent of the items had the correctly assigned inventory level to service level requirement. The buyers were focused on the 20 percent of the items that were understocked, and management was focused on the 70 percent of the products that were overstocked. The key to the proof of value was finding items that were deemed part of both the 20 percent understocks and 70 percent overstocks, but the icing on the cake would be to find items that had a problem with markdowns. However, you couldn't be too obvious about the markdowns as to create a negative reaction from the buyers.

It must be remembered that buyers always need to be included in inventory optimization engagements. Management has the purse strings to order the software, but buyers can stonewall the engagement if they feel their needs are not met. Oftentimes, engagements are circumvented when huge savings are found. The reason was not that the buyers were negligent; they were doing the best they could with the resources at hand. The problem was they were threatened by the optimization and revolted against it. We will see that problem very soon.

Setting up the Proof of Value

This retailer had over 400,000 stock-keeping units (SKUs) in over 500 stores nationwide. In this instance, the stores were important, but the focal point of the proof of value was at the distribution center. Both management and the buyers felt the emphasis of the inventory problem centered on the warehouse, and most of the time the buyers and management spent on inventory issues was in the distribution center while the stores were a merchandising issue that did not cross over into the buying. In other words, the stores were not having the overstock and understock issues except having to deal with demand problems. At issue was holding the correct inventory at the distribution center (DC) to support the merchandising plans.

The best way to set up the proof of value was to take 118 weeks of sales and inventory history. The idea was to make the first 52 weeks as a baseline. From that basis the forecasting, inventory optimization, and replenishment could be applied on a weekly basis so that two sets of results could be shown; the first would be the retailer's ongoing results, and the second would be the optimization results. This would be able to show the classic z-curve results but a wrinkle needed to be added. A *z-curve* is something that always shows up in inventory optimization engagements. The 20 percent of items that are understocked get ordered. This creates an upward spike in inventory costs. After the initial order, the overall inventory bleeds off. Once the inventory reaches an optimal level, it holds steady in what is known as the *steady state*. The graph looks like a giant Z, hence the name z-curve. By taking out pricing information, the new forecasting would not be swayed by the event estimates positioned by the buyers, and the new results would only factor in statistical shifts of demand presented to the system. By doing this view of overstocked items, there would be a shift in the inventory reaction. If done correctly, the increased demand from a markdown would show up as an uptick in inventory if the old inventory had bled off already and did not need to be marked down.

The final action was to cull the products down to an agreed-upon number and focus. A total number of 11,605 SKUs were chosen that represented buyer-monitored understocked items and management-monitored overstocked items. Another requirement of the data was that there would be no "new items" positioned. Each of the items in the test needed to be in circulation the entire time, even if they were intermittent-demand products. The overall weekly inventory for the selected group was $785,000. This represented about 7 percent of the total weekly inventory carried by the retailer.

The Results

As shown in Figure 8.1, the results are driven out over weeks 53 to 117. Based on the previous 52 weeks as a baseline the beginning inventory for both strategies started at $750,080. The actual inventory levels following the retailer's inventory policies held relatively flat, but started to rise after week 75. This rise continues with various increases and decreases until week 95 where there is a dramatic reduction of inventory. After week 99, the inventory starts to creep up again and, finally, there is a decline after week 113.

What was happening with the inventory in the actual retailer's strategy?

Upon review with the retailer's buyer/management team, it was uncovered that a significant group of items in the sampling had not done well during their promotional periods, and strategies helped drive the inventory into an overstock situation. A decision was made to

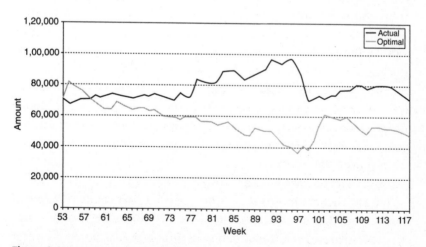

Figure 8.1 Inventory Profile over Time

have a markdown strategy to get rid of the excess inventory at the DC. During the discussions with the retailer, it was clear that management wanted to introduce the need to focus on working capital and the reduction of markdown strategies.

What was the reaction when the optimal inventory line was introduced?

Over the years, I have found the overlay of the time-phased optimal inventory graph to be the great eye-opener of every engagement, and this was no different. Everyone expects the optimal to be lower, but there are always two focal points: Why is there a blip at the beginning, and why are there anomalies somewhere on the graph? This engagement was no different.

Whenever there is a group of buyers witnessing an inventory optimization presentation, the best way to level-set the discussion is to go back to the days of supply versus service level requirements and the old Goldilocks analogy. This helps the buyers understand that, in many ways, they have been fighting the battle with one hand tied behind their backs. This level setting also introduces the concepts of optimization versus replenishment so that they do not feel intimidated by so-called policies.

The optimal graph shown in Figure 8.1 followed the classic optimization z-curve process toward optimal settings. The inventory jumped between 7 and 10 percent as items that were understocked were assigned more appropriate inventory levels and were replenished. This is always a tough point in every *proof of value (POV)* because the system is doing something that is contrary to common thought about optimization. Optimization is not just about reducing inventory—it is about making the inventory optimal. As discussed in the Goldilocks situation, some 20 percent of the items are usually understocked and cause buyers headaches that have to be handled via expedited orders. The uptick in inventory reacts first before there is any bleed-off of inventory.

At the same time the understocked products are being replenished the overstocked items are getting new policies that create new, lower thresholds of inventory. Now comes the inventory bleed-off process. Depending on the velocity of demand, this bleed-off could take a few weeks, months, or, in some cases, years. Yes, years, but in most cases about 95 percent of the inventory comes into line within months, and the majority of return on investment (ROI) occurs quickly.

From weeks 55 to 100 the inventory bleed-off is in full swing. Anyone who has gone through a short-term ratcheting down of days of supply knows how nerve-wracking it can get, but the Goldilocks problem is not in effect. The 20 percent of the inventory that is usually in short supply and first to go out of stock has been optimized correctly. We do not have short-supply problems while this bleed-off is occurring.

Here comes the eye-opener. Everyone in the room has been looking at the drop in actual inventory, and the upswing in optimized inventory, and wondering about the correlation. The actual inventory drop was due to a markdown strategy to get rid of overstocked product. If you look closely, there is a lag of about three weeks before the optimal inventory spikes up. What happened here is that the optimal inventory was following the statistical forecast, but when actual sales took off due to the markdown (remember, while working with management we purposely did not use pricing as an input?), the optimization engine reacted and replenished product. It replenished it because in the optimal solution the product that was marked down was already within optimal thresholds; it didn't need to be marked down.

In the real world, this outlier would have been handled via pricing information in the forecasting so the spike in ordering would not have occurred. Management was delighted at this point. They had one of those teaching moments: By not having excess stock capital was saved and revenues were increased by selling at the regular price instead of at a markdown.

The POV had a two-pronged benefit. The buyers would see how problem products that they had been focused on had been rightsized, and the system was holding the products with natural overstocks in check. Both buyers and management were happy with the process, but would the proof bear out?

The goal of the POV was to increase overall service level by 2 percent and keep inventories at the same level.

As shown in Table 8.1, the net result of the POV was a 2.5 percent increase in service level and a 27.2 percent decrease in inventory.

Table 8.1 The POV Results

	Actual Profile	Optimal Profile
Weekly Inventory Cost	$785,148	$571,823
Nonstockout Percentage	96.3%	98.8%

THE BAD: WHEN PROOF OF VALUE ENGAGEMENTS DON'T WORK

A catalog retailer in the United States prided itself on having exciting new offerings each month to tantalize its consumer base. Most of its business centers on computers, but it also caters to customers needing just about any household electrical product.

A key component of its marketing message is that a customer can order from the website and have the purchase delivered anywhere in the continental United States within three days. This promise had put a tremendous burden on the company's inventory positioning. To accomplish the delivery promise, the company uses a three-warehouse system. Depending on where the order originates, the closest warehouse will fulfill the order. When an order comes in and the primary warehouse is out of stock, one of the alternative two warehouses would be tapped to supply the order.

Due to the short life cycles of retail electronics products and parts, and the need to deliver the customer orders in three days, the company was running into a triple-edged sword: (1) high inventory costs, (2) high logistics costs, and (3) high levels of product obsolescence.

VIEWING THE POV FROM A PROJECT MANAGEMENT PERSPECTIVE

From kickoff to final presentation, the POV was six weeks. We had weekly status meetings with the customer. The team consisted of the inventory optimization consultant and a data consultant. In the end, the data consultant played a smaller part in this project, with the inventory optimization consultants performing most of the work.

The project milestones were:

2 weeks	Data assessment
2 weeks	Execute inventory optimization analytic routines
1 week	Analysis of inventory optimization results
1 week	Final results and knowledge transfer

The data preparation by the customer took place before the data assessment phase started. It took one week for the customer to gather and send us its initial set of data.

The goal was to show value by:

- Proving inventory optimization can reduce shipping costs
- Proving inventory optimization can reduce inventory costs

Viewing the POV from an Analytical Perspective

In a normal inventory optimization POV, the customer would provide a two-year demand history with the corresponding inventory/replenishment information. What we would do, then, is use the first year as a baseline, and the second year demand forecast would be created using a forecasting system. Once the inventory policies are positioned, the replenishment process is driven to mimic daily purchasing. The customer provided the information needed, but it was quickly realized that the short life cycles found in consumer electronics were difficult to forecast and the team needed to come up with agreed-on business rules to get better results.

Individual electronics tend to have extremely short life cycles. For instance, a 40-inch plasma screen TV from a certain vendor might only be stocked for three to four weeks at a time. It made forecasting that specific TV very difficult. We looked at aggregation alternatives and found product groupings to be the best way to aggregate. In this case, all 40-inch TVs were grouped as an ongoing category for both time-phasing and aggregation. This technique provided a way to extend the life cycles of categories and give a more accurate forecast than the ones used by the customer.

As the project continued, it was found a significant business rule that was assumed by management was not actually followed. For instance, management assumed that since the warehouses would react to an order placed close to their proximity all warehouses would have the identical SKUs stocked. This was not the case. We had to whittle down the number of SKUs so we had a representative number stocked in all locations for the POV. In some ways the team became more of a trusted adviser to the customer at that point. We were able to point out how the logistics costs were elevated due to orders being supplied out of a distant warehouse and they had to be expedited to meet the three-day delivery. These costs were not completely understood by management.

A large percentage of the business revolved around special, unplanned onetime buys they might make from a vendor. Once the purchase was received, they advertised to their end users using a hot price. For instance, a vendor might come to them with a special-deal price if they purchase 10,000 lamps. The purchases are extremely random and could be on any product. There were several issues in this type of behavior, creating problems for the POV team. First, the randomness of the product being purchased and the timing made it almost impossible to forecast. Second, since it was a onetime buy, the inventory policies and replenishment planning processes were rendered moot. Third, the size of the purchases was usually a decision made by a buyer who, in most cases, used tribal knowledge to come up with an inventory amount. Lastly, due to the obsolescence factor found in short-life-cycle products, if the special sale did not move the inventory, the company was stuck with product that had to be written off the books at huge discounts.

Forecasting demand requires some kind of pattern to be accurate. When products are purchased and advertised on a planned basis, it becomes much easier to forecast demand correctly. Furthermore, in situations where the product is consistently stocked rather than made with a onetime buy the forecast and replenishment can be synchronized for best results. It was found that if the buyers would use a system of product group aggregation as stated earlier to analyze the projected demand of the product against other like items, they would have a better number to negotiate with than the tribal knowledge process they were using. However, this was not part of the scope of the POV.

The Results of the POV

The overall results were met with a lot of excitement (see Table 8.2). The management team could see an immediate opportunity to reduce costs and stockouts. This is what the POV was all about.

When it came to presenting the underlying data in a category review, the meeting quickly fell into a conversation about "what constitutes a successful POV" (see Table 8.3). Since buyers were present, there was a lot of turf protection. For instance, if there was a significant improvement, the buyer didn't want to be second-guessed and took offense at the solution. If there was no or little improvement, it was seen as a referendum against the solution.

The lamp category was highly advertised, with the buyer making at least three onetime purchases, far beyond the projected demand information. "The deal was just too good to pass up," explained the buyer. The result of the buyer activity was good service levels, but inventories were extremely high. However, no amount of inventory capital expenditure and markdown loss versus revenue generated would sway the buyer from his decisions. He was proud of his purchases and stood by his decisions. Conversely, the buyer working on the washer and dryer categories was almost giddy to see that he was outperforming the so-called optimization. What he didn't see was that the out-of-stock numbers made his products some of the worst in terms of revenue generation. If he would raise his inventory instead of artificially holding it down, he might have slower inventory turns, but less out-of-stocks. Finally, management did not have a communicated goal of improvement so when it was questioned by those doing the work there was

Table 8.2 Overall Results of Inventory Optimization POV

Daily Average KPI	POV Results	Historical Results	Improvements
Stockout Percentage	9.3%	31.7%	22.4%
Total Inventory Cost	$15,448,794	$19,512,248	$4,063,454
Inventory Carrying Cost	$8,465	$10,692	$2,227
Total Shipping Cost	$18,728	$25,382	$6,654

Table 8.3 Breakout by Buyer Category Portfolio

Category	Item Count	Daily Stockout Percent			Daily Inventory Cost			Daily Carry Cost		Daily Ship Cost		Total Carry & Ship Costs		
		POV	History	Improve't	POV	History	Improve't	POV	History	POV	History	POV	History	Improve't
Boxes	497	6.7%	39.5%	32.8%	$1,914,472	$2,503,404	$588,932	$1,049	$1,372	$6,965	$8,014	$8,014	$10,509	$2,495
Walkers	85	11.6%	30.1%	18.5%	$3,155,176	$3,752,566	$597,391	$1,729	$2,066	$3,297	$4,315	$5,026	$6,371	$1,345
Washers	9	24.0%	20.2%	-3.7%	$79,133	$107,071	$27,938	$43	$59	$159	$228	$202	$286	$84
Plasma	28	10.9%	9.2%	-1.7%	$1,710,713	$737,550	$(973,163)	$937	$404	$1,284	$1,704	$2,221	$2,108	$(113)
Eyeglasses	32	16.5%	19.3%	2.8%	$394,329	$1,023,359	$629,031	$216	$561	$741	$1,130	$967	$1,691	$734
Widgets	18	8.9%	15.1%	6.3%	$140,653	$230,402	$89,749	$77	$126	$357	$399	$434	$525	$91
Canes	128	16.8%	18.0%	1.2%	$3,833,390	$3,438,202	$(395,187)	$2,100	$1,884	$940	$1,185	$3,041	$3,069	$28
Lamps	151	11.9%	10.9%	-1.0%	$3,170,465	$6,930,957	$3,760,492	$1,737	$3,798	$4,527	$6,606	$6,264	$10,404	$4,140
Dryers	126	8.3%	48.5%	40.2%	$778,993	$500,223	$(278,770)	$427	$274	$379	$544	$806	$818	$13

no clarity of direction so that, in the end, the buyers made it clear that they were happy with the way things were and not inclined to have something like optimization looking over their shoulders.

This POV did not result in the account going forward with implementing inventory optimization. Indeed, once the engagement was completed, the account tried to do some internal efforts to clean up the forecasting methods, but the hot ads on onetime buys continued unabated.

Looking Back

In retrospect, there needs to be an understanding of the results and how the viewers might react. When it comes to massive improvements using improved forecasts and scientific algorithms to help project inventories, some precautions must be taken to improve the reception of the numbers. For buyers, making decisions with incomplete or inaccurate information will always be a tough thing to do. Given what this group had to work with, they actually did a very good job. In turn, it should be noted on the other side of the numbers that without strong pricing and promotion information, it was difficult to improve on a heavily advertised category. If the inventory optimization solution had been better positioned as a way to help buyers make better decisions upfront, it might have made for a better reception of the detailed results.

THE BEST: A COMPLETE PROOF OF VALUE ENGAGEMENT

A manufacturing organization, on the recommendation of its IT department, adopted an ERP supply chain planning and execution module to manage their repair and operations (MRO) inventories. The ERP system produced a strong return on investment (ROI) and was deemed a successful installation by the organization.

Over time, however, managers found that the MRO buyers were spending a disproportionate amount of time reviewing inventory levels and making emergency purchases. The result of this behavior was that the MRO staff had grown to accommodate the increased workload, and the cost of rush orders—coupled with high inventories—had put a strain on the budget. While the staffing and cost increases were of concern, it was felt that the ERP module was not at fault. It was still producing an acceptable ROI, and service levels were within acceptable ranges.

However, as the organization's business increased, the trickle-down effect on the MRO inventories compounded the now common unacceptable inventory positions. Emergency purchases had become almost a normal business practice. During a fact-finding meeting with consultants, the organization's supply chain management team shared the MRO staffing concerns and cost overruns.

Enhance versus Replace

As the fact-finding sessions proceeded, it became clear that three issues were very important to the participating executives:

1. The installation of the ERP system and the supply chain management (SCM) module had been a huge endeavor from both a cost and time perspective. This investment needed to be justified, and, even more important, it needed to be protected.

2. The results that had been coming out of the system since it had gone live had provided a good ROI from the previous method of supply chain management. If the results were not as good as they should be, the management team needed to know why.

3. If a decision was made to purchase an analytical enhancement to the ERP system, the management team needed a POV assessment that would be both compelling and defendable.

The POV Assessment

Interviews with the MRO management team and buyers produced telltale signs of problems with demand signals (forecasting issues) and the resulting supply responses (inventory policies). Due to the misaligned signals, the system was producing mixed results. The buyers were forced to develop workarounds and/or emergency buy procedures.

The POV team recommended improving the demand and supply signals with a combination of advanced forecasting and multiechelon inventory optimization. This combination would replace the demand and supply variants so the resulting outputs of the ERP system would be more efficient. The effect of the better outputs would be reduced inventories, fewer emergency purchases, and a more productive buying staff.

The organization's management team came up with a set of acceptable hurdles or goals the inventory optimization solution needed to overcome in order to be deemed successful in enhancing the ERP system. The team defined the acceptable levels of improvement and expressed those improvements not only in monetary values but also in a reduction in MRO buyer activities.

The Goals of the POV

The goals of the POV engagement need to be measurable and relevant:

1. Reduce working capital invested in inventory by a minimum of 15 percent.
2. Maintain a service level of 98 percent while eliminating appropriate inventories.
3. Reduce the time and improve the quality of the management of materials requisition.

PROOF OF VALUE STEPS THAT LEAD TO SUCCESS

A truly comprehensive off-site POV can take one to two months because of the effort needed to ensure all relevant information is examined and validated by everyone involved. There are many high-speed POVs that are promised to organizations as an incentive to take the first step, but the pragmatic buyer requires more than just a cookie-cutter POV. There needs to be a customized view that gives the organization a platform for collaboration. This platform ensures that everyone is comfortable with the process and the results (see Figure 8.2).

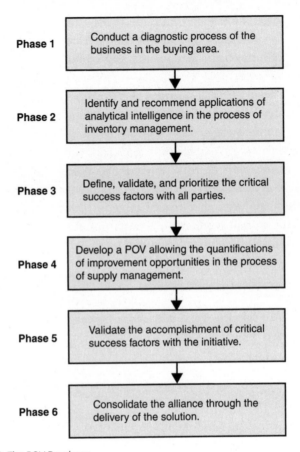

Figure 8.2 The POV Roadmap

The POV Process

In this example of the POV process, the collaborative team gathered the relevant data, analyzed the data, built the optimization models, validated the results, measured the gains, and developed a final presentation showing both the gains and the business benefits.

The following is a high-level outline of a collaborative POV process:

1. Gather the following data to facilitate both demand and supply information for the products:

   a. History of consumption of each part/product in the MRO inventory

  b. Unit of measure of each part/product
  c. Hierarchical classification to mimic the organizational system
  d. Part value or cost
  e. Desired service levels
  f. Cost of maintenance
  g. Cost of ordering
  h. Other costs, such as transportation options extra handling or special storage processes
  i. Historical lead times and actual performance to compare variance
  j. Current/historical stock policies for each item
2. Analyze the data (much of this was done as part of the interview process):
  a. Segment the parts into quadrants:
    i. Critical vs. noncritical
    ii. Availability
    iii. Variability of the demand and supply
3. Build the model:
  a. Create a naïve model for use as the baseline.
  b. Once the model is validated and run, pay particular attention to the buyer problems of products or parts:
    i. What is creating the outlier effect:
      1. Demand variability?
      2. Supplier variability?
      3. Both?
4. Optimization modeling:
  a. Demand side:
    i. Align the proper forecasting method to reduce the variance.
  b. Supply side:
    i. Sharpen inventory costs and replenishment costs:
      1. Cost of processing orders
      2. Opportunity cost of capital invested in inventory
      3. Warehousing costs

4. Handling and counting costs

5. Other costs, such as insurance and taxes

ii. Additional lead-time information:

1. Take into account the review time costs of the buyers.

5. Validation:

a. Beyond the results:

i. To alleviate the mystery, it is important to show how the policy calculations can have a huge effect on how inventories react to demand signals:

1. The ERP module policy structure in action

2. The optimization policy structure in action

6. Return calculation:

a. Inventory differential snapshot:

i. Some parts will have adjusted inventories upward with optimization:

1. The buyers were reviewing unnecessarily due to a bad policy.

ii. Some parts will have adjusted inventories downward with optimization:

1. Unnecessary or redundant safety stocks were on hand to achieve the required service level.

b. Inventory time series:

i. The z-curve correction: With the demand flow in place, the inventories will begin to adjust. Because some inventories are below required levels, an order will result. This will create an immediate uptick in the inventory levels. However, as the other inventories bleed off, the overall inventory will decline.

1. The correction timeline: It is critical that the pragmatic buyer understand the time it takes to achieve the optimized inventory level. The projected demand flow will provide the input to show the graphical drop in inventories to the net levels. The return can be shown in an expected time.

7. The final presentation:

a. There is no silver bullet to delivering the perfect final presentation. The key when it comes to solving the inefficient ERP module is to give the organization a transparent view into the results. This means that not only is the information understandable and reliable, but the organization can participate along the way and can validate any and all points because the organization has made a collaborative investment with the POV team.

A DIFFERENT PRODUCT PERSPECTIVE

The organization used a basic ABC classification to align products into various critical levels of need to the success of the MRO department's goals. As with most ABC assignments, the A items were deemed to be the most critical to the health of the department and their resulting service agreements to other segments of the organization. Interestingly, the MRO buyers explained that the troublesome products did not adhere to the ABC assignments.

In fact, there did not seem to be any correlation between the ABC classification and the troublesome products except one: Because they were classified as A items they received more review attention, while B and C items were either reviewed on an ad-hoc basis or had their safety stock levels raised arbitrarily. To get a clear picture of why some items required more review time than others, a different, quantitative approach was needed that went beyond the present ABC system. To delve deeper, the POV team worked with the organization to classify the products into four quadrants that were graded by:

1. Critical importance to the company (high to low):

a. Operational continuity: Would the operations stop if this part were to be out of stock?

b. Environmental impact: Would the environment be hurt if this part were to be out of stock?

c. Human life risk: Would people be adversely affected if this part were to be out of stock?

d. Extra risks: Do any operational risks exist that would not be covered by b or c?

2. Product availability (based on demand accuracy and replenishment variability):

   a. High demand accuracy and high replenishment speed
   b. High demand accuracy and low replenishment speed
   c. Low demand accuracy and high replenishment speed
   d. Low demand accuracy and low replenishment speed

This exercise gave the buyers a way to see products from a different perspective from the classic ABC banding methodology. The quadrant is shown in Figure 8.3.

As the products were placed onto the map, the buyers began to translate the way they treated the products within each of the quadrants. This naming may align to the way your organization treats the data:

- **Quadrant I: Exception focused.** These items tended to score high on one of the critical risk areas and had a high level of forecast accuracy and a fast replenishment cycle. They were easy acquisition items with minimum levels of inventory. The buyer only had to review the information on an exception basis.

- **Quadrant II: Attention focused.** These items also had a high score for the critical risk area and had high levels of forecast

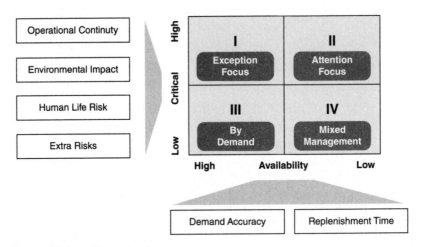

Figure 8.3 Buyer Focus Quadrant

accuracy. However, because they tended to have a slower replenishment cycle the items required high safety stock levels to cover the critical nature of the product.

- **Quadrant III: Demand focused.** These items were low on the organizational risk scale and had a high level of forecast accuracy and a fast replenishment cycle. In this case, the buyer could easily anticipate when and how much to purchase. Safety stock needs were quite low.

- **Quadrant IV: Mixed management.** This quadrant was an odd grouping since the operational risk was low, forecasting had a high level of variability, and the replenishment cycle was slow. As a result, the items tended to be lumped together by inventory costing factors. This means for low-cost materials the safety stock was raised and managed automatically. In turn, the high-cost items would be manually reviewed.

THE EYE-OPENING MOMENT: DISCOVERY AND INSIGHT

As the MRO product portfolio was placed into the quadrants in a hit-or-miss pattern, the organization's executives and buyers uncovered two surprising factors. The first was that there was no correlation between ABC classifications and the placement of products on the quadrant. Each quadrant had A, B, and C items. The second factor allowed the team to uncover why so much time was spent reviewing the data: 86 percent of the products were in quadrants II and IV. See the chart in Figure 8.4.

WHY THE ERP SYSTEM HAD TROUBLE WITH MOST OF THE MRO PRODUCTS

Rather than relying on random assumptions to explain why the POV team could do a better job of providing superior analytics and, thus, better results, the POV team set out to show the steps the ERP system took to produce the numbers. In turn, once that information was explained, the optimization methodologies could be integrated into helping the ERP system do a better job.

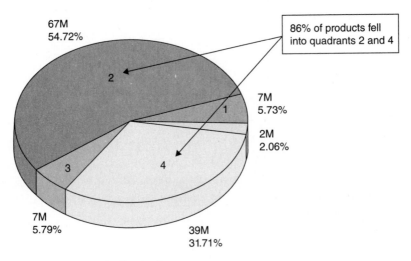

Figure 8.4 Inventory by Quadrant

SIMULATION OF THE REPLENISHMENT POLICIES

In looking at the forecasted demand versus the actual demand shown below, one can see the dilemma of the buying staff on the reviewable items. The forecast tends to over- and underamplify the demand. Over time, this will push the buying staff to raise the inventories beyond their already inflated quantities. Since products are banded as like items, a one-size-fits-many method of assigning inventory levels will be used. This is represented by the maximum inventory levels, order points (reorder level), and the order-up-to levels.

A telltale sign of a production optimization system (remember ERP planning systems had their start in product planning) is a large gap between reorder levels and the order-up-to levels. This type of inventory policy is called "min-max" or "s, S." In most cases, this policy will require a strong, historical demand pattern to support it adequately from an optimization viewpoint. In fact, the reliance on the strong history will promote a "demand smoothing" that cancels out anomalies. In Figure 8.5, one can see how the forecast on the MRO products did not take into account four major anomalies.

Service parts and/or MRO products tend to have highly variable demand patterns and are ordered in small lot sizes, requiring a quick turnaround time. This means that a different type of forecasting technique that accounts for these variances might be more applicable

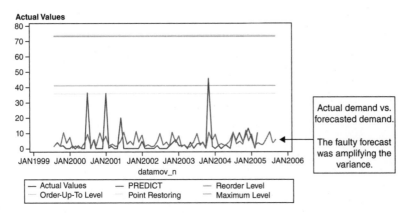

Figure 8.5 Using Min-Max Inventory Policies, the Inventory Reaction Was Lagging

(see Figure 8.5). Conversely, an inventory policy that adapts to a fast replenishment cycle would allow the system to adapt to the true demand and supply signals. This means that the proposed system, if it is to help reduce inventories and help better manage the ordering process, needs to maximize the response time to the demand signal. The problem in the ERP system was creating the buyer's workaround.

SIMULATION OF THE ERP/SCM MODULE REACTION

The SCM module uses demand inputs to set the inventory policies. By using min-max reorder points based on the demand information provided, the system can hold the service level. However, as shown in Figure 8.6, the system is letting the stock fall way below the reorder points during anomaly periods because of the length of the replenishment cycle. In three instances, the SCM module let stock fall far below the out-of-stock level. Since there is a large gap between order-up-to and reorder points, the system will promote the inability to adapt to fluctuations.

SIMULATION OF THE OPTIMIZATION SYSTEM

The optimization system used forecasting methods (Croston's and exponential smoothing) to help with the slower-moving products or products with intermittent demand. Indeed, in some cases aggregation needed to be used to find better demand patterns. However, given

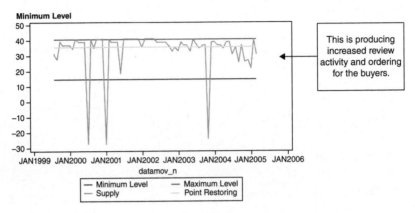

Figure 8.6 Inability to React to Anomalies in Time

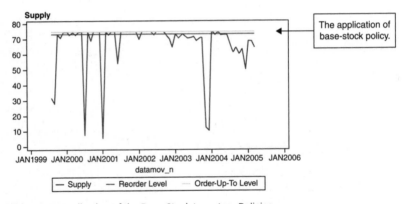

Figure 8.7 Application of the Base-Stock Inventory Policies

the amount of inventory and the lot sizes required to support service and/or MRO parts, speed is more important than large amounts of inventory to support the service level requirement. Therefore, the inventory and ordering process will be tightened to provide speed to the replenishment process. As viewed in Figure 8.7, the optimization system will be tied to a base-stock policy that will allow for a faster reaction time.

THE EFFECT OF POLICY

Rather than a one-size-fits-all inventory policy parameter, the POV team used a business rule format to assign specified base-stock policies when needed. In quadrants II and IV, there was a tendency for the products to react better to a base-stock format rather than a min-max format. The base-stock format provides a more reliable way to create a policy on products when the fixed ordering cost is insignificant with slow replenishment.

How Big an Effect Can This Policy Change Have?

Indeed, the product/SKU results in Figure 8.8 show that the affected items were scattered across a range of very slow moving to regular moving volumes. However, the items tended to have a corresponding low frequency of demand in relation to the total volume:

- Very slow moving: 18 percent of the affected items
- Slow moving: 50 percent of the affected items
- Regular moving: 32 percent of the affected items

As stated in the previous section, the products in this area react better to a base-stock policy. By using business rules to identify the product

Yearly Demand	Frequency of Demand						Total
	0–2	2–4	4–6	6–8	8–10	10–High	
0–1	Very Slow Moving		18%				7,395
							18.01%
1–5							14,463
							35.22%
5–10	Slow Moving						4,916
	50%						11.97%
10–50				Regular Moving			7,904
				32%			19.25%
50–100							2,122
							5.17%
100–High							4,268
							10.39%
Total	11,695	9,364	4,656	2,920	2,050	10,383	41.068
	28.48%	22.80%	11.34%	7.11%	4.99%	25.28%	100%

Figure 8.8 Inventory Velocity Review

need and applying the appropriate policy format, the POV team could better align the needed policy and replenishment requirements.

Consider the earlier findings about the two quadrants that had the most review.

Quadrant II: Attention Focused

These items also had a high score for the critical risk and high levels of forecast accuracy. However, because they tended to have slower replenishment cycles the products required higher safety stocks to cover their critical nature.

Quadrant IV: Mixed Management

These products had low operational risk, forecasting had a high level of variability, and the replenishment cycle was slow. As a result, the products tended to be lumped together by inventory costing factors. This means for low-cost materials, the safety stock inventory was raised and managed automatically while high-cost items were manually reviewed.

The stochastic or random nature of the demand, coupled with the corresponding supply variance, produces a problem with the production-based inventory policy generated by the SCM module. The SCM methodology is based on systems grounded in production. Production systems require stable and historically strong demand and supply data to produce accurate inventory thresholds. The resulting product style inventory policy would be min-max rather than the more efficient base-stock format. The result of the methodology is that policies would create inventory and ordering structures outside the service-level requirements.

The critical product case of quadrant II, the speed or variance in which the replenishment side could react, made the policy one of (1) rush order—this added cost and buyer review time to the system, or (2) raising the policy levels. However, for the production methods of the policies in place, there was already more than enough on hand. Since the organization had put a premium on inventory levels and inventory turns, the rush order became the activity of choice.

In the mixed management case of quadrant IV, since the demand variability was high and the replenishment cycle short, the buying staff developed a process for handling the products using a cost methodology of segmentation. This system divided the products into the same two areas that we found in quadrant II. If the product was high cost, it was rush ordered. If the product was low cost, the inventory thresholds were simply raised to overcome any safety stock issues due to demand fluctuations.

In the process of adaptation, the organization's buyers had created a workaround to overcome an inherent flaw in the SCM module. However, in this case the workaround took the incorrect policies and amplified the cost to the inventory levels, the extra logistics costs, and the overall MRO buying staff workload.

POV RESULTS: INVENTORY OPTIMIZATION ENHANCES THE ERP SYSTEM

The improvement found by using advanced forecasting and inventory optimization methods provided a 37 percent reduction in inventory. Moreover, the 98 percent service level was maintained even with the 37 percent drop in inventory (see Figure 8.9). This means the organization could realize a return of over $18.5 million. This creates a win-win situation because the POV shows the benefit

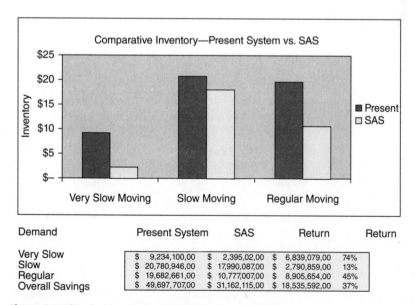

Demand	Present System	SAS	Return	Return
Very Slow	$ 9,234,100,00	$ 2,395,02,00	$ 6,839,079,00	74%
Slow	$ 20,780,946,00	$ 17,990,087,00	$ 2,790,859,00	13%
Regular	$ 19,682,661,00	$ 10,777,007,00	$ 8,905,654,00	45%
Overall Savings	$ 49,697,707,00	$ 31,162,115,00	$ 18,535,592,00	37%

Figure 8.9 Historical Comparison to SAS Inventory Optimization

of purchasing the system used in the POV, but more important, the original money invested in the ERP/SCM system would be realized at a quicker pace.

HOW LONG WILL IT TAKE TO ACHIEVE THE REDUCTIONS?

Using the projected demand information, the organization can now better understand how fast the excess inventory would bleed off to achieve the ROI. Due to the slow and very slow volume of many of the items, the bleed-off will take over a year. However, half of the change will occur in the first three months. See Figure 8.10.

WERE THERE IMPROVED BUYER EFFICIENCIES?

By increasing the trust in the inventory and ordering outputs, the buyers could expect to reduce the amount of time they were using to review and use it for more value-added activities. By applying estimates from the buying staff and management, the collaborative team estimated that the reduced time and improvement in quality

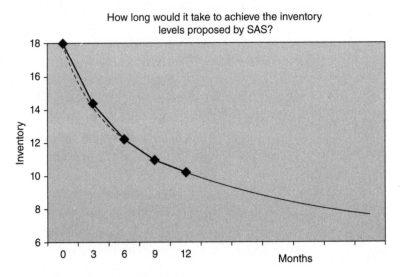

Figure 8.10 Inventory Bleed-Off Schedule

of materials requisition would allow for the same five resources to process up to 15,000 transactions per month, as compared to the current level of 8,000.

Measurement of Success of the POV

- Reduction in inventory?
  - Projected goal for success: 15 percent reduction.
  - Realized: 37 percent reduction.
- Maintain a 98 percent service level?
  - A 98 percent service level was realized with a savings of $18.5 million in freed-up working capital.
  - One half of the savings would be realized in the first three months.
- Improved buyer efficiencies?
  - Dramatic decrease in order review time.
  - Projected to move from 8,000 orders a month to 15,000 orders a month.
  - No increase in headcount.

LOOKING BACK

The ability to reduce inventory in a real-world organization requires more than just an application of algorithms. There are all kinds of factors that come into play, none of which is more important than overcoming time, money, and manpower spent making the current system viable. This last POV example and the subsequent official rollout of an installation led to an active collaboration between the inventory optimization consultants and the assigned project personnel from the client.

Participation was the key to this highly successful engagement. Too often, inventory optimization is the idea of someone close to the inventory, but the virtues or benefits are not sold to upper management. When potential projects are hidden, almost all inventory optimization engagements fail completely or wither on the vine. Never hide the benefits of inventory optimization.

In our first example, the POV results were incredible and exciting, but it took a tremendous amount of effort to move the engagement to a small test rollout. Why would something with so much potential cost saving and revenue generation literally limp along? In retrospect, the dueling goals of management and buyers almost derailed the POV and subsequent rollout. Management had a completely different agenda focused on overstocks, while the buyers were focused on out-of-stocks and lost sales. In the end, it took a benefits summit meeting to align their goals into a workable plan. However, once that plan was put into action, the rollout of inventory optimization into the organization was extremely successful.

The second example was a classic one of corporate infighting. A collaborative team was never an option here. The POV team tried to pull the combatants together, but from the beginning the inherent rogue-buyer mentality was very prevalent, and no amount of inventory planning was going to sway a buyer from making those special purchases. In the end, the client did not buy an inventory optimization solution, but many of the assumptions of inventory management that were held by the management team needed to be reevaluated. This led to some changes, and, at last report, there have been improvements.

The last example of a POV engagement shows the potential opportunity to dig deep into the inner workings of an inventory and replenishment operation. Too often inventory optimization is just thought of as a way to reduce inventory and free up working capital. It is that, but in reality it is all about optimizing the total inventory to meet a customer satisfaction need. Indeed, in the last example the initial focus was to reduce inventory and keep the same service level. Reduction of working capital was the driver. However, as I often see, the actual benefit comes from the secondary requirements. No one really thinks about the effect out-of-stocks have on company revenues until after the fact. In virtually all installations I have been a part of, there is a revenue gain during the same time as an inventory reduction, and this installation was no different. The final surprise is the streamlining of buyer functions. Without all of the tactical problems buyers have to face with following up on delayed shipments or expediting orders, they can spend more time in strategic planning. The POV showed the buying staff could almost double their order capacity with the same staff. They didn't do that. In the end, the staff looked at taking on more strategic planning and collaboration with their partners in the organization, dealing with things like preventative maintenance and better forecasting capabilities.

CHAPTER 9

Inventory Optimization in the Real World: Matas A/S

We started our examination of inventory optimization by exploring the inherent shortcomings found in company enterprise resource planning (ERP) systems and the resulting inefficiencies flowing through the supply chains. We have looked at how inventory optimization can correct these shortcomings by evaluating the costs attributed to service-level requirements down at the granular item/location pairing. Finally, we have seen how organizations have tested the theories found in inventory optimization on their own data.

As we have moved along this pathway, we uncovered that leading-edge organizations have found tremendous results. In many cases, inventories have been cut by 20 to 30 percent while service levels increased. Countless proofs of value (POVs) have been done, and yet inventory optimization comes across as something only visionaries have access to. Why is it that a tried-and-true technology with proven results gets placed into the "interesting, but I don't know if it will work here" point on inventory management project lists?

In all my travels and interactions with inventory management professionals, I continually come down to a single, pervasive question that splits into two directions:

The question:

> "We have tried to reduce inventories, or we have tried to increase our customer satisfaction levels, but in almost every case it was a temporary action that withered away over time. What proof do I have that this solution will provide ongoing results?"

What that really means:

1. "I have heard that inventory optimization can help, but I have a long history in inventory control that tells me most reductions in stock or increases in service levels are temporary. How do I know if I am really getting long-term inventory reductions?"

2. "Technology can only take me just so far. After that the majority of benefit comes from change management. In addition to installing the software, what changes do I need to make in my processes in insure this project's success?"

In the end, the decision maker is left with concerns for (1) the confidence of companywide success and (2) the company's willingness to accept change. Honestly, when it comes to most inventory optimization rollouts, this is the tipping point, and most software companies do not understand this decision-making transition. As trusted advisers, inventory optimization software vendors need to help the organization by (1) explaining inventory optimization in layman's terms, (2) making sure the goals of your project align exactly with the company's goals, (3) making sure those goals are measurable and achievable, and (4) above all, making sure one of the requirements is to make people's jobs easier.

Given this simple roadmap for success, let's take a look at an inventory optimization project as it went from company vision to rollout to maintenance.

MATAS A/S: AUTOMATED FORECASTING AND REPLENISHMENT

Matas is a Danish drugstore chain founded in 1949. The store motto is *Good Advice Makes the Difference*. The Matas chain has 297 stores all over Denmark and employs about 2,500 people. The annual revenue is approximately D.Kr 2 billion ($360 million in U.S. dollars). Matas sells a broad range of items related to personal hygiene and cosmetics, such as Lancôme, Clinique, L'Oréal, and Gillette, along with a host of private-label products. Interestingly, most, if not all, of the Matas shops have a chemical department where the shopper can find both household chemicals and more exotic chemicals for the home chemist. Other things sold in the stores include vitamin supplements and herbal remedies such as ginseng extracts and licorice root.

In 2007, the private equity fund CVC acquired more than 250 of the Matas stores. The goal of the acquisition was to help Matas management transform the company into a top-performing retailer in the European marketplace. At the time of the acquisition, Matas was experiencing the same problems that many retailers around the world were dealing with. In an effort to compete in a troubled economy, extra focus was placed on ensuring customer satisfaction and customer loyalty.

WHAT WERE THE PROBLEMS AT MATAS?

The problem was that over time, inventories in both the stores and distribution center were becoming bloated, and yet out-of-stocks were a common occurrence. This was in direct conflict with the Matas effort to maintain customer satisfaction and loyalty. As a result of these diametrically opposed problems of high inventory and out-of-stocks, store management took extraordinary measures to review store inventory and process weekly orders and send them to the distribution center. Indeed, the average time it took store personnel to complete an order cycle was 15 man-hours. This meant over 3,750 man-hours a week out of store management time. Jacob Sand, the supply chain manager at Matas, said, "Stores more or less guessed need, when they ordered manually. And it is clear that the fear of getting an out-of-stock led to unnecessarily high stock levels, but at the same time one should not underestimate all the experience store personnel have collected as they reviewed the inventory."

In addition, Matas had developed an ABC-style classification hierarchy to help managers focus on products that meant more to the Matas image and profitability. In this instance, an A-type item was most important to keep in stock for customer-satisfaction purposes. Even with the extra review and time spent by store personnel to process the orders, a large percentage of high-value A items were out of stock. This out-of-stock issue on A-type items certainly will cloud customer satisfaction issues, but most important, it can have a huge impact on unrealized revenue.

Finally, as with any kind of manual process, errors occur. One of the big problems at Matas was known as the *forgotten order*. Even with all of the checking and rechecking, store managers would invariably forget to purchase a certain percentage of products for the store. Two things would then happen. The first was that a natural out-of-stock would occur in the store. The second would be a critical "extra" order the next week. The critical second order would have an added effect on the warehouse stock as additional orders were coming in above and beyond actual sales numbers. This bullwhip effect would create an out-of-stock ripple up the chain.

DC REPLENISHMENT

Let's review some of the issues that Matas is dealing with, in addition to the acknowledged problems of receiving manually created orders from store managers. Remember, Matas is using a transactional system that has inherent island of efficiency problems found in multiechelon supply chains.

- The upstream warehouse does not see any store demand information. The demand is created by store orders with no visibility into the actual demand. In fact, the response to the downstream demand is actually an interpretation of the store manager's view of the last 31 days of sales.

- The demand that is provided is somewhat disjointed. Orders to the distribution center (DC) are generated over a five-day period. Groups of stores have order days where they have a designated day (or night) to transmit their orders to the DC. Given this process with no downstream vision into the actual demand, the demand signal is lagging as it is being communicated to the DC. This lag in demand signal creates extra safety stock requirements.

- Even with the ABC classification of products, the assignment of weeks of supply inventory measurements will create the Goldilocks effect across the assignments. The more the DC might try to improve the in-stock percentage of an A item that had a problem, the more the inefficiencies of the weeks-of-supply assignment would make other products overstocked. In turn, in an effort to reduce stocks the reduction of inventory would create even more out of stocks on the high-volume items. Matas was in a whipsaw problem in an attempt to harmonize the inventory at the DC.

- The final issue is the manual processing of the orders. As you can imagine, with a manual process there are huge opportunities for errors. The DC personnel are reviewing orders for authenticity and accuracy. The demand information for the DC cannot be completed until this step is taken and validated.

The Matas DC is in a tough situation. It must supply product efficiently with a muffled and inaccurate demand signal. Without a solid predictive signal, the DC-to-vendor orders are based only on DC sales. This creates the second lag point in the order process. These two lag points in demand signals flowing through the DC make the need for extra safety stocks even more amplified.

As we have seen in our examination of the effects of redundant safety stocks, an upstream inventory location positioned in a multi-echelon supply chain creates a bloated and unresponsive distribution center. Matas was exhibiting all of the classic signs of a problematic upstream DC being bullwhipped by conflicting inventory and demand signals that were filtering in over a week from the stores.

STORE REPLENISHMENT

Oftentimes when inventory optimization is introduced, the buyers get defensive. Actually, it is truly amazing what buyers can accomplish when they have so many factors weighing against them. Going all the way back 30 years to my humble beginnings to examining how buyers of today deal with faulty information, I am shocked at how good buyers do in overcoming the odds. Let's look at what is stacked up against these store managers at Matas as they go about doing their jobs:

- In normal ordering in a transactional system, the downstream location has to always assume 100 percent service level on all items purchased. The normalized tables in the ERP system dictate that relationship. Now, add to that, human nature. The store managers are attempting to create their own islands of efficiencies. They are taking a look at 31 days of sales history and providing a gut-feeling order. If human nature is consistent, the response is to always order a little bit more. The DC has the same 31-day history, but the orders that are accumulated from downstream always come in a little bit higher.

- The DC can't provide 100 percent service level, especially on those A items. This creates a bullwhip effect. When the store managers begin to have a gut feeling about supply consistency, they will order more and more. This creates temporary out-of-stocks as the false demand signal travels up the chain. In most situations like this, there is a rolling in-stock/out-of-stock problem even though inventories might have the correct inventory weeks of supply.

- The space constraints placed on the end-of-supply-chain, customer-facing location create the added problem of balancing sales against excess inventory. You can't sell something while it sits in the back room. Oftentimes the service parts industry is pointed out as the key industry with intermittent demand problems. Without a doubt, retail can rival that problem. In many cases, the store manager is ordering something that has a lot size of 12 or 24 and only sells one a week. Constrained ordering at the store level is an art and a science. If the DC is looking at a store selling four units in a 31-day period and suddenly gets an order for lot sizes of 12 or 24, it can create out-of-stocks.

As you can see, Matas is in a difficult situation, but this is not unique. This is, actually, an extremely common occurrence in the retail industry. The customer-facing location demand is not correctly communicated through the supply chain, and the store managers are using tribal knowledge to overcome the problems. The store managers work alone in their island of efficiency and do not communicate with other managers to get a better cumulative understanding of the problem. At the other end of the spectrum, the vendors are reacting to a DC with no visibility to predictable demand. The result is an extremely inefficient supply chain that suffers from, as described by Matas, bloated inventory, an unacceptable out-of-stock problem, and, finally, an extremely costly ordering process. Once again, if you want to experience this kind of activity, you can go to the MIT Beer Game at www.beergame.org.

A PROJECT IN INVENTORY OPTIMIZATION

The Matas automated ordering project is an example of four key ingredients to a successful installation engagement. First, management had a clear idea of the issues they wanted to solve. This was not a situation of a mid-level manager wanting to recreate a purchasing system.

Management understood that the present system was not working and aggressive steps needed to be undertaken to solve the problems. Second, management spent time reviewing different solution sets and how each rationale was viewed with pros and cons to achieve the goal. Once management had decided on the forecasting and inventory optimization route to accommodate the automated ordering, they were confident the solution would achieve the results they were looking for. Third, management communicated to all parties of the engagement, both internal and external, how the goals would be measured and reviewed. They understood the old human nature process in change: "People gripe, then they grope, then they grow." Management were preparing everyone for change and fostered an open door to the process to vent any frustration or concerns. Finally, management reviewed the progress and weighed internal feedback to the final goal. They made adjustments, but the final goal never wavered. Management stayed firm to the final goal of an automated ordering system that would be more accurate and timely and would save the company money and employees a lot of wasted time.

Following is an illustration of a successful inventory optimization engagement.

The Matas Requirements

So often an inventory optimization engagement is defined by the statement, "We have a problem with our inventory." It is up to the client and technology company to define and solve the various issues that make up the inventory problem. In the case of Matas, the management team had a vision of what they wanted solved in addition to the inventory dilemma. This holistic vision allowed the account teams to align the solution so that it enabled Matas to incorporate change management with the addition of technology.

A Coherent Replenishment Flow

Often, inventory optimization comes across as an extremely complicated activity that only the PhD can understand. In the case of Matas, it wanted to see a rational replenishment process that could be understood and acted on. Since the stores were segmented out into five equal batches throughout the week, the same staggered ordering would be maintained. The initial flow would simply be from the store-level hierarchy so that the DC could fulfill those store orders. Once this was signed off on, the DC could implement a similar process for vendor sourcing of product. Thus, a complete ordering system could be implemented.

Automated Orders

An ordering environment needed to be created where the system took into account the relevant time-phased demand so that the last 31 days were taken into effect, but the most recent were weighed at higher levels. The goal is to reduce the number of man-hours required to process the orders. Indeed, the reduction should be at the store side (producing the order) and at the DC side (reviewing the order).

Higher Turnover Rate

Most of the time, a customer gets wrapped up in the ability to reduce inventory and places undue focus on getting rid of overstocks. As we found in the last chapter's proof of value (POV) with the computer catalog operator, the reduction could backfire. In this case, Matas was extremely smart. Inventory turnover is a recognized inventory key performance indicator (KPI) tied to inventory health. When overall inventories are rightsized, meaning both increased to cover understocked items and reduced to cover overstocks, the inventory turnover, in general, speeds up. This is an excellent KPI, but it must be understood that it tends to be a delayed KPI that does not react immediately. Finally, being a delayed indicator, management needs to understand the z-curve effect of right-sizing the inventory. Most inventory optimization engagements actually have a slowdown in inventory turns in the beginning as low-stock inventory is replenished before the overstock bleeds off. Matas understood the right-sizing problem and waited for the inventory bleed-off to take effect before reviewing the inventory turn rate.

Fewer Out-of-Stock Situations

Again, Matas is smart. Inventory optimization has a strong effect on cutting the overstock problem, but in the majority of cases, the real growth and what gives executives the *ah-ha* moment is when out-of-stocks are reduced and revenue or market share increases due to increased sales. The fact that customer satisfaction is tied up in the customers' belief that they can get their choice of product the first time is important to the retailer. However, one of the key focuses of the Matas requirements was not just a simple reduction in out-of-stocks. Matas wanted it to be a controlled reduction where the focus was placed on A-type items. This would allow for complete rationalization of stock-keeping units (SKUs) instead of simply an out-of-stock number attained.

The Requirements of Matas

Any time there is an interaction among an inventory optimization software company, consultants, and the customer, there needs to be a strong understanding of the following: First, there needs to be precise inventory information at both the store and DC levels. Second, there needs to be a strong view of master product data information, space management, and assortment structures for inventory con-straints. Finally, there needs to be a good understanding of the order management process.

However, there are two important aspects of the data, so that everyone is on the same page going forward. When it comes to inventory optimization projects, one game everyone loves to play is, "Let's see what you can do with this garbage data scenario." In this case, the customer will give the software vendor and consultant every tough forecasting product with loads of intermittent-demand problems. This doesn't do anyone any good. The time invested on intermittent-demand products—unless they are extremely expensive and have long lead times—brings little in the way of benefit. It is extremely important to get a good cross-section of products in an assortment so the customer can see the benefits. As indicated earlier, it is far more important to right-size an A-type item with understocked inventory and lost sales than to reduce an intermittent-demand prod-uct from an overstock position of three down to a correct inventory of two—unless the product is worth $1 million each. Therefore, having a good cross-section of items is extremely important if you are going to compare options. The second requirement is to ensure that stores you might be comparing are truly representative and equal. Therefore, equal products and equal stores and the access to the Matas system would allow for the best possible start to the project.

A PILOT PROGRAM VERSUS A PROOF OF VALUE PROCESS

The software industry tends to work with two different "proof" processes to provide the customer viability of a solution. The vast majority of engagements deal with the POV process. In this situation, an agreed-on set of product and location data is provided and the software provider assembles the data into a time-phased output offsite. The various KPIs that have been agreed to are measured and, if the information is persuasive enough, the project moves on to the next level. Another technique that is used is called the *pilot program*. In this process, the client and the software provider work onsite to assemble a mini-verison of the solution to test the results against the present processes. In the case of inventory optimization the pilot program has a lot of benefits. First, the mini-install does not create a duplication of effort. The pilot becomes the basis for the rollout to the entire organization. Second, the engagement teams get an opportunity to work together on a small scale onsite. This can be a huge benefit as the pilot allows everyone to get on the same page and agree to the working conditions and outcomes. Finally, the pilot program enables the focus to be aligned to agreed-upon locations and products so that there is a true test of both inventory KPIs and workflow processes.

Matas and the software provider decided to take the pilot program process over the proof of value direction because they felt the potential duplication of effort was too costly and the ability to focus on agreed-on stores and products allowed for a better understanding of the solution's true potential. In the case of the Matas pilot program, the consultants and Matas chose 400 representative products and eight stores:

- The 400 products were represented in each store, and the stores were in similar locations and had the same overall volume.

- The stores were divided into two groups. Four stores would maintain the status quo ordering process and submit the orders to the DC on their respective days.

▪ The second group of four stores would use forecasting with point-of-sale inputs that would integrate with inventory optimization to develop inventory policies for the products and generate orders as required. The second group of stores could review the orders, but unless there were wild inconsistencies the order was submitted on the day normally done for ordering.

▪ The side-by-side comparison pilot would be maintained for three months, and the respective inventory positions and ordering times would be measured.

Matas and the consulting team put in place an escape clause to the pilot program that would allow Matas to exit the project if the results were not to its liking. You can imagine that a lot of eyes were on the outcome.

The results were strong over the three-month pilot as shown in Figure 9.1. The automatic ordering showed potential to reduce inventory levels by 15 percent, overall revenues increased by 13 percent, and the inventory turnover increased by 29 percent at the end of the pilot. Moreover, the ordering time was significantly reduced. Interestingly, reports came back from the auto-ordering stores that store managers wanted to override the orders generated, but over time they stopped when the results were so strong. This was something that came back to resurface later in the project.

These results inspired Matas to move the project to the entire chain. Given the results in four stores Matas could, potentially, realize multidigit millions in savings. True to form in the case of Matas, the savings were important, but at this point the management was more interested in the time savings. To them, a believable and supportable automated ordering system was more important to the growth of Matas than short- to mid-term inventory savings. Having store managers focused on strategic activities would allow for solid company growth. Therefore, at this point, the whole engagement was not defined as a savings project; the overall aim was—and is—to save shop staff time to inventory management, so they can concentrate on advising and delivering experiences to customers.

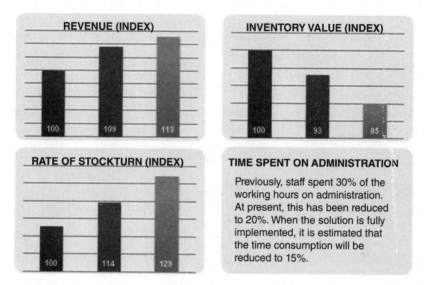

Figure 9.1 The Matas KPI Metrics over a Three-Month Period

ROLLING OUT THE PROJECT TO THE ENTERPRISE

The first step is to integrate the inventory optimization process into the forecasting and replenishment cycle of Matas. To do that, the consultants worked to create a best practice process of aligning the optimization so that inventory optimization could gather the inputs from the Matas data warehouse and push the output to the ERP system.

As noted in the chart in Figure 9.2, the normal store ordering process would come directly from the stores into the ERP system. With the addition to the Matas structure, the inventory optimization would be able to pick up both store and DC stock levels and the POS and demand information from the Matas data warehouse and process this information and optimize the results. Once the information had been updated, the inventory optimization system would generate order proposals for both the stores and the warehouse. After this process had been completed, the automated orders would go out to the stores for review. The store managers had the option of overriding the automated orders. The orders were turned around and sent back to the ERP system for processing. Now that the store and warehouse orders were synchronized,

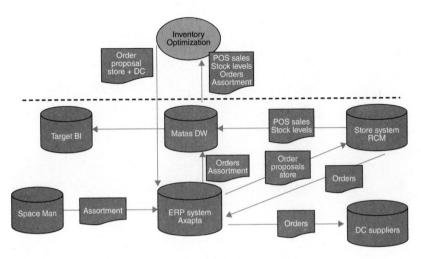

Figure 9.2 Where Inventory Optimization Fit into the Matas System

the warehouse orders did not have to wait for the full order sequence to be completed over the week to properly order from the vendors.

From a change management standpoint, this is an extremely important juncture. As we saw before, buyers, at any level, tend to push back when confronted with what they believe are black-box technology purchases. From the beginning, the focus of Matas was to simplify the ordering process while improving it. If the streamlining of the ordering process was to take place, it had to have acceptance from the store managers in the field. Matas management felt there needed to be, in place, a method where the store managers had the ability to edit the orders so they would feel comfortable with the results. Management felt that over time the editing would naturally be reduced as the store managers became comfortable with the automated orders. The ultimate goal would be to shut off the editing at a point where there were no measureable improvements from the editing or when management felt the time had come to simply shut it off.

THE MATAS NETWORK

As shown in the mapping diagram in Figure 9.3, the primary network flow is for vendors to ship orders to the Matas warehouse for

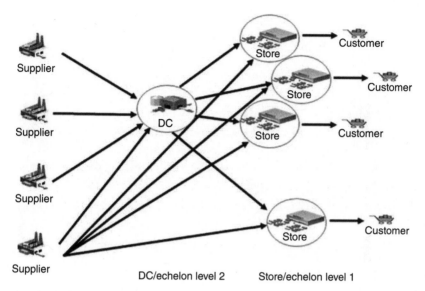

DC/echelon level 2   Store/echelon level 1

Figure 9.3 The Matas Distribution System

dispersal to the stores. However, a secondary network flow was set up to accommodate products that had an ongoing direct-to-store delivery system or to bypass the warehouse when specific ordering requirements were instigated. These requirements might be to support a major advertising event or when direct store shipping was more advantageous. Here comes another *ah-ha* moment in the engagement. The direct-to-store shipments had a lot to do with vendor salespeople cutting special deals in the stores for extra product shipments. This created a faulty inventory number in the system and directly contributed to overstocks in the stores. Once the auto-replenishment process started, the vendor-driven overstocks stopped immediately.

Within the Matas network, the stores were considered to be the first echelon of optimization, and the warehouse was the second level of optimization. Up until this time, Matas had looked at the stores and the warehouse as separate entities and managed them separately. The only way the warehouse understood the downstream demand was to aggregate the store POS and ordering into a single demand signal. As you remember, this classic sequential optimization was part of the island of efficiency model. Now that inventory optimization was going to occur, the primary demand signal was going to be the granular store/product demand pairing. The system would recognize each pairing signal and react as a network rather than individual parts. As a last step, the warehouse's ability to see downstream to the store-level demand enabled it to aggregate the demand and react to it in a much more timely fashion. This systematic approach would allow better demand communication back to the vendor by allowing a better view of the demand across the network. The result of this store-warehouse-vendor visibility was a much more adaptable supply chain. It could easily recognize changes in demand faster than the previous store ordering process. A good example of this occurred during the bird flu pandemic in 2009. The pandemic set off increased demand for hand disinfection liquid. It was automatically detected by the auto-ordering system, which reacted to increased demand before the staff realized the increase in demand had occurred. The ability to automatically recognize the uptick in demand for the hand sanitizer actually provided enough stock for the stores to take care of demand and created added sales that would not have been realized in the old system.

The goal of the rollout is to optimize both the stores and the warehouse in a dual-echelon inventory optimization process and simplify the overall ordering experience.

A CLOSER LOOK AT THE OPTIMIZATION PROCESS

Let's take a closer look at the flow of information, so that we understand the steps being taken in the optimization process (see Figure 9.4). So often I am asked, "Can I do optimization out of the box?" To that I almost always say, "Yes, but . . . ." Let me explain. A better demand signal and a better, more uniquely assigned inventory policy will provide more accurate results, but most companies are very different from each other in the way they want to proceed once the optimization has occurred. Even though the optimization will deliver a better result, most companies want to have products handled differently. This end is where out-of-the-box meets customization. Therefore, it is important to make a distinction in out-of-the-box. I have found very few inventory optimization companies that have

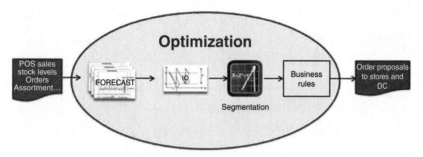

Figure 9.4 The Optimization Process Flow

been successful in applying a generic code to all products and gotten acceptable results. The best usually help the company by collaborating on how the optimization is applied. In the case of Matas, the optimization is out of the box—but also out of the box are the abilities to use sophisticated operations research segmentations capabilities and business rule applications so Matas could apply its own flavor to the optimization.

Forecasting

The first step in any optimization process is to have the best forecast available. In the case of Matas, special methodologies were used not only to allow for the best forecasts, but also to allow for the proper sequencing so the stores and warehouse were aligned and working as one entity or network flow.

The store-based, level-one echelon forecast created 2 million SKU/store combinations. These forecasts were based on a weekly level extrapolated on 52 weeks and a rolling three years of data. These forecasts rolled up to the warehouse where 26,500 forecasts were produced each day and reconciled on a daily basis. It was very important, as it is with all retailers, that event variables were introduced to account for promotional activities and seasonal shifts in volume. Prior to this level of forecasting sophistication, Matas had been using a lot of gut-feel ordering from the store managers, and, as we had seen, it took long, tedious hours to develop orders with limited success.

Here are some of the various event inputs that would be used in the Matas example:

- Flyer event
- Newspaper event
- Specific campaign beauty products
- Christmas seasonal activity
- Family discount, like a BOGO (buy one, get one free)
- Segmenting the campaign into weeks for proper consumption

Once the forecasted demand is produced at both store and warehouse level, the demand output for projected sales at the stores will be sent to the optimization engine. It is important to note that one of the *ah-ha* moments of the engagement was seeing the aggregated store demand without the aggregated demand variance. This for Matas showed some of the power of optimization. In previous situations, the safety stocks at the warehouse were calculated using a formula to cover the accumulated store demand and created a huge amount of redundant stock. The new demand signals coming from the forecasting engine now harnessed the extra demand variance, thereby reducing the needed stock. Right out of the blocks Matas was seeing the power of optimization.

Inventory Optimization

The key goal of the inventory optimization run was to find the optimal reorder levels and the optimal order-up-to levels. The ordering threshold is important because it matches the order timing with the demand expectancy so the minimum amount of safety stock is required and the product will not run out of stock. As we have discussed in previous chapters, these numbers are effectively called the min-max.

As part of the constraining process, products with higher ordering costs and higher fluctuations of demand will be assigned the s, S or min-max policy, and products with lower ordering costs and lower demand fluctuations will get a base-stock policy. This type of policy assignment was coordinated with the Matas team to ensure the proper alignment of ordering to the product type. In many cases, stores would

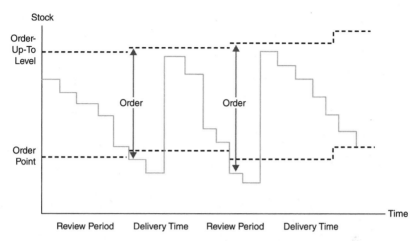

Figure 9.5 Capturing the Min-Max Ordering Process

have lot sizes of a 12-pack, but the product sold one or two a week. This constraining functionality, coupled with the store space, enabled the inventory optimization system to match the ordering logic needed to move from warehouse to store, but also to translate aggregated inputs for the vendor purchases moving into the warehouse.

In the example shown in Figure 9.5, the inventory optimization s, S or min-max policy is in effect for a product in a Matas store. In the case of lead time, it should be noted that in all inventory optimization calculations the lead time is computed with both ordering time and delivery time. Finally, another important point to Figure 9.5 is that s and S are recalculated each time it is possible to make an order and therefore makes s, S not only individual but also dynamic.

Operations Research Segmentation

One of the specific areas that Matas wanted to explore as part of the ordering and inventory optimization was the effect that limited supply might have on its system. From a retailing situation, this is extremely important. Oftentimes, a product supplied by a vendor is in short supply and needs to be allocated in a logical and informative fashion. If this were to occur in a basic inventory optimization system, the process flow would simply indicate an out-of-stock and a reduction in service level. Matas wanted to understand the best way to position products in short supply so that stores with the highest need came first in the pecking order. Moreover, it wanted to ensure that customers requiring the product most got the product to increase customer satisfaction. This process stops the "trying to sell fur coats in Hawaii when people are freezing in Minneapolis" problem and puts the product in the right place for the best return on investment and customer satisfaction.

A second use of operations research inputs was to align vendor orders from the warehouse so they could be aggregated into full-truck quantities. By taking into account tie and tier counts for pallet quantities and weight and cube information, trucks could be built to accommodate minimum weight and cube requirements. This enabled Matas to maximize vendor ordering for best pricing options.

Last, the operations research (OR) functionality also gave Matas the ability to adhere to space management requirements in the stores by aligning constrained orders to minimum presentation stock levels and maximum order-up-to levels pressed by shelf depth and height. This would allow for the constraining of an order so that it fits the parameters of the store requirements and frees up the store manager from trying to adhere to those constraints by tribal knowledge.

Business Rules

One of the distinct problems found in industries as diverse as spare parts and retail is intermittent demand or extremely slow movers. When products get to the end of the supply chain, sometimes volume just slows to a crawl. In those kinds of situations, especially in constrained inventory locations, space allocation and SKU rationalization is important. Oftentimes, inventory optimization will overstate inventory needs when the forecast is looking at intermittent demand. In the case of Matas, the management wanted to reduce the amount of complexity required to fully forecast and push business rules implantation to products when feasible. For instance, if an item is moving only one every other month and the cost is below a certain threshold, the total inventory might be positioned at "2" with a base-stock order policy of "1" if something is ordered. In the situation where there might be a bit more seasonality involved, the presentation level might be raised during seasonal times and backed off during the out-of-season periods.

THE ULTIMATE MATAS GOAL

As inventory optimization and replenishment were rolled out from the pilot to a full chainwide system, Matas maintained its original vision of creating a fully automated process of ordering that would replace gut feel and tribal knowledge with high levels of forecasting coupled with advanced inventory optimization routines. The automated system would create order proposals that would reduce the amount of time store managers were spending doing mundane activities. It would greatly reduce the number of SKUs that were forgotten during the ordering process. Finally, it would effectively reduce the out-of-stock problems at Matas in a rational way so that those products that were most important had the highest service levels and were able to maintain customer satisfaction on important stock. The expected results were as follows:

- **Reduce inventory.** The reduction of working capital invested in inventory would allow for an improved balance sheet and income statement. Most important, it would allow Matas to be a much more nimble retailer.
- **Reduce out-of-stock situations.** The increased revenue from the reduction of out-of-stocks is an important segment of the project. The return on investment (ROI) of the engagement will depend on revenue enhancements and will have the highest impact on the company balance sheet and income statement. In many ways, this would be the leading indicator of the project success.
- **Increase efficiency of store and warehouse personnel.** Freeing up expensive labor from doing heavy, manual, and recurrent labor will allow store managers to work on strategic activities.
- **Reduce the bullwhip effect.** In addition to the classic ordering problems occurring between warehouse and stores, the warehouse was dealing with huge redundant inventory issues by having extra safety stock. However, one of the critical issues was the cost of expedited orders. Matas wanted to calm the supply chain down and reduce the cost of doing business.

THE MATAS RESULTS

Inventory optimization is not just about technology. Change management is a tremendously important segment of any project. As we found in the catalog company, the buyers revolted at the idea that they were being questioned about their buying habits. Many an inventory optimization engagement has ground itself to a halt because management did not allay fears and stay the course. Matas had to change the way it viewed ordering. Up until this time, the ordering system was built on a human process that was fraught with error. The use of high-powered analytics and optimization overcame the human errors, but it took time to slow down the fears and get the personnel to trust the system. As you can see from Figures 9.6 and 9.7, Matas moved from a system of ordering by gut feel at the store to a process of accumulating aggregate orders to send off to the vendor. In Figure 9.7, you can see the analytics and optimization set up in a circular improvement cycle. In addition to simply starting off well, the system continued to learn and improve.

So, how did Matas do? Management stayed the course and got its improvements, but there were *ah-ha* moments along the way:

- Total inventory stock value was reduced by 10 percent.
- The out-of-stock situation was reduced by 2 percent to a service level of 98 percent.

    This was another *ah-ha* moment: By using the unique store/SKU pairing functionality of inventory optimization and

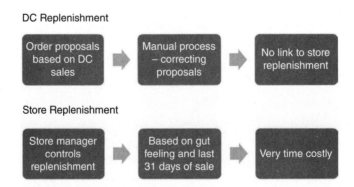

Figure 9.6 The Old Matas Ordering System

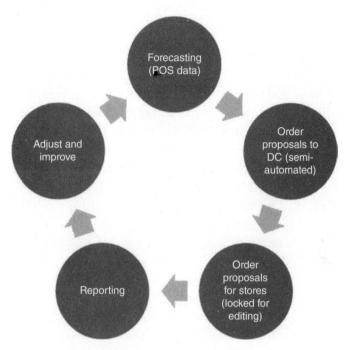

Figure 9.7 The New Matas Ordering System

replenishment, Matas was able to fine-tune the service level requirements on its A, B, and C items so that the out-of-stocks could be controlled by SKU classification.

The 2 percent (98 percent service level) out-of-stock factors equated to the following:

- 0.1 percent were A-type items.
- 0.4 percent were B-type items.
- 1.5 percent were C-type items.
- Man-hours spent on replenishment activities were reduced by 70 percent.

REFLECTIONS ON THE PROJECT

From an operational standpoint, the project was and continues to be a rousing success. However, it is never easy to introduce change into an organization. It needs to be moved through an organization with care.

Jesper Amsinck Børsen and Jacob Sand, executives at Matas, sum up the results well.

Børsen, Matas's supply chain manager, said, "We told the board of management that we could reduce the inventory by 10 percent, but we hoped that the actual figure would be 20 percent. So far, the results show that we are close to 50 percent." On introducing inventory optimization to Matas, Sand had this to say: "You have to be careful not to describe the kind of change as too rosy, because it is not easy to introduce an innovative new technology in a chain that is also in a number of other major changes. Having said that, there is no doubt that the automatic ordering is a success."

My hat is off to a great organization that took the dual approach of technology and change management to a successful conclusion. It is a roadmap for success.

CHAPTER **10**

The Strategic Value Assessment

LOOKING BEYOND THE REQUEST FOR PROPOSAL

Requests for proposals have gotten a bad rap lately. What ends up happening is a fashion show competition breaks out when someone should have simply asked the question: What really is your business problem and what do you see as a success? What is lost is the true understanding of what the company in question is trying to accomplish. It is great that a company might want to entertain the upgrade of their forecasting or replenishment system, but what was the problem with what they were doing in the first place and why do they need this upgrade? Let's face it, a software upgrade is a complicated and uncomfortable process, and it can be a particularly arduous one if you don't have some kind of vision of what the benefits will be at the end of the journey.

This is why I always push for a software provider to do a strategic value assessment (SVA) while working with the customer. Obviously, there should be some kind of qualification, because the last thing anyone wants to do is waste time researching and validating information to a customer who has no intention of moving forward. The SVA is an opportunity to spend a day with the customer to get a complete understanding of what is in the *vision*.

THE STRATEGIC VALUE ASSESSMENT

So, what is a *strategic value assessment*?

I have been involved in more SVAs than I care to count, but every one of them takes on a strange ritual dance of trust building and expectations. It is far more than speed dating and far less than a marriage proposal.

As a software evaluator, imagine yourself sitting down with a group of people who you know are there to sell you software. You have to explain how your business is coming up short in their efforts and now management wants to dramatically improve the company's bottom line with your project. Your career is hanging in the balance! On the flipside, you have the software vendor who has been pigeonholed by past experience as a "seller of snake oil." Indeed, you, by definition of being a software vendor, have never seen a round hole you couldn't drive a square peg into! There are some serious trust issues going on here.

The goal of the SVA is to develop a common understanding of how the project will fit within the goals of the company. Just simply saying the company wants to achieve a specific metric or group of metrics does not meet the financial hurdle points required when projects are being evaluated. There needs to be a short-, medium-, and long-term financial view, along with a common understanding by all parties. In the end, the SVA is used to show management how the project will play out and provide the needed results. It is imperative that software evaluators trust the SVA. The ritual dance is designed to get everyone on the same page so that the evaluator and vendor share their knowledge and experience.

The Lynchpin

Remember our discussion about how proofs of value can be derailed by those not included in the process? This is even truer during the SVA process. An SVA is being built with one thing in mind—to enable "someone" to put real numbers in front of decision makers so that the project can be greenlit. That someone is the *lynchpin,* or executive sponsor.

It is imperative to have an executive sponsor for the SVA to be successful. The sponsor sets the tone and the vision. For what it's worth, I have yet to see a successful outcome to an SVA done without a strong executive sponsor.

There are three key roles of the executive sponsor:

1. **Provide the overarching context for the software and the project.** Oftentimes, a project is not an isolated activity, but one activity in a broad-based, companywide initiative.

2. **Give perspective and insight into the company dynamics.** Egos abound in most organizations. Although the final decision may not be a democratic one, the group needs to be heard, understood, and acknowledged. The executive sponsor gives the team a better understanding of the political atmosphere and a guidance of how to deal with it.

3. **Allow for honest feedback and guidance during the process.** Invariably, mistakes are made on both sides. The ability to see, recognize, and react to the ongoing process enables it to move to a coordinated and successful conclusion.

The First Step in the SVA: Setting the Stage

The executive sponsor needs to set the tone for the SVA engagement. During the opening comments of the meeting, the project needs to be positioned within the larger context of the organization's charter. People in the room need to understand the seriousness of the process and the need to share both the company's vision and the vendor's limitations/strengths. I say *limitations/strengths* because, as I said in Chapter 1, people who enter into an inventory optimization SVA have preconceived ideas about what it can do and how it does it.

The Second Step in the SVA: Understanding the Supply Chain Network

It sounds easy, but understanding the current and future vision of the way product flows through a company supply chain can be a daunting task. The process begins with the breakdown into the flow of the products/SKUs/parts through the organization. From this point, there needs to be a shift to the *as-is decision-making process*. The next step is to understand the metrics and value opportunities so that there is an agreement as to the value of the engagement. There needs to be a deep dive into the IT systems so that there is a common understanding of where the optimization would fit and what systems would be enabled to complete the engagement. Finally, there must be a common vision of what, if any, changes need to take place in the supply chain so that it mimics the future. We don't need to get into "in the weeds" type analysis, such as how much order cycle times should be postponed or tightened. We need to get a basic view from the team if there is to be a future state, and what it would look like.

The Material or Product Flow Process

What kinds of product/SKUs do you deal with?

Business Discovery

- What lines of business are you dealing with, and what is their associated revenue? In essence, what are the important lines of business, and what are you most associated with?
- How is your business changing? Is it growing or declining? Is this the same as the industry?
- Describe your product/SKU population. How big is it? Are the products fast or slow movers? What categories would you put them in?
- What are the classification schemas?
- Characterize your product life cycles for your lines of business.

System Discovery

- Is there a consistent master data system for the product/SKUs?
- Where is the master data system kept?
- What are the product life-cycle assignments? Where are they kept?

What does your inventory network structure look like?

Business Discovery

- Describe your inventory network. What are the inventory levels? Inventory values?
- How is demand met? Is demand a consistent flow, or are there alternative routes to meeting it?
- Describe the way you source product/SKUs.
- Do you have a rate of obsolescence? What is the yearly write-off?
- Describe areas where you might have an opportunity to optimize. Where does the demand occur? How do you meet demand? What is the sourcing?

System Discovery

- What systems do you use to record demand occurrences and fulfillment?
- Where are the records of "ship to and ship from" held?
- What SCM, ERP, and WMIS systems do you use? Describe their interactions.

The Third Step in the SVA: Understanding the Current Processes

Supply and demand goes through a systematic process. Each company is the same, but wholly different. Oftentimes, an SVA can get short-circuited by assumptions being made in the area. It is imperative to make sure everyone is comfortable at the end of this step in the process. The SVA needs to understand how demand is assimilated and if there is a process of review and consensus to get the demand information correct. Once the demand information is positioned, how does the supply chain react to the information? This is where the SVA begins to understand the mechanics of the company and the maturity of the supply side. Does the company rely on simple KPIs and metrics, or are there other triggers in place to create the inventory needs? Finally, the SVA will uncover the replenishment tactics and how the organization treats uncertainty in the supply chain. Overall, when this step has been completed, the developer of the SVA and the participating members of the team will understand how decisions are being made and to what metrics they are held when the supply chain is in motion.

As-Is Decision Flow

Demand Planning

Business Discovery

- How many different forecasts are developed?
- What level do you forecast at?
- Who is responsible for creating forecasts?
- What methodologies do you use to measure forecast accuracy, and at what level?

- What influences your forecasts?
- Do you use POS data?
- Do seasonality, intermittency, and life cycle come into play?
- How many years of demand data are available?

System Discovery

- What tools do you use for forecasting?
- What do you see as strengths and weaknesses?
- What data sources do you use for making forecasts?

Inventory Planning

Business Discovery

- Describe how forecasts translate into inventory plans.
- Who, what, and how are inventory plans generated?
- How are safety stocks calculated?
- What is the process for estimating stockouts and holding costs?
- What are the order fulfillment times and cycle times in your supply chain?
- Do you redistribute stock from time to time? How?

System Discovery

- What systems are used to check inventory availability and fulfillment?
- How do you integrate planning systems to the forecast system?

The Fourth Step in the SVA: Understanding the Metrics of Measurement

If there is one area of the SVA I enjoy the most, it is understanding the metrics of success at an organization. Companies start with an idea, but are run on efficiencies. Inventory optimization has a history of reducing inventory, but that is usually not the sole reason for adopting the methodology. In fact, most companies discount inventory optimization because the so-called short-term reduction of inventory is not a highly valued goal. In most cases, a company is having trouble attaining a level of competitiveness or has lost profitability over time. Different silos of the supply chain are looking for ways to reinvigorate the business. The result can be a hodgepodge of starts and stops—whipsawing the business between feast and famine. In fact, a reduction of inventory might be viewed as the last thing anyone wants to do! Understanding the metrics of the business and how success is measured allows everyone to visualize the current and future state. When delivered by way of the executive sponsor and the supporting staff, the collaborative team can put into perspective how they can help attain organizational goals—and how inventory optimization fits into the business plans and processes.

Metrics and Value Opportunities

Performance Metrics

Business Discovery

- Describe the main KPIs that you use to manage the business.
  - This may require a view and discussion about the current dashboard if available.
- What is the level of detail of these KPIs, and how do they roll up to the executive KPIs?
- What is your performance toward your current KPIs:
  - Forecast accuracy
  - Inventory turns
  - Days of supply
  - Costs associated with inventory
  - Expediting
  - Obsolescence
  - Shortages
- What is your revenue?
- What is the margin?
- What is the cost of goods sold?
- Describe the KPIs you would desire if you were not limited to current capabilities.

System Discovery

- What is the current reporting system?
- What kind of effort is required to generate the KPIs?
- What is the process for sourcing data for generating KPIs?

The Fifth Step in the SVA: Against Whom Do You Measure Yourself?

Oh, the problems with being best in class!

Best in class are few and far between, and, quite often, do not stay in that position for long periods of time. People need to stay at the top of their game and constantly review themselves to their peers. Obviously, comparing yourself year after year will give you a benchmark against yourself. The key to best in class, and the key to shareholder value, is how you compare to your peers.

During this last part of the SVA evaluation, the team needs to get a handle on where they want to be in 6 months, 12 months, and 36 months. Nobody gets excited about a 2 percent reduction in out-of-stocks or *nimble inventories* unless it contributes to the overall health of the company. Executives get excited about revenue gains, customer retention, and increased net profit, especially when they are advances beyond those of their peer competitors.

The final step of the SVA is to get out the yardsticks and see where everyone wants to be in the future:

1. Internally, what do you want to attain?
2. Whom do you compare yourself to in your peer group?

Measuring for Success

Business Discovery

■ What are the priorities of your metrics for success?

■ What is the executive importance?

■ What companies do you measure yourselves against?

■ What do you perceive as their strongest and weakest attributes?

■ Do you have a stock price evaluation process?

■ Do different KPIs have weighted values over time? Short term/long term?

System Discovery

■ How do you get the information to evaluate peers?

■ Are there specific analysts that you look to for information?

THE RESULTS OF THE SVA

As indicated earlier, inventory optimization is usually viewed as a way to reduce inventory. For years, that was done by reducing days of supply to a point where out-of-stocks started to climb and holding it there for as long as needed. This put a tremendous amount of strain on procurement, because any deviation from the norm on supply or demand would throw everything off—and result in high out-of-stocks on key items. Most organizations can do this for one to six months, but sooner or later, they must go back to previous levels of inventory. This is why many CFOs refuse to recognize inventory reductions as a sign of long-term efficiencies—they usually go away. In fact, while inventory optimization can provide long-term inventory reductions, the true benefits are not all about the initial reduction. Figure 10.1 illustrates the short- and long-term benefits of inventory optimization. The SVA presentation to executives is usually the first time they can see and appreciate the short- and long-term benefits that go beyond the cost of goods reduction. As you will see, the primary benefits of increased

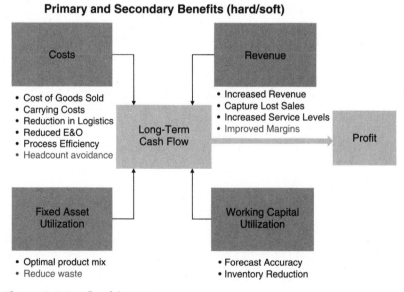

Figure 10.1 Benefits of the SVA

revenues and secondary benefits of reduced waste and headcount efficiencies far outweigh the inventory cost reductions in the long term.

STRATEGIC VALUE ASSESSMENT BENEFIT ANALYSIS

Before going into the SVA presentation, the team needs to get buy-off
on *assumptions*. The SVAs that I have done usually take what I have
been able to do in the past and go conservative. Figure 10.2 shows the
types of assumptions that can be made to assimilate the information
and have it be understandable and defendable. Indeed, I will discuss
with the executive sponsor the benefits that inventory optimization
has provided to peer-type companies to theirs and tell why I am dramatically reducing the assumptions. This is not to get away from "pie
in the sky" projections. I am making sure expectations are held to a
reasonable level and the sponsor has wiggle room if the subordinates
do not follow through on promises of support.

One of the key aspects of the SVA is to hold off on inventory reductions from increased forecast accuracy. First of all, it is hard to prove
that so-called *improved* forecasts can be believed. Second, the improvement falls into the ERP people's view that IO is just improved safety
stocks and not a true improvement of inventory positioning and network actions. Taking this off the table helps everyone look at the whole
picture instead of trying to defend the undependable "best" forecast.

Finally, the chart on the left allows for the discussion of the *efficiency frontier*. We are looking at one view. Moving the metrics to reflect
another view simply moves the results to a different part of the frontier. For instance, if you wanted a much higher service level that might
improve sales and margin, the cost would be higher, but still within the
range and perfectly attainable—simply a different result *and* open for
discussion.

Let's face it, this is an eye opener for most first-time viewers.
Reduce inventory? Sure, but it is only about 17 percent of the total
benefit! The cumulative three-year benefits of this SVA are almost
$56 million (Figure 10.3). However, only about $8.7 million was from
inventory reduction. In this SVA, the reduction would have occurred
in the first 9 months, and once it had attained the optimal inventory,
the savings would go away. That's classic inventory optimization. The

Benefits	ROI Model
Reduce Inventory	50% Theoretical maximum 10–30% reduction typical 20% in business case
Reduce Non-capital Carrying Costs	Relative to inventory levels
Increased Sales	Conservative 2%
Reduced Logistics/Freight	Conservative 1%
Reduced Premium Freight/ Expedite	25% Reduction
Reduced E&O	33% Reduction
Margin Improvement	Conservative .5%

Not Qualified	
Inventory Reductions	Increased forecast accuracy
Sales Increases	Potential for component inventory reduction
POS Data Leverage	Compliance, visibility, collaboration
Increased Process Efficiency	Automation

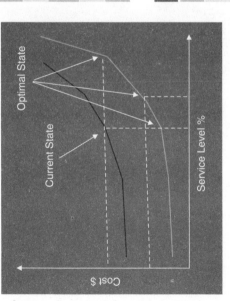

Figure 10.2 Projection Assumptions

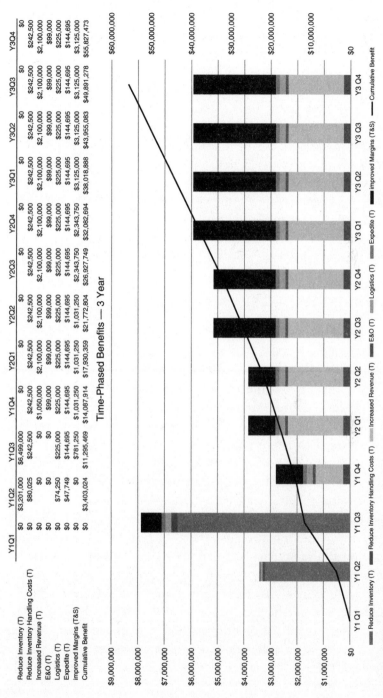

	Y1Q1	Y1Q2	Y1Q3	Y1Q4	Y2Q1	Y2Q2	Y2Q3	Y2Q4	Y3Q1	Y3Q2	Y3Q3	Y3Q4
Reduce Inventory (T)	$0	$3,201,000	$6,499,000	$0	$0	$0	$0	$0	$0	$0	$0	$0
Reduce Inventory Handling Costs (T)	$0	$80,025	$242,500	$242,500	$242,500	$242,500	$242,500	$242,500	$242,500	$242,500	$242,500	$242,500
Increased Revenue (T)	$0	$0	$0	$1,050,000	$2,100,000	$2,100,000	$2,100,000	$2,100,000	$2,100,000	$2,100,000	$2,100,000	$2,100,000
E&O (T)	$0	$0	$0	$99,000	$99,000	$99,000	$99,000	$99,000	$99,000	$99,000	$99,000	$99,000
Logistics (T)	$0	$74,250	$225,000	$225,000	$225,000	$225,000	$225,000	$225,000	$225,000	$225,000	$225,000	$225,000
Expedite (T)	$0	$47,749	$144,695	$144,695	$144,695	$144,695	$144,695	$144,695	$144,695	$144,695	$144,695	$144,695
Improved Margins (T&S)	$0	$0	$781,250	$1,031,250	$1,031,250	$1,031,250	$2,343,750	$2,343,750	$3,125,000	$3,125,000	$3,125,000	$3,125,000
Cumulative Benefit	$0	$3,403,024	$11,295,469	$14,087,914	$17,930,359	$21,772,804	$26,927,749	$32,082,694	$38,018,888	$43,955,083	$49,891,278	$55,827,473

Time-Phased Benefits — 3 Year

Figure 10.3 Time-Phased Financial Benefits Analysis

true benefits of this opportunity are in the increased revenues from reduced out-of-stocks and improved margins due to efficiencies. This is where inventory optimization shines.

In this particular company, the executive sponsor was the one to say, "The revenue improvement and efficiencies would have put an increase of 15 percent to our net income last year!"

I couldn't say that kind of statement and get away with it, but the executive sponsor got everyone's attention!

The key is cumulative benefits. Inventory optimization is not put in place to show what a bad job the buying staff is doing. They have been doing a yeoman's job with faulty inputs and metrics designed to create inefficiencies. Inventory optimization is put in place to help the ERP system do a better job and enable the buying staff to do their jobs easier. The cumulative benefits are staggering.

SO, WHAT DOES THE SVA ACCOMPLISH?

Requests for proposals (RFPs) will always be part of the software decision-making process. There is no getting around that. However, very few RFPs are positioned for inventory optimization. In almost every case, inventory optimization is a checkbox to the RFP, with little emphasis. Indeed, there are far more questions and requests to make sure the RFP respondent has all of the reports necessary to continue doing the replenishment processes like they've always done in the past and not look at how to do things better. Inventory optimization is not an RFP product. It doesn't generate that kind of inspection.

Inventory optimization needs to go beyond the realm of innovator product and get into the mainstream of business—not for the project, but for the long-term benefits. The SVA gets the entire corporate team onto the same page. First, it allows the executive sponsor to have a readymade presentation to take to management for product cost and benefit analysis. The information has been agreed to and is defendable. Second, the team has developed a vision of how inventory optimization fits into their business and system processes. It is no longer an outlier project that will be scrapped once the funding is completed. Third, both the executive and subordinates developed the vision of how it will integrate into their day-to-day activities, insuring the ongoing support. Finally, inventory optimization becomes more than just a reduced inventory. It helps drive efficiencies that are measurable and defendable.

Almost 97 percent of all of the inventory optimization engagements I have participated in have continued on. Some are now 10 years and counting. That is not the case in the vast majority of competitive engagements. They tend to be short-term fixes to an inventory problem. The benefit is reached, the sponsor gets promoted, and the system is scrapped. I am firmly convinced that the SVA process is a significant reason behind the long-term acceptance of inventory optimization at the accounts I have dealt with.

CHAPTER 11

A View of an Inventory Optimization Installation

WHAT DOES AN INVENTORY OPTIMIZATION PROJECT LOOK LIKE?

Inventory optimization software installations tend to be created in eight distinct steps.

1. Software implementation
2. Design of the system and deciding on the scope
3. Data integration (creation of analytical base tables [ABTs])
4. Creation of the forecast process (if not supplied from another system)
5. Creation of the inventory process
6. Post-processing of results (evaluation of output and implementation of business-specific factors)
7. Test of the results
8. Automation and commissioning

As can been seen in Figure 11.1, project management is not forgotten in a standard implementation, but it is also not considered a classical stage like the others but rather an ongoing one. I will return to the project management aspect later.

Regarding the implementation time, this naturally depends on the scope of the project and also on the availability of the data. From experience, it will be possible to start up and be up and running with a limited scope in 8 to 12 weeks. By *limited scope,* I mean a small assortment of products and starting with one echelon in the network and then expanding from there. I like to take this type of engagement process because so-called big-bang engagements can take months, if not years. The smaller, project-based process can provide information to the client quickly for executive buy-in purposes. Once the limited-scale project is in place, it is simply an expansion of the scope after that. The client has actionable information it can deal with in a two- to three-month period of time that will be replicated as the project expands. This is extremely reassuring to everyone involved and gives everyone the opportunity to fine-tune where there might be issues before jumping in with both feet.

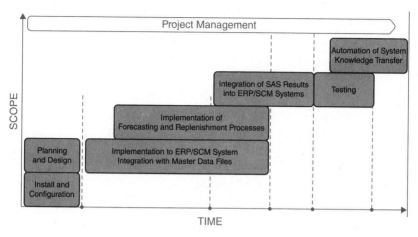

Figure 11.1 Project Management Workflow

How Is the Project Split Up for Best Results?

As already indicated, a good way to look at inventory optimization implementations is to let them grow with the time and the need.

By this I mean that if you start with a limited scope, you will get up and running much faster than if you want to include the whole network from the beginning. However, this does not mean that you should not have a master plan and include the whole network. Splitting the project up into smaller steps and taking one at a time provides faster results (see Figure 11.2).

I see four reasons for this:

1. The company gets a better feeling for what it means to let the machines take over the ordinary replenishment process, and

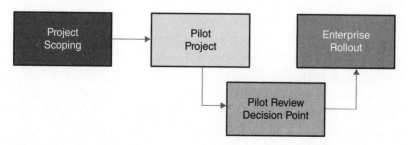

Figure 11.2 Pilot Decision Point

gains confidence/trust in the implementation as the results start to show.

2. The implementing consultants get a better understanding of the company and the specific characteristics of the market that the company is operating in.

3. You reduce the implementation risk, since you can escape the implementation at each step.

4. And last, but not least important, why wait for a full implementation when you can start harvesting the easy fruits at an early stage?

Some might say that if you do not include the whole supply chain (or at least the part of the chain that the company can control), you will have islands of efficiencies, which is in part correct. Because if a warehouse is empty, you can have the best replenishment calculation, but the downstream chain will still not get resupplied. Hopefully, it is not the majority of stock-keeping units (SKUs) that are out of stock, and therefore you will be able to benefit from all the rest of the products, and then as the project is expanded the islands of efficiency are eliminated, creating even more value for the rest of the chain each time an echelon is added. And like walking up stairs—if everything is easy, you can take two steps at a time. Do not look at the limitations for a small group of SKUs, but look at the value added for the majority of SKUs.

How to Create Trust When Installing Inventory Optimization

It is easier to be successful when the implementation team is involved at an early stage in the decision process. The reason for this is that the implementation team often has a deeper knowledge of the product than the account managers/sales representative, without meaning any disrespect. That way, you can avoid having huge expectation gaps between the company and implementation team, which is a bad way to start an implementation.

Furthermore, it is very important to have a holistic focus on project management. The reason for this is that the projects have a tendency to develop along with the implementation. By this I mean that there are many possible ways to improve the system by using more advanced options and/or new, improved information, so people have a tendency to continuously increase the scope as the project moves with the plan. I consider this a good thing. However, without a lot of focus on aligning expectations and keeping track of what is in scope and what is out of scope, there is a risk that deadlines will not be kept and the project will be delayed. Another thing about project management is that implementation will benefit if the project manager has some knowledge about inventory optimization. For instance, while I have not been involved in such a project, there have been instances where a project manager lacking in domain expertise can be swayed by the customer to accept more and more requirements as the project runs its course. Since the project manager does not have the expertise, the added requirements come across as reasonable and acceptable, but they are getting in the way of a mutually acceptable and successful engagement project.

Besides the focus on project management, there is also a great need to focus on change management. As stated before, don't estimate that the conceptual change of going from days of supply to a service level target is usually a big thing. The task with change management, in regard to an implementation, is naturally placed with the company. However, the company could benefit from sharing the experience of the implementation team, since they have done this type of implementation before. The project team members need to understand their role in providing guidance in change management. Most technical solution projects don't have a consultant focused on change management, but the discussion of past learnings can help the client move in a direction where the change is pushed at their end, but instigated from the project team—as our experience with a particular problem.

Documentation sometimes has a tendency to be lowered as a priority if there is a lot of pressure on the implementation to reach the deadlines, which is okay as long as it is not forgotten in the quest for completion of the implementation. It is critical to have a well-documented system, because if some persons are changed later on, others will be able to take over where they left off. This creates a much faster ramp-up cycle so they don't feel like they have to rediscover everything themselves.

In connection with the documentation, another lesson from my implementations is that businesspeople and implementation people often talk two different languages, so even if people are using the same words, they can mean very different things. It is, therefore, important to be aware of this and create a common understanding of important terms in implementation.

A good way of doing this is to open the black box of these implementations. This can be done relatively simply by making a report that shows what kind of information has been used as input in the different stages of calculation. This can help businesspeople get a better understanding of what is going on in the black box and, therefore, enable them to be more constructive in the testing phase. Another benefit of this kind of information is that businesspeople will be able to create the first level of support without involving the implementation team and therefore reduce company dependency on and cost of the implementations team/consultants.

As I have dealt with various business/technical people on the client side, this input/output discussion can really help the technical people in the client's organization see how the solution integrates with and improves the overall performance. Oftentimes, the technical team will look at the solution as a review of bad information coming out of the technical team from the business users. That could not be further from the truth. Sitting down with all parties and discussing the data flow, interactions with data, and the ultimate improvements gives everyone a much clearer picture of the end game and lets everyone know they are all on the same page.

What Kinds of Information Are Required from the Customer to Ensure a Good Installation of Inventory Optimization?

In order to look at the required data, you need to have a little understanding of what the target of inventory optimization is. What does it optimize? Inventory optimization is about minimizing the cost associated with inventory under certain constraints like a desired service level.

There are three basic kinds of information you need in order to start with inventory optimization. The first kind of information is the expected demand at the different locations in your supply chains, also called *nodes*. The second kind of information is data about how the different locations in your supply chain are linked together. And, finally, you need data about your SKUs (which can be different from location to location).

If we start by looking at the SKU data and the minimum information that you can start with, this is:

- The cost associated with your SKUs—what does it cost to hold the inventory?
- Information about how you want to measure your service (fill rate, ready rate, backorder ratio) and what your target should be.
- Information about the normal lead time for each SKU at each location.
- The kind of calculation method that should be used: (B, S) base-stock policy or (s, S) policy (min-max policy).

The minimum information that is required about the demand data is:

- Average demand per time period (day, week, month) for each location in your supply chain
- The variance of average demand

The minimum information required regarding the network, which location is linked to which location, will align the node costs with the arc costs to create the links.

This information will provide a reorder level and an order-up level. If inventory information is added, it will therefore also be possible to create order proposals that can be loaded into an ERP system instead of just the inventory policy information.

Of course, the minimum requirements are just that, and a lot of extra information can be added, if available. This could be adding ordering costs, variable lead time, or minimum order quantities and so forth. All this extra information will make the model more and more complex but also closer and closer to the real world, which is pretty complex.

What Happens If the Customer Lacks Certain Data Requirements?

Oftentimes, you don't have all the required data when you start off on a project. For instance, the client might not have a policy calculation method to use for each SKU, what the holding cost should be, or even the variance of demand information. The implementation team should be able to help you in order to find the optimal setting for the company. If the implementation team is involved at an early stage, the team will be able to identify where there might be shortcomings in data. This is why you need to have the implementation team involved at the very beginning. Some information can also be generated by making assumptions.

For instance, it is sometimes hard to calculate the exact cost of making an order or splitting the costs between various SKUs. These assumptions can have a huge effect on the output and performance of the system. I would like to make a point here: It is very important to be aware of what is modeled and what is not, indeed, even to the point of understanding what assumptions have been made and how they interact with the calculations. This way it will be possible to make adjustments if things are not modeled correctly. It is times like this when the implementation team has the knowledge and understanding of what the model is producing, so that it can communicate why the outputs are not reacting as expected. The key point I am trying to make is that assumptions must be understood by everyone on the team—both client and consulting—so that the adjustments are correctly mimicked for best results. The last thing anyone needs is changing inputs to satisfy an initial POV, but completely missing the mark when it comes time to roll out the model to the entire enterprise.

What Creates Complexity in Doing an Installation?

The task of keeping track of assumptions and different parameter settings is one thing that can increase the complexity in an implementation, especially if these are not documented. There-fore, it is important to keep the documentation updated, which should be no big surprise. What can be a little surprising is to be aligned on what the documentation should contain.

There can be a technical documentation and a business documen-tation. The technical documentation is often made by the implementa-tion team and contains technical information regarding placement of data, programs, description of program flow, and so forth, but some-times the business documentation is forgotten because the company and the implementation team expect the other part to keep track of business-specific modifications, but no one keeps track of them. There-fore, be sure to align who is updating the business documentation. This is normally not an issue as long as it is the same person who is involved; however, when new people are introduced or taking over, this infor-mation has to be learned again, and it is faster if it can be read/looked up instead of having to be discovered as one is working with the sys-tem. Imagine, if you will, once the project is completed. If the technical and business documentation are not coordinated, the business user group will be left in the dark regarding key outputs and/or results. This kind of situation can, literally, grind an install to a halt as information is questioned.

The number of SKUs is normally considered an indication of how complex a supply chain is. From my point of view, there is some truth to that, not because of the number of SKUs itself, but because of the number of groups of different SKUs that need special modifications. And the more SKUs, the higher is the probability of having more groups that need special attention. An example of this would be inexpensive, slow-moving SKUs where from a cost perspective it can be more optimal to order large quantities (compared to the demand) but where you don't want to fill up the store or warehouse space. In this case, instead of jamming up the optimization process, you can use a business rule. For instance, the client uses a funny rule like "one to go and one to show." Looking closely, you realize that it means your goal is to always have two on hand, but the first one is for a purchase and the second is to hold the space as a buffer to be sold if needed, but the real need is to get the second one back on the shelf. In the nomenclature of inventory optimization, that business rule would be: "Inventory should be two. Use a base-stock policy replenishment process regardless of demand." On the flipside, there might be a problem with erratic demand patterns in a product group. Here you need to smooth the demand before being able to generate a good forecast; however, this is only treating the symptoms, not the actual cause. Indeed, here is a classic example of when technical and business documentation need to be coordinated. Oftentimes, the technical documentation will provide a rule-based response to this activity, but the business documentation will be looking into the business activity in place causing the technical problem, such as the bullwhip effect being driven by price fluctuations, shortage gaming, and so on.

The complexity of the supply chain that is modeled is also something that adds to the complexity of implementation because there are more things that have to be accounted for. My point of view is that the more levels/echelons there are in the supply chain, the more complex it becomes, not as much from a data point of view, but more from an explaining point of view. This means that the different levels in a supply chain require the same kind of information, but to explain on a detailed level why different factors at other locations in the supply chain affect the present order proposal can be rather complex. This complexity problem is found all the time when dealing with multiechelon inventory optimization replenishment. The people tasked with doing this have always worked in an environment where inventory and orders are generated using island-of-efficiency viewpoints; they have to get out of their comfort zone. This means they have always seen the inventory and orders from a single-node position. Trying to explain and document this kind of technically advanced process to business users sitting in one location in a network can be daunting. However, it is the central theme of inventory optimization, and once explained, the concept of a coordinated (albeit complex) network is understood.

So there are lots of theoretical things that, seen alone, are not that complex, but when added together create great complexity. This is also why it is difficult to get the complete holistic overview and understanding of the supply chain. The sheer complexity of the models make evaluation extremely difficult without inventory optimization methodologies. A study by Croston (2005)[1] supports this statement. By using the MIT-developed BeerGame, it was shown that people had a tendency to underestimate the inbound SKUs even though the demand was known and constant. The problem is that the buyer will almost always underestimate, trying to "optimize" her own environment. The reason for this, according to Croston, is the human limitation on seeing outside of one's own sphere of influence. This limitation can be overcome with an objective system using analytics and optimization.

There are other factors that can cause complexity with an implementation besides just theory.

Let's take a look at two particularly humorous examples of how conceptual differences can gum up the engagement:

1. There could be cultural/conceptual differences between the company and the implementation team. This means that there might be a natural gap in knowledge about the solution, which can lead to misunderstandings. Here is an example of a misunderstanding we found in discussing something about forecasting. When the implementation team talks about forecasting, it will normally be about various forecasting models like Arima or exponential smoothing model. It must have taken three days to finally understand the client was saying their order proposals were their "forecasts." As you can imagine, this led to some pretty funny conversations and weird facial expressions until it was discovered that two very different things were being discussed.

2. A particular grocery client was adamant about making sure that *inventory turns* would be a key performance indicator. The client wanted to make sure this important inventory measurement would be included in all buyer performance windows. The implementation team was deep into developing the hooks to go grab inventory quantities and the expected demand to be able to create the inventory turn numbers for each and every product. However, the client kept talking about *turn orders*. Due to the conceptual differences, it took several days to finally understand that the client was talking about "everyday orders" the system would generate. Since the implementation team was so immersed in turn calculations, there was a belief the client wanted to create some kind of ad-hoc draw of the

inventory turn numbers so they could figure out what the key performance indicator (KPI) was at any moment. The conversation between the two groups, literally, got to the point of saying things louder and slower just to get their points across. When the poor implementation team finally figured out what turn orders were, it was a definite head-slapping moment.

Typical Problems and Hurdles to Overcome When You Are Dealing with Forecasting

Besides the fact that *forecasting* can have different meanings depending on the person who is talking, here are some classic issues regarding forecasts:

- Focus on the bad forecast
- Lack of trust in forecasting
- New/replacement product/short time series
- Sparse data
- Volatile data
- Lacking information/knowledge of sales drivers
- Master data

Focus on the Bad Forecast

One of the hurdles that are typical in inventory optimization implementations is where one bad forecast makes everyone think all of the forecasts are bad. Of course, you should focus on the forecasts that are considered out of tolerance. You should investigate why it is wrong and, if possible, add information that will correct the issue. This will certainly improve the system. However, it is also worth keeping in mind, if you are making 1 million forecasts in an automated way, there will always be some forecast that is not acting as expected. This is normally around 5 percent. The problem is that not trusting all forecasts because a few are off will keep you from generating value for 95 percent of the SKUs. Therefore, there will be a need to monitor the forecast, but the point here is that the forecast should be managed by exception, so you only need to spend time on those SKUs that have strange forecasts.

Lack of Trust in Forecasting

Another nontheoretical issue is that often, a part of this kind of implementation is that there has been a lack of trust from business users. They don't believe a computer can predict the demand better than they can, based on all the experience they have. They think they are being accused of being wrong. They may in fact have knowledge or information that is not modeled in the forecast, so there can be some value in allowing business users to adjust the forecast. However, this should be monitored very closely by calculating the forecast added value in order to follow up on whether the business users are adding value to the forecast. It is a known fact that the more a forecast is touched, the more inaccurate it becomes. Measuring added value to forecasting activities allows everyone to better understand that (1) the actual forecasting should be trusted in the majority of cases, and (2) tribal knowledge can only take a buyer so far. In the majority of cases, the tribal knowledge employed by the buyers just created more or less inventory than what was really needed. It was found that when a forecast was simply "touched" to increase so-called value, all that was done was to make it less accurate. Measuring the forecast added value is also a good way of showing the business users that the system works, thereby gaining trust in the system. However, if the lack of trust is originating in the business users being afraid they are expendable, it is more a change management issue.

New/Replacement Product/Short Time Series

New products are often hard to forecast. This is especially true if you only have the actual sales and have a short time series where each sales observation can have a large impact on the forecast. This leads to very volatile forecasts that can have large changes from period to period. When there are large shifts in the forecasts, there will also be large shifts in the output of the inventory optimization calculation.

In order to avoid these wild fluctuations, use other ways or information to make the forecast for these kinds of products. This could be by actually working with a new product forecasting process or by simply using a reference product. Using a reference product is an easy shortcut to make a new product forecasting judgment. The key, though, is to take the time to pick proper reference products.

Sparse Data

Time series with sparse data due to limited sales observations are another classic example of a forecast issue related to inventory optimization. In many cases, there will be long periods of "0" demand and either a "1" or "2" ordered, then back to "0." These time series are often classified as slow movers or items that have long periods with no demand at all, otherwise known as *intermittent-demand products.* You can use intermittent demand models like Croston's to generate a forecast. However, demand is often so low that it can cause issues with the inventory optimization calculations. If this is the case, then it is up to the consultant to create some kind of agreed-on business rule for these SKUs.

Volatile Data

Volatility is often like poison to inventory models because of the service level constraint. If there are highly volatile products (which there almost always are), you can do the following:

- Set a limitation to the variance coefficient so that the variance is limited.
- Lower the desired service level of these volatile SKUs in the realization that it is too expensive to carry the inventory needed to meet the demand in the spikes.

Investigate if the origin of the volatility can be located; perhaps it is simply because there is a large bullwhip effect hidden in the demand data.

Lacking Information/Knowledge of Sales Drivers

Another issue that can cause the forecast to have bad quality is that the actual sales drivers are missing or unable to be identified. Examples of this might be commercial campaign information, either because it is not available in a structured way or because the information is invisible to you. In most cases, that kind of information might be further down the supply chain and needs to be applied, but at first it simply is not available. Often, though, the campaign information is registered in the wrong way, and it will reduce the quality of the forecast instead of enhancing it.

Master Data

In general, keeping the master data related to the product characteristics found in the ERP system as correct as possible is always important. This is both in regard to forecast calculations and also in regard to the inventory optimization calculation. It is my experience that 70 to 80 percent of the support-related issues could have been avoided if master data had been corrected. An excellent way of countering the master data error problem is to create an error report for specific products. Then take the products through the steps of calculation from initial data entry to final results. The implementation teams can examine the data and uncover the problem area—most often, it is in the initial master data. This will reduce this kind of question to the implementation team and thereby reduce the time/cost spent on support, which can be saved or used to improve the system.

How Do These Problems Translate into Inventory Optimization?

The expected demand, with its corresponding uncertainty, is a very important input to inventory optimizations, and any error or large fluctuation in this will have great impact on the quality of the output from inventory optimization calculations. So, if the above hurdles are not handled, it will naturally affect the output of the inventory optimization step in the process, and it is no surprise that if you use input data of bad quality, your output will also have poor quality.

Therefore, it is also a good idea to keep your common sense, on both the business side and the implementation team side, and if the output of inventory optimization (IO) does not correspond to what can be expected and cannot be explained, it might be a good idea to involve the product's software engineers. Indeed, over the years we have provided SAS with many requirements focused in intermittent demand models. While Croston's method is used in the majority of intermittent demand situations, it is still, at best, an estimate. With the addition of lumpy or sporadic demand, Croston's model can be compromised. With our ability to interact with the SAS inventory optimization product management and engineering staff, we were able to upgrade the way the multiechelon optimization process handled the intermittent demand problem and greatly upgrade the way the optimization handled the intermittent forecasts. This was a win-win for everyone involved.

What Happens When the IO Output Has Problems at the Start of the Project? What Needs to Be Done?

An obvious reason for this can be that there is an error in the IO calculation. Any time we are on an install, we have direct input to research and development (R&D) through proper channels. When this happens, we can have an immediate fix. This kind of communication benefits everyone and gets the customer the best possible product as quickly as possible. We don't run into miscalculations very often, given the number of installs out there. However, when we do, the response is fast. Another reason a problem might crop up can be traced to the fact that an IO calculation has some limitations. An example of this could be when you try to make IO calculations where the input is extreme. For instance, this could be regarding extreme slow movers, where an approach could be to make a workaround and business rules. The implementation team/company also has to communicate these issues back to R&D in order to continue to improve the IO calculation. Another example of this was that one time the output of the IO calculation was very volatile, even though there were only small changes to the input data; this problem was quickly solved in cooperation between R&D and the implementation team.

Close cooperation between R&D and implementation teams has other advantages, because it often links the scientist's world and real-life challenges of the actual implementation, and through a close cooperation there will automatically be a knowledge transfer from R&D to the implementation team and the reverse.

A learning point here is to make close cooperation between R&D and the implementation team a parameter when selecting the vendor to implement an inventory optimization system.

How Much Time Is Spent Onsite versus Offsite When Developing a Project?

The more time you can have onsite the better, because the two parts of the team will get to know each other, and increased interaction leads to an increased knowledge transfer. The business will get a deeper insight into the black box of inventory optimization, and the implementation team will get a deeper knowledge/understanding of the company, especially of the conditions of the market in which the company operates. This is accomplished by more open communication where there is not a long gap from thought to action. When you are onsite it is easier to show things and how these affect the output at different steps in the installation process. All in all, it is my opinion that the implementation will be faster and better if the whole implementation is done onsite. However, keep in mind that these benefits are only achieved if the company has also allocated the necessary resources to implementation.

Often, it is not possible to make the full implementations onsite. This could be because the implementation team is not physically placed near the company, so the team would have to travel a lot, which would increase the cost of the implementation. In order to reduce the cost of the implementation, travel may be kept to a minimum in this situation. Indeed, the company personnel also have other tasks, like continuing the current inventory processes, and therefore don't have the time to be fully allocated to the implementation project. Another reason can be that the company does not have the space to house the implementation team.

When It Is Not Possible to Be Onsite the Whole Time, Where Should You Focus Your Onsite Time?

It is very important to be onsite a lot in the scoping and design phase of the implementation, as well as in the test phase. The reason is to minimize the risk of misunderstandings at critical points in the project. In order to minimize the risk of misunderstandings during the project, status meetings should be held with persons physically present—perhaps not every time, but when there are important issues to be discussed.

What about Project Management in IO Implementations?

Project management has been mentioned several times during this chapter. It is very important and should not be underestimated in any project. Project management is so important in IO implementations because:

- IO implementations often have a high degree of complexity, due to:
  - Cultural differences
  - Knowledge gaps
  - Black-box approaches instead of a fully functional user interface
- The scope of the implementation has a tendency to increase as the project progresses.
- The IO implementation often has a large impact on the whole company, and therefore there is a need for change management as well.

IN CLOSING

Inventory optimization is a strange animal when installing it at a customer site. The output is going to impact both company goals and individuals throughout the supply chain. In the majority of cases, the company and the individuals have been doing things their way for years and years. Suddenly, a bunch of so-called experts show up onsite and are going to teach them a thing or two about inventory control. It is only natural to push back, especially if there is no prior education of the people involved in the project.

Successful implementations are all about collaboration between the client and the consulting/installation team. The knowledge gap must be addressed and kept at the forefront throughout the project. Moreover, as the inputs and outputs are being worked on, the people dealing with the results need to be kept informed. Their understanding of the results is of the utmost importance. In the vast number of cases, these people are either forecasters or inventory buyers/planners. In my experience, when they see how the problem of human nature gets in the way of optimized results, they have a better appreciation of how inventory optimization helps them do their jobs.

Above all, the team effort where the onsite personnel are in tight coordination with product management and engineering enables constant communications and resolution of most problems. The more the install people are onsite and in front of the customer, the more the relationships blossom and the overall project is kept on track to a successful conclusion.

NOTE

1. R. Croson and K. Donohue, "Behavioral Causes of the Bullwhip Effect and the Observed Value of Inventory Information," *Management Science* 52, no. 3 (2005): 1–14.

CHAPTER 12

Inventory Optimization in Supply Chain Verticals

Out-of-stocks in the distribution chain are usually thought of in three ways.[1] The first is *shelf*—"last 100-foot problem." The stock is in the store, but due to the lack of foresight, the product has not been restocked and an empty shelf is in play. The second is *store*. The store has mis-ordered and stock is not in the store. The third is *distribution*. There is a lack of stock in the distribution system. The first is a distinct problem of retail execution. The latter two are attributable to a combination of oversight and a lack of acceptance of demand and supply variance. The latter two are completely solvable.

Several years ago, I was at a supply chain conference, listening to various industry experts talk about the problems they were having with regard to inefficiencies. It made me kind of smile because you could have taken each of the expert's points and just changed the date of a supply chain conference to 5 years, 10 years, or even 20 years prior! Each of them were talking about the grave situation with out-of-stocks, fill rates, inefficient forecasts, lack of collaboration, and on and on. All you had to do was update the buzzwords to make sure you were in 2014 instead of 1994. Supply chains are so much like forecasts. You know they're going to be wrong! You just had to make sure they are less wrong and plan for the inefficiencies in such a way that you reap the advantage you have over your competition in the space.

What I found odd at this conference was the shifting of the narrative. In the vast majority of supply chain discussions prior to this one, it was the manufacturers voicing the need to work closely with their retail partners for best results. Now it was the retailers discussing the problems they were having in getting product to the final customer. This was something new I had not heard before in a public forum. I was hearing this out in the field often as a lament to everyone in the supply chain: Retailers had driven their inventory risk back onto the vendor. The problem was that the vendor having accepted the supply chain risk simply had no visibility to the customer demand until it's too late. This left the retailer on an island to fend for themselves.

What created this mess in the supply chain?

As we had discussed earlier in this book, the just-in-time (JIT) inventory processes swung through the distribution supply chains in the early 1990s. At that time, retailer and vendor inventories were similar in the number of days of supply and in the 30- to 45-day range.

In Table 12.1, you can see the result of 15 to 20 years of JIT activities in various industries. This study of average days of supply by industry, done by *Gartner and Supply Chain Digest,* shows the 5-year period running from 2005 to 2010. Look closely at Retailing and Vendor Segments compared to the various industries supplying that retail sector.

Industry Segment	Change since 2005	Average
Various Retailing Segments	−0.8 to −5.2%	−4.5%
Various Vendor Segments	−7.2 to +20.5%	+15.7%

In virtually every segment that has a retailing customer-facing environment, the supply chain shifts risk back onto the vendor. Is that all bad? No! It's only bad when the inventory positioning and mix are incorrect. This is especially true when it occurs in the retailer's warehouse. In a groundbreaking study done by the Grocery Manufacturer's Association (GMA) and the Food Marketing Institute (FMI) in 2002, it was discovered that worldwide out-of-stocks run at 8 percent and promotional products run out of stock at a rate of 17 percent due to the fundamental replenishment practices of the retailer—not the upstream vendors. This resulted in a total reduction of revenue of 4 percent for everyone involved: retailers and vendors![2]

Suddenly, everyone was off to the races trying to get a handle on the out-of-stock rates and how to solve the problem. The same study was redone two more times at four-year intervals in 2006 and 2010. Guess what? The out-of-stock rates of 8 percent and 17 percent remained the same in each study. All of the inventory management techniques and smartest minds came up with the same out-of-stock rates over an 8-year period of *improvement.* Here is the kicker: Remember the illustration of the MIT Beer Game? Over the thousands and thousands of times that game has been played online and in classrooms, a little-known fact comes out: The retailer in the MIT Beer Game suffers from 8 to 10 percent out-of-stock rate and a 15 to 20 percent promotional out-of-stock rate (as shown by the initial reaction to large orders).[3]

What is going on in today's supply chain where extremely smart people with decades of experience are performing at the same level as

Table 12.1 Supply Chain News: Inventory Performance by Industry 2005 to 2010 / July 27, 2011

Days Inventory Outstanding (DIO) 2005–2010 Various Industry Groups

Industry	No. of Companies	Example Companies	Lowest 2010 DIO in Group	Highest 2010 DIO in Group	DIO [FY 2010]	DIO [FY 2009]	DIO [FY 2008]	DIO [FY 2007]	DIO [FY 2006]	DIO [FY 2005]	Change 2005 to 2010
Aerospace and Defense	21	Honeywell, Raytheon, Goodrich	5.3 Raytheon	252.24 BE Aerospace	67.9	64.6	60.3	52.8	49.9	42.4	60.1%
Auto Components	13	Johnson Controls, TRW, BorgWarner	13.4 Tower Int'l	62.8 Cooper Tire	33.1	33.1	35.7	31.9	32.5	33.2	−0.5%
Automobiles	3	Ford, GM, Harley–Davidson	19.2 Ford Motor Co.	32.6 General Motors Co.	26.3	27.0	27.0	15.6	14.6	13.0	102.2%
Beverages	7	PepsiCo, Molson Coors, Hansen Natural	15.6 Coca-Cola Bottling Co.	42.9 Hansen Natural	24.3	22.8	21.9	22.1	22.6	19.6	23.7%
Biotechnology	7	Amgen, Cephalon	22.4 Biogen Idec Inc.	159.3 Talecris Biotherapeutics	57.6	56.9	53.0	50.2	53.7	56.5	1.9%
Building Products	8	Masco, USG, AO Smith	35.2 Masco Corp.	75.8 Griffon Corp.	46.0	40.9	50.5	43.9	43.3	33.6	36.7%
Chemicals	46	Celanese, Dow Chemical, Olin	14.8 Praxair Inc.	107.8 Sensient Technologies	53.4	56.8	56.5	57.2	57.7	60.6	−11.9%
Communications Equipment	12	Juniper, Tellabs Ciena	4.7 EchoStar	77.2 CIENA Corp.	30.8	27.5	31.8	27.1	26.8	24.8	24.1%
Computers and Peripherals	9	HP, Apple, Dell, Lexmark	5.9 Apple Inc.	57.5 Diebold, Inc.	31.7	35.0	37.1	37.9	36.8	32.1	−1.1%
Containers and Packaging	16	Crown, Ball, Smurfit-Stone	29.3 Smurfit-Stone Container	60.3 Silgan Holdings Inc.	44.7	42.2	43.1	41.6	39.5	38.9	14.9%
Electrical Equipment	14	Emerson Electric, Acuity Brands	27.3 Roper Industries Inc.	123.4 GrafTech Int'l	55.5	55.9	46.3	50.9	51.8	53.9	3.4%
Electronic Equipment, Instruments and Components	22	Corning, Tech Data	11.2 Dolby Laboratories Inc.	109.6 AVX Corp.	46.5	44.0	42.2	44.3	47.5	42.9	8.5%
Food and Staples Retailing	19	Walgreens, Supervalue	7.8 Susser Holdings	69.6 The Andersons, Inc.	31.1	29.8	29.6	32.2	32.7	32.8	−5.2%

Food Products	21	Kraft, Hershey, Chiquita	12.8 Dean Foods Co.	70.6 Green Mountain Coffee	40.3	37.0	38.9	39.6	39.9	33.5	20.5%
Healthcare Equipments and Supplies	21	Baxter, CR Bard, Hologic	22.4 Intuitive Surgical, Inc.	71.8 The Cooper Companies	49.8	50.0	49.6	52.7	52.3	48.6	2.4%
Household Durables	14	Mohawk Industries, Whirlpool, Newell Rubbermaid	17.1 Sealy Corporation	116.0 Fortune Brands Inc.	56.7	53.9	54.7	55.4	54.2	58.4	−3.0%
Household Products	6	Kimberly-Clark, Colgate-Palmolive, Energizer	28.2 Church & Dwight Co. Inc.	75.4 Spectrum Brands	51.3	47.7	50.4	54.9	54.2	55.2	−7.2%
Industrial Conglomerates	4	3M, GE, Seabord, Carlisle	28.8 General Electric Co.	62.2 Carlisle Companies Inc.	45.2	44.6	44.7	43.3	45.7	42.1	7.1%
Internet and Catalog Retail	4	Amazon, HSN, Overstock, Netflix	10.4 Overstock.com	36.1 HSN, Inc.	29.7	24.2	25.9	28.0	28.8	25.3	17.3%
Leisure Equipments and Products	6	Mattel, Brunswick, Eastman Kodak	28.9 Mattel Inc.	101.3 Callaway Golf Co.	51.8	46.7	48.6	46.0	48.3	48.6	6.6%
Life Sciences Tools and Services	11	Thermo Fisher, Bio-Rad, Illumina	0.7 Pharmaceutical Product Dev	142.9 Bruker Corporation	48.6	47.3	51.5	50.1	46.0	44.9	6.6%
Machinery	43	Caterpillar, Deere, Danaher, Timken	24.5 PACCAR Inc.	119.7 Tenex Corp.	59.1	59.5	56.6	58.0	59.6	56.0	5.5%
Metals	15	US Steel, Alcoa, AM Castle	42.5 Schnitzer Steel Industries	107.1 Allegheny Technologies	64.9	74.6	57.3	60.3	64.8	54.0	20.2%
Multiline Retail	15	Sears, Target, Big Lots	36.8 Nordstorm Inc.	88.0 Saks Inc.	62.0	61.3	61.2	65.1	66.9	72.9	−14.9%
Office Electronics	2	Xerox and Zebra Tech	16.7 Xerox Corp.	43.4 Zebra Technologies	30.1	29.0	31.5	31.7	32.9	30.5	−1.5%
Paper and Forest Products	7	Wausau, MeadWestvaco	32.4 Verso Paper Corp.	65.7 Wausau Paper Corp.	49.7	49.4	51.3	46.8	48.1	36.5	36.1%

(continued)

257

Table 12.1 (Continued)

Industry	No. of Companies	Example Companies	Lowest 2010 DIO in Group	Highest 2010 DIO in Group	DIO (FY 2010)	DIO (FY 2009)	DIO (FY 2008)	DIO (FY 2007)	DIO (FY 2006)	DIO (FY 2005)	Change 2005 to 2010
Personal Products	4	Avon, Alberto-Culver, Nu-Skin, Revlon	27.2 Nu Skin Enterprises Inc.	39.1 Alberto-Culver Company	34.2	33.1	37.0	39.3	44.3	81.1	-57.8%
Pharmaceuticals	13	Pfizer, J&J, Hospira	17.0 Allergan Inc.	89.0 Hospira Inc.	44.7	53.3	42.8	40.2	51.0	49.4	-9.6%
Restaurants	13	McDonald's, Panera Bread, Texas Roadhouse	1.4 Chipotle Mexican Grill, Inc.	18.5 Starbucks	4.9	5.2	5.5	6.3	5.9	6.4	-22.4%
Restaurants w/o Starbucks	12	McDonald's, Panera Bread, Texas Roadhouse	1.4 Chipotle Mexican Grill, Inc.	6.3 Domino's Pizza, Inc.	3.6	3.9	4.6	4.0	4.3	6.4	-43.5%
Semiconductors	22	Intel, TI, RF Micro	26.5 ISI Corporation	76.2 Micron Technology	45.0	45.0	47.9	46.6	42.4	45.9	-1.8%
Specialty Retail All	55	Broad Mix	23.8 Aeropostale, Inc.	192.3 Tiffany & Co.	60.6	59.7	61.2	63.0	62.1	60.5	0.1%
Specialty Retail - Apparel	30	The Gap, Chico's, Buckle	23.8 Aeropostale, Inc.	84.5 The Men's Wearhouse	49.9	48.3	48.9	52.2	51.7	49.2	1.5%
Specialty Retail - Auto Parts	4	AutoZone, Pep Boys, O'Reilly's Advanced Auto	118.0 Pep Boys	138.4 O'Reilly Automotive	126.4	128.2	131.8	120.0	120.2	115.8	9.1%
Specialty Retail - Electronics and Household	11	Best Buy, Lowes, Pier 1	37.7 Systemax Inc.	82.1 Bed Bath & Beyond	58.0	58.1	58.8	61.7	59.2	60.5	-4.2%
Specialty Retail - Office Products	3	Office Max, Staples, Office Depot	35.1 Staples, Inc.	43.2 Officemax Incorporated	39.0	37.5	37.8	40.9	39.9	39.3	-0.8%
Specialty Retail - Other	6	PetSmart, Dick's Sporting Goods, Tractor Supply	39.5 PetSmart, Inc.	192.3 Tiffany & Co.	86.5	86.6	93.5	94.8	94.3	92.8	-6.7%
Textiles, Apparel and Luxury Goods	16	VF Group, Jones, Sketchers	42.3 Liz Claiborne Inc.	111.6 Hanesbrands Inc.	61.7	53.1	61.0	59.2	54.0	60.9	1.3%
Tobacco	4	Phillip More Int'ls, Lorillard, Altria, Reynolds	43.5 Lorillard, Inc.	111.6 Phillip Morris Int'l	65.6	74.6	68.4	72.2	110.7	77.3	-15.1%
Trading Companies and Distributors	11	Grainger, Interline Brands, Kaman	42.4 WESCO International	143.3 Tital Machinery	69.4	72.8	66.6	65.2	69.2	68.5	1.3%

Source: Hackett Group/ REL and SCDigest Analysis

first-year college students playing a supply chain simulation game for the first time?

Retailers tend to use a supply chain formulation called *aggregate and buy*. The turn and promotional ordering is done using an aggregation of the demand and the addition of a number to create a *days of coverage* or *days of supply*. There is very little stock positioned for the variance of demand and supply. Finally, the upstream trading partners are seeing an "interpretation" of the customer demand via an order. In Figure 12.1, we begin to see the problem. The store is seeing an instantaneous view of customer demand. However, each level upstream is delayed. The retail DC is 3 to 10 days (7 to 20 if you add a distributor). The vendor/manufacturer is 10 to 20 days (20 to 45 days, if you add a distributor). The raw material suppliers are 20 to 60 days (45 to 80 days, if you add a distributor).

As you can see, the demand signal delay, coupled with interpretive demand, creates massive opportunities for inventory mismatches. Let's look at *how* inventory optimization can help in each of these situations in the chain. Then we are going to take a look at *the projected results* each segment could attain with inventory optimization.

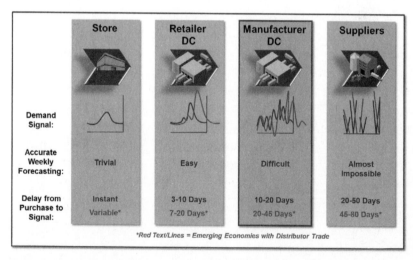

Figure 12.1 Inventory Optimization Study / Supply Chain Insights / Lora Cecere / May 2015

RETAIL: LIFE AT THE END OF THE CHAIN

Retail offers a special problem for inventory optimization. In almost all engagements, the focal point of inventory optimization is on inventory reduction and the corresponding improvements in having a nimble and effective inventory. However, as indicated over the past 30 years, retailers have effectively shifted a lot of the inventory burden onto upstream vendors and reduced their days of supply to some of the lowest of any industry! This shifting of inventory risk and the positioning of retail at last step of the supply chain creates a unique problem. With extremely tight inventories and vendors with no visibility into customer demand, the retailer has trouble reacting to unforeseen demand.

When it comes to retail, the focus is on out-of-stocks, customer satisfaction, cash-to-cash cycle time, and lost revenue!

Right product, right place, at the right time is the mantra of the industry, but OOS and lost sales at the shelf is a constant battle. The days-of-supply KPI leads to a mismatch of inventory at both the retailer and the vendor. Since the vendor has no visibility to the customer demand, it will overreact in a classic *bullwhip* fashion when the retailer unexpectedly expedites an order. However, the damage has already been done—at the very least, the lag time from vendor to retailer allows for an out-of-stock for 3 to 10 days. Worst yet is when the vendor has no way of anticipating the unforeseen demand and is also caught with an out-of-stock. Now the lag time to the shelf could reach 20 to 40 days. The former is most often seen in regular turn merchandise, but the latter happens often in promotional merchandise. The retailer has lost sales and the vendor will have increased inventory since it reacted too late for the demand increase. The out-of-stock and lost revenue problem was cited to be upward of 4 percent of revenues according to the GMA/FMI study.[4] This worldwide out-of-stock problem equates to billions of dollars!

The Long-Tail Problem

There is a deeper issue in play than just a lack of visibility. With the proliferation of products and the positioning of those products closer and closer to the final customer, the granular nature of the demand makes it

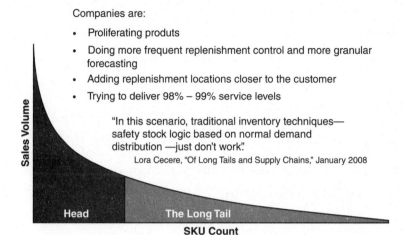

Companies are:

- Proliferating produts
- Doing more frequent replenishment control and more granular forecasting
- Adding replenishment locations closer to the customer
- Trying to deliver 98% – 99% service levels

"In this scenario, traditional inventory techniques— safety stock logic based on normal demand distribution —just don't work."

Lora Cecere, "Of Long Tails and Supply Chains," January 2008

Figure 12.2 Long-tail products are slower moving and more difficult to forecast, resulting in higher-than-normal safety stocks.

extremely hard to forecast (see Figure 12.2). The slower-moving products in the long tail tend to have extremely large safety stocks due to demand variances. Not only do they have large safety stocks, the actual forecast could be grossly incorrect so that no amount of safety stock can cover. If both the retailer and vendor are in low stock levels, there is an obvious problem, but we have found in the majority of cases that the retailer could have helped themselves with better analytics. Indeed, if the correct demand and supply variances had been understood by the retailer, the entire vendor/retailer interaction could be calmed. We are not talking about increasing your days of supply and accepting more of the inventory burden. We are talking about arranging the days of supply for better performance!

How does the retailer's activity amplify the problem?

Reaction Time

The retail reaction time to unforeseen demand is the shortest in the supply chain. The stores have an instantaneous view and the distribution center has a one- to three-day reaction. Since the vendor has little, if any, visibility into the short-term demand at the customer level, it would seem prudent that the retailer would have increased safety stocks to cover that problem at the DC level. The problem is that retailers don't do that. They tend to treat their warehouse as a waystation between the stores and the vendor. This is where the supply chain is out-driving the headlights. The reaction time has been artificially shortened due to extremely low safety stocks.

Safety Stock Buffer

Most retailers have extremely low safety stocks compared to vendors. Over the years, vendors have taken on more days of supply inventory, but the reaction time between retailer and vendor negates the extra inventory. Indeed, the bullwhip effect at the first-line inventory position on the vendor tends to be larger than any other supply chain due to the inability to see customer demand effectively. The vendor will overreact with extra inventory positioning *after* the retailer sends the expedited demand signal. The OOS is already occurring, and the vendor missed out with lost sales during the expedite period.

Retail tends to downplay demand variance in their planning process. A planning number is positioned and the retail order is placed against that number with the *aggregate-and-buy* mentality. There is no upper or lower confidence level. Unless there is an automatic overestimation, the number will come in less than the *required inventory* to hit 98 to 99 percent service level. In turn, little emphasis is placed on lead-time or fill-rate variance. Transaction replenishment systems do not compute this. This creates an assumption of 100 percent fill rate and 0 percent lead-time variance. These two factors literally negate adequate safety stocks at the retailer level.

The Result?

Retailers tend to be much more receptive to OOS than just about any other participant in the supply chain and the *inventory alert process* and expedited ordering has not worked in 30 years of trying.

How Do You Fix It?

Optimized inventories at DCs that reflect true confidence levels and an overall strategy of service level attainment will greatly reduce OOS and maintain inventory levels!

Focusing only on what and when to buy, then sending it up the supply chain, is a hallmark of the bullwhip effect. This *rapid replenishment* process assumes the vendor has a 100 percent SL and can expedite when required. While it creates excess inventories at the vendor level, it leads to extensive out-of-stocks at the retailer. Inventory optimization creates something called the *efficiency frontier*. In simple terms, let's say you have a 95 percent SL with a $2 million on-hand inventory and pipeline. The optimization will allow you to have the 95 percent SL at $1.4 million or a 99 percent SL at $2 million. This range is the front side of the efficiency frontier. All of the space between the old cost curve and the new cost curve allows you to fine-tune for best results. This is the *frontier!*

RETAIL BENEFITS OF INVENTORY OPTIMIZATION

According to a recent study done by Lora Cecere at Supply Chain Insights, 70 percent of the installations of inventory optimization have been done in the process and discrete manufacturing verticals. This was done to negate the bullwhip effect and reduce redundant safety stocks in upstream locations. In most cases, this was successful and continues to be a great opportunity to process manufacturers. It has been my experience to see a different view of inventory optimization over the past 15 years. I have been involved in inventory optimization installs from process manufacturing to distribution to retail. It has always amazed me at the benefits attained by retailers. Their success is not so much in curing the bullwhip effect, because there is very little at that end of the chain. For the retailer, it's in making the inventory work smarter! The retailer finally gets its warehouse to act as a buffer instead of a simple transfer point. It reduces the amount of out-of-stocks and increases revenues.

The retailer has a long history of reducing inventory at the end of quarters and end of the fiscal year to make its numbers look good on the balance sheet. This reduction would always lead to a rebound of inventory after the books are closed; otherwise, out-of-stocks will soar. With inventory optimization, the inventory safety stock is repositioned for better results. The 70/10/20 split would enable the reduction of inventory, but there were far more benefits.

Table 12.2 Time-Phasing Inventory Benefits for a Retailer

Benefit	Increase/Decrease	When?
Inventory Reduction	20% reduction	Bleed-out occurs over 3–9 months
Inventory Carrying Cost	2–4% of the reduction	Stays constant to the reduction
Increased Revenues	2% conservative estimate	Starts at month 2–3 and increases
Reduced Freight/Logistics	1% conservative estimate	Immediately
Increased Service Level	1–3% conservative estimate	Immediately
Margin Improvement	.5% to 1% increase	Immediately

Table 12.2 shows the types of benefits a retailer can expect when using inventory optimization.

Moreso than anywhere else in the chain, the retailer has the benefit of massive improvements in revenue and margin. Elsewhere, the upstream collaborators to the retailer are looking to streamline the supply chain and gather benefits from the internal performance. The retailer holds the key to the entire chain's revenue and margin improvements by selling product at the right place and right time. If the retailer drastically reduces the 8 percent/17 percent out-of-stock rates on turn and promotional product, the retailer, distributor, and manufacturer greatly enhance their bottom line. With a 4 percent revenue improvement opportunity, billions of dollars are at stake—everyone benefits!

DISTRIBUTION: BEING IN THE MIDDLE OF SIBLINGS WHO DON'T PLAY WELL WITH EACH OTHER

As indicated in Figure 12.3, the addition of the distributor or emerging economies can have an effect on the length and complexity of the distribution supply chain. The distributor's function is to hold inventory for specific customers/clients. Oftentimes, the distributor is working with unwieldy spreadsheet-based planning systems rooted in tribal knowledge, extended lead times, and gut feel. This type of planning might have worked 30 years ago, but in today's fast-paced supply chain, this type of process is going to overwork the best of plans. Furthering the problematic nature of the distributing business, the requirement to carry products for specific customers extends the

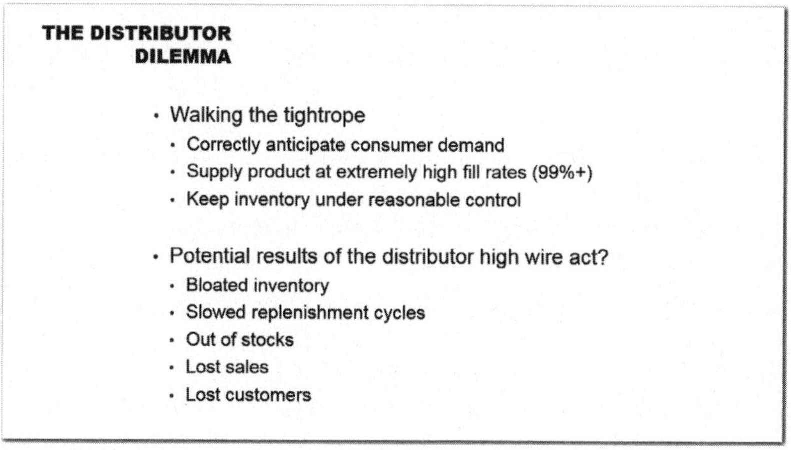

THE DISTRIBUTOR DILEMMA

- Walking the tightrope
  - Correctly anticipate consumer demand
  - Supply product at extremely high fill rates (99%+)
  - Keep inventory under reasonable control

- Potential results of the distributor high wire act?
  - Bloated inventory
  - Slowed replenishment cycles
  - Out of stocks
  - Lost sales
  - Lost customers

Figure 12.3 Retailers have effectively pushed inventory risk back onto the vendors.

long-tail phenomenon. Instead of all products going to all "stores," the distributor must divide the inventory into groupings of stores or banners.

Whereas most vendors and retailers can manipulate the product volume by way of demand shifting and shaping, the distributor must anticipate and react to short-term demand sensing as a way of coping with the variation of demand. New products, end-of-life products, and supersession play key roles with the distributor because they have little hands-on effect and have to deal with the obtuse behavior of downstream customers.

Key Distribution Problems

Anticipating Downstream Demand

A distributor is much like the vendor in reacting to the retail aggregate-and-buy process, but they have to deal with less inventory buffer and an added one to three weeks of lead time. Just like in the wholesale warehouse I was dealing with as a buyer back in the 1980s, we find distributors watching the downstream withdrawals of product at the one- to four-week demand window. The reaction to the demand shifts will, most likely, be based on a rule-of-thumb inventory requirement or a forecasted demand number with little demand variance. Since many of the products in the distributor portfolio are long tail in nature, the forecast will become more and more suspect. This leads to a large number of overstocks in the distributor system.

The Expectation of Extremely High Fill Rates

To amplify the distributor problem, the downstream customers are expecting at least 98 or 99 percent fill rates and, in many cases, their systems are expecting 100 percent due to single-stage calculation techniques of their replenishment models. They will also want 0 percent tolerance of lead-time variation. As indicated in Figure 12.2, they want the impossible! Imagine the long-suffering planner/buyer in a distributor trying to manage an inventory with little visibility to the actual demand, relying on the ability to anticipate the demand without having the ability to shape it and keep the inventory in line with target KPIs. That is a daunting challenge.

The Result?

Most distributor inventories are running 20 to 30 percent above needed levels to attain the 98 percent fill rate required of them. Given the tight profit margins on the industry vertical any improvement to providing a nimble and supportive supply chain should be the goal. Yet, we are seeing more and more pressure being exerted on the distributor for better and better customer service. Distributors are literally choking themselves on inventory in an effort to support fill-rate expectations. The noose around their necks is the cash-to-cash cycle. The cash-to-cash cycle is imperative to the survival of the distributor. Keeping cash tied up in inventory is the death rattle for a distributor working in a small margin industry vertical.

How Do You Fix It?

Just like in retail, the distributor needs to view its inventory as a buffer against unanticipated demand and supply problems instead of as a simple waystation for product flowing to the end customer. Days of cover or days of supply management techniques will not work, as indicated in Figure 12.2. The distributor needs to recognize the variation of supply and demand and build inventory based on flow of products and not just the snapshot of inventory gained by days of supply.

DISTRIBUTOR BENEFITS OF INVENTORY OPTIMIZATION

I have actually seen extensive improvements in inventory control by simply using point-of-sale information and an extrapolation of demand at a distributor. Indeed, using inventory optimization as an extension of the regular distributor forecast is going to dramatically improve the majority of long-tail products and produce results in normal volume items. The best of all worlds is the combination of accurate forecasting, coupled with inventory optimization.

It used to be that most demand planning and forecasting experts saw that the only way to improve inventory was to implement high confidence forecasting first. The idea was to improve your forecasting horizon with confidence levels. This would give you the majority of improvement; then you could come in behind with inventory optimization to fill in the gaps. We are beginning to find the opposite to be true. The inventory optimization can produce a much faster and deeper improvement to a company inventory than increasing the accuracy of the forecast. Indeed, a recent installation of forecasting and inventory optimization proved that every 1 percent improvement of mean actual percent error (MAPE) provided a 2 percent reduction in safety stock. However, at the same time, inventory optimization generated a savings of 30 percent of the total inventory and did it in 60 days for an ROI of less than 40 days![5]

The distributor offers a unique challenge. Given the need to improve the forward planning horizon and position the correct inventory, the forecasting option is a great fine-tuning opportunity when given the ROI from inventory optimization. This $1 + 1 = 3$ option is perfect for the distributor industry vertical.

Table 12.3 shows the types of benefits a distributor can expect when using inventory optimization.

The key deliverables to the distributor industry vertical are the reduction of inventory and the margin improvements. The reduction in the cash-to-cash cycle is a huge benefit. When a company is dealing with a 2 percent 10-day or 30-day discount period, being able to turn

Table 12.3 Time-Phasing Inventory Benefits at a Distributor

Benefit	Increase/Decrease	When?
Inventory Reduction	10–30% reduction	Bleed-out occurs over 3–9 months
Inventory Carrying Cost	2–4% of the reduction	Stays constant to the reduction
Increased Revenues	1% conservative estimate	Starts at month 2–3 and increases
Reduced Freight/Logistics	2% conservative estimate	Immediately
Increased Service Level	1–3% conservative estimate	Immediately
Margin Improvement	1–2% increase	Immediately

merchandise and get favorable accounts payable rates will pay handsomely. In an industry segment that works on a 2 to 4 percent margin, the ability to double it can be a competitive advantage. Improving the fill rates and customer service will help gain new customers. The net results will be a much more robust balance sheet and income statement for the optimized distributor.

Finally, in many of the distributor engagements I have been involved with, the inventory reduction took on a secondary advantage. The sheer size of the inventory reduction contributed to a *footprint reduction*. Once it was shown that the inventory could be held at the optimal level over time, management viewed the increased warehouse space as an advantage. It gave them flexibility to gain a competitive advantage in growth areas by providing additional SKUs when required or an added space/focus on Internet sales versus normal distribution.

CONSUMER PACKAGED GOODS MANUFACTURING: WHERE IT ALL BEGAN

In virtually no other industry is the burden of inventory pushed up the chain like it is in the retail/CPG distribution chain. CPG vendors are creating consumer forecasts with the latest in sophisticated third-party data like IRI and scanner information, but then have to react to unpredictable retail demand requests. The result can be some of the worst examples of the bullwhip effect!

The key to the CPG vendor is the ability to extend the reaction time between the expected (and unexpected) consumer demand and the unforeseen retailer reaction. As we have seen, the 8.3 percent OOS rate and expanding inventories show the old technique of warnings, reporting, and reaction do not work. High-powered analytics can make you predictive instead of reactive. It can extend the reaction time so you are able to anticipate the disconnect between consumer demand and retailer reaction for lower costs and higher fill rates.

Walking the Tightrope

The CPG vendor has devised a promo/nonpromo demand plan out into the future. However, the CPG supply chain relies on a *retail partner* to facilitate the final customer interaction. Brand loyalty and store loyalty is a jointly shared bond. If a store is out of stock, the brand and the store's customer loyalty take a hit. The last 100 feet of the CPG supply chain can be a totally unknown pathway to many, if not most, CPG companies. Is the product on the shelf? Did the retailer perform the promotion as promised? Did a competitor run a promotion prior to ours, and did it cannibalize the promotion?

Here is where it gets sticky. Since the vendor has a somewhat-opaque view down to the current customer demand the vendor will tend to hold higher-than-normal stocks to cover the lack of safety stock at the retailer. The required high level of fill rate negotiated with the retailer contributes to an even higher level of inventory. Using a single-stage inventory management plan creates bloated inventories on 70 percent of the products in the portfolio. Even with the bloated inventory, there are still 20 percent of the products close to running out of stock. Over the last 15 years, retail/CPG inventories continue to climb, but the same 8 percent out-of-stock level remains!

Why?

- The reaction time at the retail link in the chain is extremely small. Due to seasonality and/or volatile promotions, a miscalculation of demand can result in massive out-of-stocks within days, if not hours! Since order review periods are periodic, this information is not relayed until the out-of-stocks are both in the DC and most stores. The delay is further amplified by the fact that the vendor's replenishment facility is days or weeks away, depending on network requirements.

- Retailers tend to use a single planning number, given a forecast and/or a formula to project the inventory requirement. Most retail forecasts focus on a planning number with no upper or lower confidences. This means little or no demand variance in the plan. Add in the fact that very few retailers factor in supply variance—less than complete fill rate or faster or slower delivery—and the safety stock at a retailer DC is almost nil.

- Increasing rule-of-thumb days of supply to cover an inefficient supply chain creates an exponential increase in costs as you get to higher service levels in the 97 to 99 percent range. However, at those levels, the rule-of-thumb metric can't overcome the retail aggregate-and-buy rapid replenishment reaction to low stocks.

The key to the CPG vendor is to embrace the current inventory risk and use it to an advantage to evaluate the out-of-stock problem in the industry, while closely evaluating the operational excellence of your organization.

CONSUMER PACKAGED GOODS MANUFACTURING BENEFITS OF INVENTORY OPTIMIZATION

As indicated earlier, prior to 1990, both retail and CPG companies had roughly the same days of inventory outstanding. However, since that time the retail segment has embraced just-in-time (JIT) inventory control. As shown in Figure 12.4, today the CPG suppliers are now holding 60 to 75 percent more days of inventory outstanding than their retail trading partners. Yet, there continues to be the ever-present 8 percent out-of-stock rate on the retailer's shelves. While a lot of the problem is based on retail practices, there is enough blame to be shared at the CPG vendor level.

The lag time between understanding true customer demand and facilitating retail purchase orders creates a bullwhip effect around needed stock in the customer-facing distribution centers within the CPG supply chain. This redundant inventory amplifies right up the CPG chain to the plant warehouses and leads to whipsaw production. The CPG supplier needs to calm the overreaction to aggregate-and-buy

Industry Sector	Median Days Inventory Outstanding	Industry Sector	Median Days Inventory Outstanding
Aerospace and Defense	46	Food Manufacturing	45
Apparel/Luxury Goods	51	Grocery and Drug Retailers	26
Auto Parts and Components	31	Household Products/CPG	40
Beverages	20	Machinery/Industrial	52
Building Products	36	Medical Devices and Suppliers	46
Chemicals	46	Metals/Mining	51
Communications Products	27	Paper/Forest Products	39
Computers and Peripherals	27	Personal Care Products	43
Containers and Packaging	40	Pharmaceuticals	46
Department Stores/Mass Merchants	63	Semiconductors	42
Electrical Equipment	45	Specialty Retail	57

Figure 12.4 "Let's Put Working Capital to Work," Lora Cecere, August 30, 2011

techniques and get a better view on actual consumer demand in its forecasting process. Once this occurs, the inventory can take on a much closer flow pattern to the customer need.

Charlie Chase's book, *Demand Driven Forecasting*, 2nd edition, looks into this faulty shipment style forecast process. He shows how, with the addition of syndicated data, the forecast going into inventory optimization can provide a much better and much more forward-thinking demand number. The methodology is called *multitiered causal analysis,* or *MTCA*.

MTCA integrates sell-through data such as POS and or syndicated scanner data (ACNielsen/IRI) into the demand forecasting process to determine the effects of consumer demand on supply/shipments. In essence, a second model is overlaid on top of the first causal model. It measures and quantifies the lag time between shipments and actual demand. This extra visibility allows for a much better way of creating demand sensing, shaping and shifting.

Up until this time, most CPG companies have tried to create highly adaptive demand sensing processes. They are trying to anticipate demand or extend their ability to see into the future. We have all seen the marketing hype around *demand sensing* in the forecasting circles. Indeed, the "our numbers are better than your numbers" are starting to rival those old "our math is better than their math" rants about inventory optimization.

Demand sensing is extremely important, but CPG suppliers hold a trump card few other manufacturers have—the ability to shape and shift demand through customer analysis. With demand sensing, you are in a reactive mode. With demand shifting and shaping, you are in a predictive mode. Look at the example of sensing an unexpected dramatic upswing in demand. "If" you catch it in time, you have the ability to drive additional production to cover for the increase. Most sophisticated forecasting models have the ability to sense demand, but is a 1-for-1 reaction to it the ideal way to produce the highest profitability? What if that unexpected demand cannibalizes the rest of your product portfolio?

Using MTCA and demand shaping/shifting, the user has the ability to manipulate the demand for best results. The forecast overlaid with customer data allows the user to see, shape, and shift the demand for best results—not just a lot of product out the door. We want product to fly *off* the shelf—not just onto the shelf! With MTCA and optimization, the CPG supplier has the ability to profitably shape demand and the resulting distribution. Indeed, as I found many years ago, if the supplier can think and act like a retail collaborator, the distribution to the customer quandary can and will be solved.

As always, it seems that inventory optimization works best in a multiechelon inventory optimization situation like that of a manufacturer with a long, complicated supply chain. Indeed, 70+ percent of all IO installs are in manufacturing. If there is a sweet spot for inventory reduction, the CPG supplier is the best place to garner that result, but there is so much more to the optimization story than just reduction of stock.

The out-of-stock problem in the retail/CPG supply chain creates a 7.8 percent shortfall in revenue according to the research firm IHL. This equates to over $1.1 trillion globally, or $158.00 for every man, woman, and child on the planet. Just in the United States the revenues lost to out-of-stocks are equal to the combined annual revenues of Kroger, Home Depot, and Target![6]

The CPG manufacturers need to break away from the reactionary mode of inventory management and embrace the concept of predictive analytics and optimization to overcome the present aggregate-and-buy techniques. Forecasting with MTCA overlays, collaborative planning via consensus inputs, demand shaping and shifting, and a focus on out-of-stocks via inventory optimization will drive long-term growth beyond short-term inventory reductions. Almost every installation of inventory optimization I have been involved with has started off as a way to be more nimble but ended up with better service levels, better fill rates, and fewer out-of-stocks than the more robust outcomes.

Reducing the out-of-stock problem at a company like Procter & Gamble by 2 percent would mean generating $1.66 billion in revenue during their 2014 fiscal year. That would have raised their net income by 15 percent.[7] You see? Reducing inventory is nice, but the whole process of inventory optimization should be to reduce the dreaded out-of-stock problem in the CPG supply chain and drive up revenue and market share for everyone in the chain. Too often, the players in this industry have attempted to collaborate, but the collaboration will always fall short when the aggregate-and-buy process is used.

Table 12.4 shows the types of benefits a CPG vendor can expect when using inventory optimization.

Table 12.4 Time-Phasing Inventory Benefits at a Consumer Packaged Goods Manufacturer

Benefit	Increase/Decrease	When?
Inventory Reduction	20–30% reduction	Bleed-out occurs over 6 months
Inventory Carrying Cost	2–4% of the reduction	Stays constant to the reduction
Increased Revenues	2% conservative estimate	Starts at month 2–3 and increases
Reduced Freight/Logistics	2% conservative estimate	Immediately
Increased Service Level	1–3% conservative estimate	Immediately
Margin Improvement	1–2% increase	Immediately

HEY, WAIT A MINUTE: WHERE ARE YOU GETTING THESE TIME-PHASED NUMBERS?

The last step in the process of developing a business case for inventory optimization is to develop a *strategic value assessment,* or *SVA.* The idea is to meet with potential customers and spend quality time, usually one to two days, going over their business to understand the processes, expectations, and present indicators. This allows the participants to get onto the same page with what can be accomplished during an installation of inventory optimization. Refer back to Chapter 10 for the steps of an SVA.

That's where those *time-phased numbers* came from.

NOTES

1. Gruen and Corsten, "A Comprehensive Guide to Retail Out of Stock Reduction in the Fast Moving Consumer Goods Industry," 2008.
2. GMA/FMI_2002_-Worldwide_OOS_Study, 2002.
3. MIT Beer Game.
4. GMA/FMI_2002_-Worldwide_OOS_Study, 2002.
5. Recent SAS installation of Forecasting/Inventory Optimization in the United States.
6. Greg Buzek and Lee Holman, "We Lost Australia! Retail's $1.1 Trillion Inventory Distortion Problem," June, 8, 2015.
7. Procter & Gamble Annual Report, 2014.

CHAPTER **13**

Pulling It All
Together

U p until the mid-1980s, most manufacturers were entrenched in the classic push supply chain. The focus was to create long and efficient production runs designed to produce products at the lowest possible cost. The marketing of those products was based on pushing products out to the consumer and creating demand through advertising. This drove a push-pull process.

At the time, most manufacturers were the tail that wagged the dog when it came to supply chain management. The key influencer was price. Companies lowered the price to create incentives to buy. This process was called *index marketing*. For instance, by using the food industry as an example, we can make a point of this process. Indexing means the amount of consumption in an area based on a national average. The national average will be 100. An area with a high index meant that that area or city had more consumption that an area of low consumption. A good example of this would be refried beans. Due to the ethnicity of the southwestern cities of Phoenix and Los Angeles, the refried bean index for those cities might be 170 to 180 compared to a city like Seattle, where the consumption is an average 105 to 107.

Market indexing would make a refried bean manufacturer push a lower price in Phoenix and Los Angeles compared to Seattle. This index marketing worked well until the advent of computers and the Internet. It didn't take long for grocery retailers to put their product pricing on the Internet—kind of like Craigslist for retailers. All another retailer had to do was figure in the freight costs of moving the refried beans from Phoenix to Seattle and, if the price point was below the one being dealt in Seattle, the retailer would place an order to the Phoenix retailer and divert a portion of the Phoenix retailer's purchase up to Seattle.

Remember what I said in Chapter 1 about the manufacturer's view that "a happy buyer is a loaded buyer"? The retailer found the Achilles' heel of the manufacturer's push supply chain. This did not just happen in the grocery supply chain—it was happening everywhere, much to the chagrin of the manufacturer. Indeed, at first, manufacturers' sales managers were only dealing with volume as the key performance indicator (KPI) requirement. Manufacturers were rewarding key account managers (KAMs) with bonuses and trips, while those KAMs were dumping excess inventory across the country. Indeed, many times national sales managers would cut deals with a single co-op warehouse in Kansas City at the end of the fiscal year and not sell another can of product for eight months nationally.

Instead of the manufacturer, the retailer was becoming the tail that wagged the dog by taking advantage of the inefficiencies of the manufacturer supply chain. Moreover, the retailers were taking more steps to become efficient. In the early 1990s, most retailers began to act like the infamous Toyota/Kanban production facilities. They were becoming very efficient with point-of-sale information and using it to better their overall functionality. The offshoot of this was that very few retailers made any attempts to transfer that information on to manufacturing. Until Walmart began passing information on to manufacturers via its collaborative web portal in the early 2000s, most retailers put up a brick wall when it came to collaborative demand information. Most manufacturers had to rely on third-party data via Information Resources Incorporated or Nielsen.

Given the lack of information, coupled with retailers reducing overall inventory positions, the pathway was set for a Toyota/Kanban environment, and indeed that is what happened. Costs were passed up the chain to the manufacturers, and with the lack of visibility to actual predictive customer demand the bullwhip effect was rampant in most manufacturing and retailing supply chains. During this transformation period, the supply chain industry began to embrace the idea of pull supply chains as the methodology that could overcome the inability to quickly react to end-of-the-chain needs.

As Erik Kruse states, perfectly efficient supply chains were thrown out of whack in an effort to become pull focused.[1] As we pointed out in our example about candles in Chapter 2, the manufacturers were trying to do the same things as before, but simply calling it pull supply chains, by running smaller and smaller batch runs that were deemed customer focused. Now the longstanding production run–centric capabilities of manufacturers were cut short. Instead of reductions in inventory, the inventories went up because there was little or no visibility to the customer-facing demand. They were still working on the same delayed and aggregated information they had always had before.

It was in this situation that the inventory optimization process started to take hold at the same time as the gulf between manufacturers and retailers was widening. The promise was to right-size inventories, but there was an important criterion that was left out: Inventory optimization works by using one single demand signal—the customer-facing location—to synchronize the entire network reaction. The one big need of inventory optimization was lost on almost everyone: *When a supply chain network reacts systematically to customer-facing demand, it is shifting behavior and becomes a pull-based environment.*

I am not going to be so bold as to say inventory optimization is the final step in the quest to provide a pull supply chain. What inventory optimization does is allow the organization to focus its attention on customer demand and synchronize the supply chain so it delivers products to a service level at the lowest possible cost. Whether you have a totally custom product or you are making long production runs of a standard product, the principles of inventory optimization work to allow a coordinated reaction to customer demand.

There is a tendency, even when all the information is placed before you, to protect your turf. You will try to lower your inventory just as I did when I was trying to lower my inventories as a buyer. Even in the face of known volume on specific items, the buyer will shoot high. The result is a seesaw battle of low inventory, expedited reactions to correct it, and the ever-increasing supply upstream to counteract the human nature reactions of the bullwhip effect. It is hard for seasoned buying veterans to accept that analytical analysis and optimized policies will correct the human tendencies and allow for correct purchasing options and optimized inventories. If buyers accept the results, more often than not they can run on autopilot.

ALIGNING THE INVENTORY OPTIMIZATION GOALS TO CORRECT DEEP-SEATED BUSINESS ACTIONS IN A COMPANY

When everything is said and done, inventory management is all about balancing supply and demand to meet the customer need. Too little stock results in lost sales. Too much stock increases the risk of lost capital in obsolete inventory and working capital tied up in inventory that could be used in better business opportunities. The results can be a company lurching back and forth trying to find an acceptable point, only to jump from one inventory problem to the next.

The goal of every company is to find that balance where it reaches an acceptable balance of inventory costs and customer satisfaction. This is the rub—once companies begin to explore their own efficiency frontier, they need to make decisions based on company goals and aspirations. Do they want the same service levels at lower inventory costs? Do they want higher service levels at current inventory levels? Do they want to change inventory techniques like practicing more postponement activities in the wake of uncovering inventory improvement opportunities? These are the kinds of next-step options companies need to explore as they work through their inventory optimization pathway. The thing is, "Companies that can come close to reaching the illusive inventory optimization goal will have a substantial market advantage over those that can only achieve middling performance or worse."[2]

INVENTORY OPTIMIZATION CAN'T DO WHAT WAS DONE BEFORE

I often find companies that enter into an inventory optimization engagement with a technology provider have been enticed by the promise of right-sizing inventories for better customer service, but the process gets bogged down in the minutia of what I call *output comparisons*. This means that no one has taken the time to sit down with the customer and discuss the various factors that drive inventory levels or how inventory optimization helps to overcome those drivers to facilitate improvements. If this is not made clear, the customer is left wondering what black-box calculation delivered an inventory projection of "500" when her output was "600." It is quite clear that the inventory optimization engagement is not centered on making the supply chain more efficient; it ends up being focused on making this new inventory optimization do the exact same things the old system did, because that is a known outcome.

One engagement, in particular, comes to mind when I talk about this phenomenon. A particular well-known retail supply chain management system was pulling support for a hosted environment for vendor-managed inventory (VMI). The manufacturer wanted to replace that system with a new one supported by inventory optimization. During the entire engagement, the output from inventory optimization was compared to the old replenishment environment. Given that most of the in-house personnel at the manufacturer were prior employees of the hosted replenishment, it should have been expected. Given that their output was their "reality," everything was measured against that output stream. If there was a marked improvement on inventory or replenishment, it was not believed. Indeed, over time the inventory optimization calculations were relaxed again and again to the point of having no discernible effect. As indicated before, this kind of behavior can sink inventory optimization engagements and leads to unacceptable results and bad press for inventory optimization as an industry.

HOW TO CHANGE THE PLAYING FIELD

What does a supply chain executive with aspirations to improve operations with inventory optimization have to do to pave the way for a successful engagement? One of the key things, just like what was experienced at Matas (see Chapter 9), is to examine the business issues contributing to out-of-balance inventories. This can quantify the problem instead of pushing the engagement into a comparison battle.

OVERARCHING BUSINESS ISSUES IMPEDE POSITIVE INVENTORY CONTROL

The analyst firm Aberdeen created a wonderful report in 2004 that still resonates today.[3] Aberdeen laid out a strategy for an organization to become more integrated in its supply chain activities. Its contention was that organizations create functional silos in much the same way islands of efficiencies are developed between inventory locations. Although I read through the report almost 10 years ago, it continues to point me toward how inventory optimization can help break down the walls of an organization's supply chain and create a thriving distribution network.

Supply Chain Organization

Is there an integrated approach to the supply chain and inventory decisions, or are there functional silos? The less integrated, the more inventory problems are likely to occur.

How does inventory optimization help?

In specific inventory optimization solutions, the scenario analysis will have results based on both the overall view and the underlying inventory points. This gives a much better understanding of the overall decision. For instance, if a warehouse working in an island-of-efficiency mode decides to start reducing its days of supply, it will create ripple effects both up and down the supply chain. The downstream inventories might have more out-of-stocks. The upstream location might have to carry extra stock to overcome the potential expedited orders coming upstream. When multiechelon inventory optimization with advanced scenario analysis is used, the reduction of inventory is coordinated so that the overall network reduces inventory instead of simply shifting it around, which is what most often happens in a siloed environment.

Supply Chain Network Design

The greater the number of stocking points, all things being equal, the higher the level of inventory. The longer the supply chain (goods produced offshore), the higher the level of inventory.

How does inventory optimization help?

This can be a serious problem in a supply chain network. Indeed, the rollout of many inventory optimization projects in the early 2000s coincided with companies developing more and more offshore inventory requirements. Even though inventory optimization was being implemented, the overall inventory was increasing due to the uncertainty of supply coming in from South East Asian locations. As supply chains add more and more hierarchies, it is imperative to keep the levels synchronized so that the dreaded bullwhip effect is not created. This is especially true of offshore situations. The transportation link extends the lead time and the supply uncertainty increases the variance. Inventory optimization can help position safety stocks in the right locations at the lowest possible costs to overcome the lead time and lead-time variance requirements.

Customer Service Policies

The company's strategies and goals related to customer service, both generally and at an A, B, C category level, will greatly impact inventories.

How does inventory optimization help?

What often happens is days of supply and customer service get melded together into an inventory position that is not really aligned to efficiency. A general rule-of-thumb days-of-supply number is placed on a product and the overarching product group as part of an inventory plan. As indicated in the Goldilocks example in Chapter 4, over time, up to 70 percent of the products become overstocked due to this assignment of days of supply over service level. The ABC categorization can help to sharpen a focus on the more important items in a portfolio, but as long as the focus is on days of supply over the service level at the lowest inventory cost, the inventory will float higher than needed.

Inventory optimization makes the days-of-supply number an outcome of the service level/lowest-cost inventory computation. The projected service level needed is the focal point, and the calculated balance between inventory costs, ordering costs, and lead-time logistics derives a unique days-of-supply number for the product/location pairing. Moreover, the synchronized assignments up and down the supply chain enable the reduction of redundant stock because the entire chain runs on one demand signal and not a delayed and aggregated signal.

Safety Stock Policies

Relatedly, how aggressive a company wants to be with safety levels and how frequently a company revisits safety stock assumptions and stock-keeping unit (SKU)-level targets are key variables.

How does inventory optimization help?

This is one of the key results of inventory optimization, the analytically calculated safety stock requirement for each product/location pairing. The supply-and-demand variances are constantly updated to reflect the current confidence level due to ongoing performance of the system. The better the forecast and the better the supplier performance, the less safety stock is needed. In addition, the multiechelon inventory optimization process allows for the reduction of redundant safety stocks up the supply chain because of aggregated demand variance. This greatly reduces the need for vast amounts of safety stocks at plant or central warehouse locations.

One of the key attributes of multiechelon inventory optimization is the overall reduction of the bullwhip effect because there is a communication factor running throughout the supply chain where the customer-facing demand signal is the driving force. The entire chain can react to that signal in a logical and tempered manner instead of reacting to delayed signals after each downward inventory location is calculated and aggregated upward. This is the reason multiechelon inventories are more efficient with 30 percent less inventory.

Degrees of Freedom for Inventory Decisions

The more individuals who have the ability to add inventory into the supply chain, the higher the levels are likely to be.

How does inventory optimization help?

There is an old adage about forecasting: The more people who touch a forecast the more inaccurate the forecast becomes. Even before anyone does anything with inventory positioning and/or replenishment, a forecast will start the planning process. Depending on who deals with the forecast, the sheer numbers of people touching the forecast will skew the numbers away from a statistically accurate forecast. How many times has a forecast simply been morphed upward to the exact number in the sales quota by sales management? The faulty forecast is the first of many steps toward high inventories.

It is human nature to impart tribal knowledge on something. In our discussion of Matas, we saw store personnel trying to add their knowledge by overriding orders. In many cases, they were ordering higher numbers just to get their fair share of the inventory, only to be shorted. The end result of that kind of behavior is to spiral inventory up to accommodate people trying to get their fair share. In the extreme example of Matas, the entire system became automated. With no one touching the ordering system, the chain became efficient.

Management of Tradeoffs

Company-specific decisions about the traditional transportation and/or unit cost tradeoffs have an impact on inventories. The lowest total cost will usually have higher inventories than the lowest inventory cost option.

How does inventory optimization help?

Inventory optimization makes an organization take a long look in the mirror at the various supply chain techniques they have used in the past. Many times, the result of the examination is a failed inventory optimization engagement. Why?

In some ways, inventory optimization is a leap of faith to become more efficient. That leap of faith requires people to examine past practices to understand how inefficient those decisions can be. For instance, bulk purchases to obtain a lower cost might, on the surface, be enticing, but sinking working capital into that inventory might far outweigh the lump-sum truckload allowance. Moreover, the buy-off of a product's off-invoice allowance might look good according to the cost of money calculations versus the holding of the extra inventory, but the net result is bloated inventory position, slower inventory turns, and wasted working capital. Management needs to weigh the inventory efficiencies with a different vision of costs. As indicated in the statement above, if you focus on lowest total cost, the inventory tends to be higher than if you focus on the lowest inventory cost option. This shift in focus does not mean you have to throw out all of your efforts to get the lowest costs; it means you have to weigh the benefits and costs.

Inventory optimization enables the user to see when products go into overstock situations. In the past, the planner/buyer was almost totally focused on the short-supply products because of customer service needs. With inventory optimization, the entire portfolio is evaluated so that the products are right sized. The goal of inventory optimization is to enhance the inventory KPIs on the company balance sheet and income statement—not to pat a buyer on the back for buying three trucks of extra product because of a hot deal.

SUPPLY CHAIN INVENTORY STRATEGIES BENCHMARK REPORT RECOMMENDATIONS

To stay competitive, companies need to buck conventional wisdom about how to manage inventory. Companies need to redesign how they manage inventory across their supply chains to lower costs and improve customer service levels. Technology support will be critical to selecting and executing a successful supply chain inventory program. In particular, companies should seek solutions that let them optimize globally across supply chain tiers rather than locally, scale for item-location policies, and enable supplier-managed processes such as min-max replenishment. Change management and metric realignment also need to be part of the program.

Following are recommendations for action based on a company's current maturity stage in dealing with inventory optimization. Whether a company is trying to move its supply chain inventory practices from laggard to industry norm, to move from industry norm to best in class, or to remain at best-in-class status, these actions will help improve performance:

Laggard Steps to Success

1. **Increase supplier-managed practices that use lean principles.** Share more information with suppliers and give them more responsibility for keeping your company optimally supplied with inventory. Some 70 percent of manufacturing-intensive companies use supplier-managed inventory today, along with 56 percent of distribution-intensive companies. Investigate the benefits of moving to pull-based processes and just-in-time delivery as part of the program.

2. **Rethink hub-and-spoke inventory placement.** Fully 60 percent of large companies surveyed report holding highly variable finished goods inventory centrally at a hub versus at each individual spoke. This method frees up working capital while improving overall service levels. Supply chain modeling tools can uncover these opportunities.

3. **Move away from simple weeks-of-supply and ABCD inventory policies.** Simplistic methods lead to flabby supply

chains. Companies facing high customer service levels, short product life cycles, or multitier manufacturing or distribution networks have the most to gain from moving toward item-location level inventory policies. Look to advanced planning systems or multiechelon optimization solutions and simultaneously look at increasing replenishment planning frequency.

Industry-Norm Steps to Success

1. **Appoint a single end-to-end owner of inventory.** Less than a quarter of companies have created a single owner for inventory across the supply chain. Without this level of accountability, local inventory reduction and service-level programs will thrive. Locally optimized programs, despite their good intentions, almost always lead to higher working capital costs and service-level challenges. Make sure metrics are changed so that local staff members are measured on how well they follow the optimal supply chain inventory and service-level policies that have been set, while central inventory planners are compensated on how much they have been able to improve customer service levels and take out cost from the total supply chain.

2. **Act on merge-in-transit, postponement, and risk-pooling opportunities.** The competition is becoming much smarter in how it pools inventory and flows product, so every corporation should be reexamining its product portfolio for additional opportunities. Nearly a quarter of manufacturing-intensive companies, for instance, say they plan to adopt new postponement or merge-in-transit strategies in the next 18 months. Inventory optimization tools that allow for scenario planning help define and quantify the opportunities. Third-party logistics firms are being used by 41 percent of respondents for execution and planning support for strategies such as these.

3. **Accelerate lean supply chain benefits with collaborative technology.** Implement a supplier collaboration platform that uses a red-blue-green or similar metaphor to enable information sharing and proactive exception management. Also look at the benefits of moving to a min-max supplier replenishment

model, without requiring consignment inventory. In addition, remember to readjust metrics—suppliers should be measured in red-blue-green percentages rather than on-time delivery percentage.

Best-in-Class Next Steps

1. **Actively manage in-transit inventory.** Enterprises with long transit times should investigate the different ways to use in-transit inventory as a virtual inventory bin to lower safety stock levels, reduce total delivered costs, and maximize revenue opportunities.

2. **Use a commercial multiechelon optimization solution.** The new generation of commercially available multiechelon optimization solutions will enable companies to properly account for variation in the supply chain. Companies with multiechelon manufacturing or finished goods distribution networks should not delay in investigating these solutions.

3. **Make supply chain inventory goals part of the product design process.** Maximize inventory flexibility and efficiency by designing products specifically to support potential risk pooling and postponement strategies. Component-based design should be a tenet of your organization.

IN CLOSING

Almost since the first commercially viable inventory optimization solutions arrived on the scene in the early 2000s, the industry has been overhyped. It has been truly amazing to see the number of focuses placed on inventory optimization by various analyst organizations. Just pulling them up on a search engine shows the metamorphosis from a broadly defined space that covered everything from network design and constraint theory to the current focuses on inventory policies. Throughout it all, many companies, in their search for optimization, simply searched for ways to mimic what they were already doing with this newfangled thing called inventory optimization. Executives who have attempted to explore options are inundated with promises too good to be true and, in most situations, shown not to be true.

However, it is too easy to blame the overhyping. Every new software solution process goes through a trough of disillusionment. Visionaries start off the process with proof of value engagements. The software providers cut their installation teeth in places that might not be the best fit, and, over time, word gets out that the promises are not being met. The result ends up being a period of time where inventory optimization starts to fall from the fashionable new business opportunity.

As we have examined in this book, inventory optimization is a viable option for the organization that understands the business problems it is suffering from and why it is leading to mismatched inventories. Inventory optimization is not a technological magic pill. You don't simply install it and step back, expecting miracles. We saw how the infighting between buyers and management stopped a perfectly good engagement in its tracks. In turn, we saw how management's ability to overcome the objections and carry on resulted in a fully automated replenishment system powered by inventory optimization.

Simply saying that inventory optimization will lower inventories can turn an industry like retail away from ever trying inventory optimization as an augmentation to replenishment planning. They know all about the short-term benefits and long-term disasters put in place by ratcheting down days of supply. However, if inventory optimization is positioned as a way to overcome the documented issue of human nature's need to overcompensate for perceived supply problems, resulting in the bullwhip effect, you might be on the pathway to a wonderful inventory optimization opportunity.

Demand-driven inventory optimization and replenishment is all about allowing the supply network to function as a synchronized entity to support the customer-facing service-level requirement. This is the baseline requirement for any supply chain wanting to move toward a pull-based model. It won't matter if you have products requiring little customization or products that are almost completely made to order. Demand-driven inventory optimization and replenishment get your organization focused on the customer.

In the end, that old adage that a happy buyer is a loaded buyer makes a lot more sense. You will have a happy buyer—the right one that you should have been focused on all along—the one at the end of your supply chain who wanted the product at the right place, at the right time, and at the right price. If you make the buyers happy, they will keep coming back and will be happy to have you continue to support their purchases into the future.

Good luck with your demand-driven inventory supply travels, and I hope to see you along the way.

NOTES

1. Erik Kruse, "From Push to Pull—Perfecting the Means," Supply Chain Resource Cooperative, September 4, 2003, http://scm.ncsu.edu/scm-articles/article/from-pushto-pull-perfecting-the-means.
2. Aberdeen Group, "Supply Chain Inventory Strategies Benchmark Report," December 2004.
3. Ibid.

Epilogue

Thank you for reading my book on demand-driven inventory optimization and replenishment. I hope that you found it to be insightful and that it will help you move your company along a successful pathway in driving a pull-based supply chain focused on synchronizing demand signals from the customer.

So, what happened with the lawyer's house in Bremerton, Washington? I have to smile at this, because I have made scores and scores of presentations about demand-driven inventory optimization and replenishment for at least 20 years, and invariably someone will come up to me and mention the lawyer's house instead of anything regarding inventory optimization. I guess the old saw is true—leave people with a picture in their minds and they will remember you forever.

When we left our little story about the lawyer in Bremerton, Washington, he and his family were the talk of the town. Everyone in their middle-class homes aspired to be just like him and have all the trappings of wealth and influence. As I said, the house was on everyone's list of places to show out-of-town visitors. People would drive by and take pictures of the beautiful house on the hill overlooking Puget Sound.

However, one night when no one was home, a fire started. Indeed, the lawyer and his family were on an extended vacation. Due to the location, neighbors did not see the flames until it was too late to save the house. The fire raged for hours while fire trucks contained the flames so that they did not spread to homes around the lawyer's property. The next day, the news of the fire had spread by word of mouth and via newspaper and television accounts. People flocked to the property to get a glimpse of the destruction.

At first, everyone was focused on the house itself. The glorious home was reduced to rubble. As they looked closer, everyone started to say the same thing: Where's the furniture? Where're the cars? Where's anything?

It was true—there was nothing inside the house. When the fire-fighters arrived to find the house fully engulfed in flames, they also learned that it was an empty house. Word spread quickly about the strange happenings.

When the family came back from their vacation, they had to confirm what the town now knew—the house was a façade to their wealth. They had very little money, and everything was tied up in being property-poor. This had been going on for years. They had sold off most of their possessions and lived like paupers inside a mansion.

I first thought of this story from my youth when I visited the grocery products paper company outlined in this book. This company had won numerous awards for customer service excellence and was a model for collaborative forecasting, planning, forecasting, and replenishment. The vendor-managed inventory personnel were doing extraordinary things with the likes of Walmart, SuperValu, Target, Costco, and so on. However, with the advice of one of the planners, I went to interview an internal logistics manager. He looked like his hair was on fire. In an attempt to provide the best possible customer service to its big clients, the company was literally burning down its house with expedited orders between warehouses to cover potential out-of-stocks.

When everything is said and done, a company is simply a giant supply chain. Things go in, and there are some value-added activities, and products or services flow out. When companies forget the basics and focus on things that are external, they lose sight of the power in their supply chain. Over the past 30 to 40 years, companies have touted the idea that a pull-based supply chain is the best supply chain. The problem is, they are getting twisted up in the nomenclature and trying to mimic custom-built actions of a pull-based supply chain without understanding that being demand driven and pull based requires that the whole supply chain be synced up to the customer demand. The basis of demand-driven inventory optimization and replenishment is to shift the focus onto one demand signal and use the supply chain process to synchronize the network reaction as one process—not steps in demand aggregation.

The metaphor of the burning house is a way of asking executives to realize that building a company without a total focus on supply chain excellence is like the lawyer building a house but having nothing inside. People pointed at the award-winning company thinking it was a model of supply chain excellence when, in reality, they were only seeing the outside of the house and thinking the inside was the same.

Now is the time to review the focus of your supply chain, before an accident happens. Don't let your company be that burning house on the hill.

Index

Note: Page references followed by *f* indicate an illustrated figure, respectively.